fodor's

MAUI

1s

Portions of this book appear in *Fodor's Hawai'i*

Fodor's Travel Publications   New York, Toronto, London, Sydney, Auckland

www.fodors.com

Be a Fodor's Correspondent

Your opinion matters. It matters to us. It matters to your fellow Fodor's travelers, too. And we'd like to hear it. In fact, we *need* to hear it. When you share your experiences and opinions, you become an active member of the Fodor's community. Here's how you can help improve Fodor's for all of us.

Tell us when we're right. We rely on local writers to give you an insider's perspective. But our writers and staff editors also depend on you. Your positive feedback is a vote to renew our recommendations for the next edition.

Tell us when we're wrong. We update most of our guides every year. But things change. If any of our descriptions are inaccurate or inadequate, we'll incorporate your changes in the next edition and will correct factual errors at fodors.com *immediately*.

Tell us what to include. You probably have had fantastic travel experiences that aren't yet in Fodor's. Why not share them with a community of like-minded travelers? Share your discoveries and experiences with everyone directly at fodors.com. Your input may lead us to add a new listing or a higher recommendation.

Give us your opinion instantly at our feedback center at www.fodors.com/feedback. You may also e-mail editors@fodors.com with the subject line "In Focus Maui Editor." Or send your nominations, comments, and complaints by mail to In Focus Maui Editor, Fodor's, 1745 Broadway, New York, NY 10019.

Happy Traveling!

Tim Jarrell, Publisher

FODOR'S IN FOCUS MAUI

Editor: Douglas Stallings, *series editor*

Editorial Contributors: Nicole Crane, Eliza Escaño, Bonnie Friedman, Heidi Pool, Cathy Sharpe, Carla Tracy

Production Editor: Tom Holton

Maps & Illustrations: Mark Stroud and David Lindroth, *cartographers*; Bob Blake and Rebecca Baer, *map editors;* William Wu, *information graphics*

Design: Fabrizio La Rocca, *creative director*; Guido Caroti, *art director*; Ann McBride, *designer*; Melanie Marin, *senior picture editor*

Cover Photo (Kanaha, Maui): Aeder Erik/Photolibrary

Production Manager: Steve Slawsky

COPYRIGHT

Copyright © 2009 by Fodor's Travel, a division of Random House, Inc.

Fodor's is a registered trademark of Random House, Inc.

All rights reserved. Published in the United States by Fodor's Travel, a division of Random House, Inc., and simultaneously in Canada by Random House of Canada, Limited, Toronto. Distributed by Random House, Inc., New York.

No maps, illustrations, or other portions of this book may be reproduced in any form without written permission from the publisher.

1st Edition

ISBN 978–1–4000–0889–6

ISSN 1943–0191

SPECIAL SALES

This book is available for special discounts for bulk purchases for sales promotions or premiums. Special editions, including personalized covers, excerpts of existing books, and corporate imprints, can be created in large quantities for special needs. For more information, write to Special Markets/Premium Sales, 1745 Broadway, MD 6-2, New York, New York, NY 10019, or e-mail specialmarkets@randomhouse.com.

AN IMPORTANT TIP & AN INVITATION

Although all prices, opening times, and other details in this book are based on information supplied to us at press time, changes occur all the time in the travel world, and Fodor's cannot accept responsibility for facts that become outdated or for inadvertent errors or omissions. **So always confirm information when it matters,** especially if you're making a detour to visit a specific place. Your experiences—positive and negative—matter to us. If we have missed or misstated something, **please write to us.** We follow up on all suggestions. Contact the In Focus Maui editor at editors@fodors.com or c/o Fodor's at 1745 Broadway, New York, NY 10019.

PRINTED IN CHINA

10 9 8 7 6 5 4 3 2 1

CONTENTS

DID YOU KNOW?

The black sand of small Wai'ānapanapa State Park on the Road to Hāna is made up of volcanic pebbles. You can swim here or hike a memorable coastal path past sea arches and blowholes.

ABOUT
THIS BOOK

Our Ratings

We wouldn't recommend a place that wasn't worth your time, but sometimes a place is so experiential that superlatives don't do it justice. These sights and properties get our highest rating, **Fodor's Choice**, indicated by orange stars throughout this book. Black stars highlight places we deem **Highly Recommended** places that our writers, editors, and readers praise again and again for consistency and excellence. Care to nominate a place or suggest that we rate one more highly? Visit our feedback center at www.fodors.com/feedback.

Credit Cards

Want to pay with plastic? **AE, D, DC, MC, V** following restaurant and hotel listings indicate if American Express, Discover, Diner's Club, MasterCard, and Visa are accepted.

Restaurants

Unless we state otherwise, restaurants are open for lunch and dinner daily. We mention dress only when there's a specific requirement and reservations only when they're essential or not accepted—it's always best to book ahead.

Hotels

Hotels have private bath, phone, TV, and air-conditioning and operate on the European Plan (aka EP, meaning without meals), unless we specify otherwise.

Many Listings
- ★ Fodor's Choice
- ★ Highly recommended
- ⊠ Physical address
- ✢ Directions
- ⌖ Mailing address
- ☎ Telephone
- 🖷 Fax
- ⊕ On the Web
- ✍ E-mail
- 🎫 Admission fee
- ☉ Open/closed times
- Ⓜ Metro stations
- ▱ Credit cards

Hotels & Restaurants
- 🏨 Hotel
- 🛏 Number of rooms
- ⟡ Facilities
- ❑ Meal plans
- ✕ Restaurant
- ⟡ Reservations
- ↘ Smoking
- 𝛾 BYOB
- ✕🏨 Hotel with restaurant that warrants a visit

Outdoors
- ⚑ Golf
- ⚑ Camping

Other
- ♺ Family-friendly
- ⇨ See also
- ⊠ Branch address
- ☞ Take note

Experience
Maui

1

WHAT'S WHERE

1 West Maui. This leeward, sunny area is ringed by resorts and condominiums in areas such as Kā'anapali and Kapalua; also here is the busy, tourist-oriented town of Lahaina, a former whaling center.

2 Central Maui. Between Maui's two mountain areas is Central Maui, the location of the county seat of Wailuku. Kahului Airport is here.

3 South Shore. The leeward side of Maui's eastern half is what most people mean when they say South Shore. This popular area is sunny and warm year-round and is home to Wailea, a beautiful resort area.

4 North Shore. The North Shore has no large resorts, just plenty of picturesque small towns like Pā'ia and Ha'ikū—and great surfing action at Ho'okipa Beach.

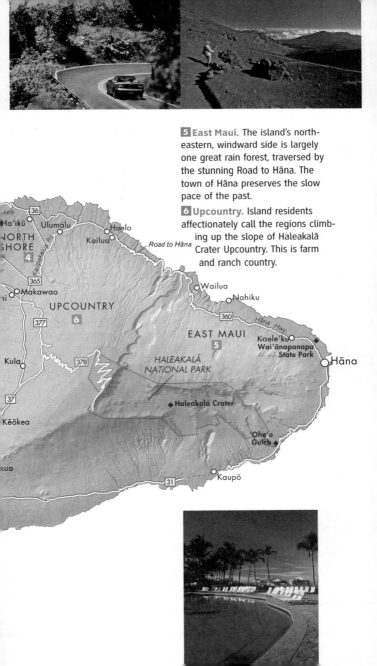

5 East Maui. The island's north-eastern, windward side is largely one great rain forest, traversed by the stunning Road to Hāna. The town of Hāna preserves the slow pace of the past.

6 Upcountry. Island residents affectionately call the regions climbing up the slope of Haleakalā Crater Upcountry. This is farm and ranch country.

PLANNER

When You Arrive

Most visitors arrive at Kahului Airport in Central Maui. The major car-rental companies have desks at the airport and can provide a map and directions to your hotel.
■ TIP→ **You may find long lines at car rental windows. If possible, send one person to pick up the car while the others wait for the baggage.**

Timing Is Everything

The humpback whales start arriving in November and are gone by early May. The biggest North Shore waves show up in winter, whereas kiteboarders and windsurfers enjoy the windy, late summer months. In high season—June through August and Christmas through spring break—the island is jam-packed with visitors. The best months for bargain hunters are May, September, and October.

Renting a Car

A rental car is a must on Maui. It's also one of your biggest trip expenses, especially given the price of gasoline—higher on Maui than on O'ahu or the Mainland.
■ TIP→ **Four-wheel-drive vehicles are the most expensive options and not really necessary.**
■ TIP→ **Parking is not always included in your room rate or resort fee.**
■ TIP→ **Booking a car as a part of a package can save you money.**

Dining & Lodging on Maui

Hawai'i is a melting pot of cultures, and nowhere is this more apparent than in its cuisines. From lū'au and "plate lunches" to sushi and steak, there's no shortage of interesting flavors and presentations. Whether you're looking for a quick snack or a multicourse meal, turn to chapter 6, Where to Eat, to find the best eating experiences the island has to offer.

Choosing a vacation lodging is a tough decision, but our expert writers and editors have done most of the legwork.

To help narrow your choices, consider what type of property you'd like to stay at (big resort, quiet bed-and-breakfast) and what type of island climate you're looking for (beachfront strand or remote rain forest). Chapter 7, Where to Stay, will give you all the details you need to book a place that suits your style. Reserve your room far in advance, and ask about discounts and packages.

| Island Driving Times | Tips for Travelers | 1 |

Island Driving Times

Maui may seem like a small island, but driving from one point to another can take longer than the mileage indicates. It's only 52 mi from Kahului Airport to Hāna, but the drive will take you about three hours. As for driving to Haleakalā, the 38-mi drive from sea level to the summit will take you about two hours. The roads are narrow and winding; it's best to go at a slow speed.

Kahului is the transportation hub—the main airport and largest harbor are here. Traffic on Maui's roads can be heavy, especially during the rush hours of 6 AM to 8:30 AM and 3:30 PM to 6:30 PM; this will add time to your drive. Here are average driving times to key destinations.

Kahului to Wailea	17 mi/30 min
Kahului to Kā'anapali	25 mi/45 min
Kahului to Kapalua	36 mi/1 hr, 15 min
Kahuli to Wailuku	6 mi/15 min
Kapalua to Haleakalā	73 mi/3 hr
Kā'anapali to Haleakalā	62 mi/2 hr, 30 min
Wailea to Haleakalā	54 mi/2 hr, 30 min
Kapalua to Hāna	88 mi/5 hr
Kā'anapali to Hāna	77 mi/5 hr
Wailea to Hāna	69 mi/4 hr, 30 min
Wailea to Lahaina	20 mi/45 min
Kā'anapali to Lahaina	40 mi/15 min
Kapalua to Lahaina	12 mi/25 min

Tips for Travelers

Advance booking of activities will ensure you get to do the activity you want; booking on-line can often save you 10% or more.

Traffic can be very heavy during busy times of day. Try to avoid driving during typical commuter hours and allow extra travel time to reach your destination.

Hawai'i has strict no-smoking laws: smoking is prohibited in all enclosed public spaces. Under Hawai'i law, hotels must designate 80% of their rooms as no-smoking.

The legal drinking age for alcoholic beverages is 21. Beer, wine, and spirits are available for sale in grocery stores, supermarkets, and other retail outlets. It is against the law to carry an open container of alcohol in your car. It's also illegal to drink in any county, state, or national park.

Do not take lava, stones, plants, or animals from the place where you found them. Much of the island's flora and fauna are are protected as endangered species.

TOP ATTRACTIONS

Hike Haleakalā

Trek down into Haleakalā National Park's massive bowl and see proof, at this dormant volcano, of how very powerful the earth's exhalations can be. You won't see landscape like this anywhere, outside of visiting the moon. The barren terrain is deceptive, however—many of the world's rarest plants, birds, and insects live here.

Take the Road to Hāna

Spectacular views of waterfalls, lush forests, and the sparkling ocean are part of the pleasure of the twisting drive along the North Shore to tiny, timeless Hāna in East Maui. The journey is the destination, but once you arrive, kick back and relax. Wave to pedestrians, "talk story" with locals in line at Hasegawa store, and explore the multicolor beaches.

The joy of snorkeling

Snorkeling is a must, by yourself or on a snorkel cruise. Wherever you duck under, you'll be inducted into a mesmerizing world underwater. Slow down and keep your eyes open: even fish dressed in camouflage can be spotted when they snatch at food passing by. Some great spots to try are Honolua Bay and Black Rock in West Maui; there are also good spots on the rocky fringes of Wailea's beaches on the South Shore.

> ### WORD OF MOUTH
>
> "I would say that Haleakalā IS Maui's claim to fame. . . . Many people take the day to drive aaalll the way up to the crater rim, climb out of the car, and stand at the rim only long enough to take some photos and get cold. I'd recommend a day hike inside the crater."
>
> —outtabed

Mākena (Big Beach)

This South-Shore beauty is the sand dreams are made of: deep, golden, and pillowy. Don't be discouraged by the crammed parking lots; there's more than enough room. Big Beach is still wild. There are no hotels, minimarts, or even public restrooms nearby—instead there are crystal-clear water, the occasional pod of dolphins, and drop-dead gorgeous scenery (including the sunbathers).

Tropical fruit at a roadside stand

Your first taste of ripe guava or mango is something to remember. Delicious lychees, mangos, star fruit, bananas, passion fruit, and papaya can be bought on the side of the road with the change in your pocket. Go on, let the juice run down your chin. No one's looking!

Resorts and spas

Indulge your inner rock star at the posh resorts and spas around the island. Sip a "Tommy Girl" in the hot tub at the Four Seasons or get massaged poolside at the Grand Wailea. Even if you don't stay the night, you can enjoy the opulent gardens, restaurants, art collections, and perfectly cordial staff.

Escape to a bed-and-breakfast

Being a shut-in isn't so bad at a secluded B&B. It's a sure way to get a taste of what it's like to live in Paradise: ripe fruit trees outside your door, late-night tropical rainstorms, a wild chicken or two. Rather than blasting the air-conditioning in a hotel room, relax with the windows open in a plantation house designed to capture sea breezes.

Whale-watch

Maui is the cradle for hundreds of humpback whales that return every year to frolic in the warm waters and give birth. Watch a mama whale teach her one-ton calf how to tail-wave. You can eavesdrop on them, too: book a tour boat with a hydrophone or just plunk your head underwater to hear the strange squeaks, groans, and chortles of the cetaceans.

Listen to Hawaiian music

Before his untimely death in 1997, Israel Kamakawiwoʻole or "IZ" woke the world to the sound of modern Hawaiian music. Don't leave without hearing it live. The Slack Key Guitar Festival (most likely at the Ritz-Carlton, Kapalua in 2009; check www.slackkeyfestival.com) features guest performers who play Hawaiʻi's signature style. The "Wailea Nights" show at Mulligan's might be the best—great dinner with unforgettable music by popular island entertainers.

Surfing on West Maui

The first thing your friends at home will ask is: did you learn to surf? Don't disappoint them. Feel the thrill of a wave rushing beneath your feet at any one of the beginner's breaks along Honoapiʻilani Highway. Ask local surf schools about the best locations for beginners. You can bring surf wax home as a souvenir.

Old Lahaina Lūʻau

The Old Lahaina Lūʻau has a warm heart—and seriously good *poke* (chopped, raw tuna tossed with herbs and other seasonings). Tuck a flower behind your ear, mix a dab of *poi* (paste made from pounded taro root) with your *lomilomi* salmon (rubbed with onions and herbs), and you'll be living like a local. Different styles of hula are part of the performance; the fire

TOP ATTRACTIONS

dancers may not be traditional, but they are fun. Reserve well in advance of your trip.

Tee off in paradise

Spectacular views, great weather year-round, and awesome, challenging courses created by the game's top designers make Maui an inspiring place to play golf. The Kapulua Resort on West Maui and the Wailea and Mākena resort courses on the South Shore, among others, offer memorable rounds. Check about twilight fees to save some money. A number of professional golf tournaments held on Maui are worth watching, too.

Tour Upcountry

Die-hard beach lovers might need some arm-twisting to head up the mountain for a day, but the 360-degree views are ample reward. On the roads winding through ranch-lands, crisp, high-altitude air is scented with eucalyptus and lavender. Stop for an agricultural tour and learn about where the island's bounty comes from.

'Ono kine grinds

"'Ono kine grinds" is local slang for delicious food you'll find at dozens of restaurants island-wide. Maui chefs take their work seriously, and they have good material to start with: sun-ripened produce and seafood caught the very same morning. Try a plate lunch, that reminder of the state's cultural mix,

at a casual spot. Sample as many types of fish as you can and don't be shy: try it raw.

Windsurfing at Kanaha or Hoʻokipa

You might not be a water-sports legend, but that doesn't mean you can't get out on the water and give it a try. In the early morning, some of windsurfing's big-wave spots are safe for beginners. Don't settle for the pond in front of your hotel—book a lesson on the North Shore and impress yourself by hanging tough where the action is.

WHEN TO GO

Long days of sunshine and mild year-round temperatures make Hawai'i, including Maui, an all-season destination. Most resort areas are at sea level, with average afternoon temperatures of 75°F to 80°F during the coldest months of December and January; during the hottest months of August and September the temperature often reaches 90°F. Higher "Upcountry" elevations have cooler and misty conditions. Only at mountain summits does it reach freezing.

Moist trade winds drop their precipitation on the north and east sides of all the islands, creating tropical climates, whereas the south and west sides remain hot and dry with desertlike conditions. Rainfall can be high in winter on those north and east shores.

Fewer bargains are available during Christmas and spring break, when room rates average 10% to 15% higher than the rest of the year.

Typically the weather on Maui is drier in summer (more guaranteed beach days) and rainier in winter (greener foliage, better waterfalls). Throughout the year, West Maui and the South Shore (the leeward areas) are the driest, sunniest areas on the island—that's why the resorts are in those areas. The North Shore and East Maui and Hāna (the windward areas) get the most rain, are densely forested, and abound with waterfalls.

Climate

The following are average maximum and minimum temperatures for Lahaina; the temperatures throughout the Hawaiian Islands are similar.

Only in Hawai'i Holidays

March 26 recognizes the birthday of Prince Jonah Kūhiō Kalaniana'ole, a member of the royal line who served as a delegate to Congress and spearheaded the effort to set aside homelands for Hawaiian people. June 11 honors the first island-wide monarch, Kamehameha I. Statehood Day is celebrated on the third Friday in August (Admission Day was August 21, 1959). Good Friday is a state holiday in spring, a favorite for picnics. Summertime is for Obon festivals and the July 4 Rodeo; the Maui County Fair and Aloha Festivals are in fall.

GREAT ITINERARIES

Maui's landscape is incredibly diverse, so while daydreaming at the pool or on the beach may fulfill your initial island fantasy, Maui has much more to offer. The following one-day itineraries will take you to our favorite spots on the island.

Beach Day in West Maui

West Maui has some of the island's most beautiful beaches, though many of them are hidden by megaresorts. If you get an early start, you can begin your day snorkeling at Slaughterhouse Beach (in winter, D. T. Fleming Beach is a better option as it's less rough). Then spend the day beach-hopping through Kapalua, Nāpili, and Kāʻanapali as you make your way south. You'll want to get to Lahaina before dark so you can spend some time exploring before choosing a restaurant for a sunset dinner.

Haleakalā National Park, Upcountry & the North Shore

Get up early and head straight for the summit of Haleakalā (if you're jet-lagged and waking up in the middle of the night, you may want to get there in time for sunrise). Bring water, sunscreen, and warm clothing; it's freezing at sunrise. Plan to spend a couple of hours exploring the various lookout points in the park. On your way down the mountain, turn right on Makawao Avenue, and head into the little town of Makawao. You can have lunch here, or make a left on Baldwin Avenue and head downhill to the North Shore town of Pāʻia, which has a number of great lunch spots and shops to explore. Spend the rest of your afternoon at Pāʻia's main strip of sand, Hoʻokipa Beach.

The Road to Hāna

This cliff-side driving tour through rain-forest canopy reveals Maui's most lush and tropical terrain. It will take a full day to explore this part of the North Shore and East Maui, especially if you plan to make it all the way to ʻOheo Gulch. You'll pass through communities where old Hawaiʻi still thrives, and where the forest runs unchecked from the sea to the summit. You'll want to make frequent exploratory stops. To really soak in the magic of this place, consider staying overnight in Hāna town. That way you can spend a full day winding toward Hāna, hiking and exploring along the way, and the next day traveling leisurely back to civilization.

For more details on any of the destinations mentioned in these itineraries, see chapter 2, Exploring Maui.

WEDDINGS & HONEYMOONS

There's no question that Hawai'i is one of the country's foremost honeymoon destinations. Romance is in the air here, and the white, sandy beaches and turquoise water and swaying palm trees and balmy tropical breezes and perpetual summer sunshine put people in the mood for love. A destination wedding is no longer exclusive to celebrities and the super rich. You can plan a traditional ceremony in a place of worship followed by a reception at an elegant resort, or you can go barefoot on the beach and celebrate at a lū'au. And there are almost as many wedding planners in the islands as real-estate agents.

The Big Day

Choosing the Perfect Place. When choosing a location, remember that you really have two choices to make: the ceremony location and where to have the reception, if you're having one. For the former, there are beaches, bluffs overlooking beaches, gardens, private residences, resort lawns, and, of course, places of worship. As for the reception, there are these same choices, as well as restaurants and even lū'au. If you decide to go outdoors, remember the seasons—yes, Hawai'i has seasons. If you're planning a winter wedding outdoors, be sure you have a backup plan (such as a tent), in case it rains. Also, if you're planning an outdoor wed-

ding at sunset—which is very popular—be sure you match the time of your ceremony to the time the sun sets at that time of year.

Finding a Wedding Planner. If you're planning to invite more than a minister and your loved one to your wedding ceremony, seriously consider an on-island wedding planner who can help select a location, help design the floral scheme and recommend a florist as well as a photographer, help plan the menu and choose a restaurant, caterer, or resort, and suggest any Hawaiian traditions to incorporate into your ceremony. And more: Will you need tents, a cake, music? Maybe transportation and lodging. Many planners have relationships with vendors, providing packages—which mean savings.

If you're planning a resort wedding, most have on-site wedding coordinators; however, there are many independents around the island and even those who specialize in certain types of ceremonies—by locale, size, religious affiliation, and so on. Ask for references—and call them. Share your budget. Get a proposal—in writing. Request a detailed list of the exact services they'll provide. If your idea of your wedding doesn't match their services, try someone else.

Getting Your License. No waiting period, no residency or citizen-

WEDDINGS & HONEYMOONS

ship requirements, and no blood tests or shots are required. However, both the bride and groom must appear together in person before an agent to apply for a marriage license. You'll need proof of age—the legal age to marry is 18. (If you're 19 or older, a valid driver's license will suffice; if you're 18, a certified birth certificate is required.) Upon approval, a marriage license is immediately issued and costs $60, cash only. After the ceremony, your officiant will mail the marriage license to the state. Approximately 120 days later, you will receive a copy in the mail. (For $10 extra, you can expedite this process.) For more detailed information, visit www. hawaii.gov or call 808/241–3498. Also—this is important—the person performing your wedding must be licensed by the Hawai'i Department of Health, even if he or she is a licensed minister.

Wedding Attire. In Hawai'i, basically anything goes, from long, formal dresses with trains to white bikinis. Floral sundresses are fine, too. For the men, tuxedos are not the norm; a pair of solid-color slacks with a nice aloha shirt is. In fact, tradition in Hawai'i for the groom is a plain white aloha shirt (they do exist) with slacks or long shorts and a colored sash around the waist. If you want formal dress and tuxedo, you should bring your formal attire with you.

Local Customs. When it comes to traditional Hawaiian wedding customs, the most obvious is the lei exchange in which the bride and groom take turns placing a lei around the neck of the other—with a kiss. Bridal lei are usually floral, whereas the groom's is typically made of maile, a green leafy garland that is open at the ends. Brides often also wear a haku lei—a circular floral headpiece. Other Hawaiian customs include the blowing of the conch shell, hula, chanting, and Hawaiian music.

The Honeymoon

Do you want champagne and strawberries delivered to your room each morning? A maze of a swimming pool in which to float? A five-star restaurant in which to dine? Then a resort is the way to go. If, however, you prefer the comforts of a home, try a bed-and-breakfast. A B&B is also good if you're on a tight budget or don't plan to spend much time in your room. On the other hand, maybe you want your own private home in which to romp naked—or maybe you want your own kitchen in which to whip up a gourmet meal for your loved one. In that case, a private vacation-rental home or condo is the answer.

KIDS & FAMILIES

Maui is a blast with kids. The entire family, parents included, will enjoy surfing, discovering a waterfall in the rain forest, and snorkeling with sea turtles. And there are organized activities for kids that will free parents' time for a few romantic beach strolls.

Choosing a Place to Stay

Resorts: All of the big resorts make kids' programs a priority, and it shows. When you are booking your room, ask about "kids eat free" deals and the number of kids' pools at the resort. Also check out the ages and size of the groups in the children's programs, and find out whether the cost of the programs includes lunch, equipment, and activities.

On the South Shore, the best bet for families is the Fairmont Kea Lani Hotel Suites & Villas where the accommodations are spacious suites. The Westin Maui is a good choice in the Kā'anapali Resort. Also in West Maui, Nāpili Kai Beach Resort sits on a crescent of white-sand beach that is perfect for boogie boarding and sunbathing.

Condos: Condo and vacation rentals are a fantastic value for families. You can cook your own food, which is cheaper than eating out, and you'll get twice the space of a hotel room for about a quarter of the price. If you decide to go the condo route, be sure to ask about the size of the complex's pool (some try to pawn off a tiny soaking tub as a pool) and whether barbecues are available.

On West Maui, all the ResortQuest Hawaii properties, such as those at the Papakea Resort, offer children's packages and have a keiki (child) activity program that ranges from sandcastle building to sightseeing excursions. On the South Shore, Kama'ole Sands is a family favorite, right across from three beach parks that are good for swimming and have grassy fields good for games and picnics.

Ocean Activities

On the Beach: Most people like being in the water, but toddlers and school-age kids tend to be enamored of it. The swimming pool at your condo or hotel is always an option, but don't be afraid to hit the beach with a little one in tow. Several beaches in Hawai'i are nearly as safe as a pool—completely protected bays with pleasant white-sand beaches.

The leeward side of Maui has many calm beaches to try; good ones include Wailea Beach in front of the Grand Wailea and Four Seasons resorts and Kama'ole beach parks on the South Shore. Nāpili Bay in West Maui is great for kids and boogie boarding. On the North Shore, at the Kahului end of Bald-

KIDS & FAMILIES

win Beach Park, check out the shallow pool known as Baby Beach.

On the Waves: Surf lessons are a great idea for older kids, especially if mom and dad want a little quiet time. Beginner lessons are always on safe and easy waves and last anywhere from two to four hours.

The gentle swells off West Maui are where the Nancy Emerson School of Surfing provides lessons designed for beginners. Big Kahuna Adventures will also show you how to ride the waves in the calm mornings off Kalama Beach Park in Kīhei on the South Shore.

The Underwater World: If your kids are ready to try snorkeling, Hawai'i is a great place to introduce them to the underwater world. Even without the mask and snorkel, they'll be able to see colorful fish, and they may also spot turtles and dolphins at many of the island beaches.

Get your kids used to the basics at Kā'anapali Beach in front of the Sheraton Maui on the island's West Side, where it's easy to get into the water and see the sea life right away. For guided snorkel tours that offer beginner instruction, try Trilogy Excursions, a family-oriented day trip from Lahaina to Lāna'i, or Maui Classic Charters out of Mā'alaea Harbor.

Land Activities

Central Maui abounds with activities for children, including the Alexander & Baldwin Sugar Museum with its interactive displays, and the hands-on Hawai'i Nature Center next to Kepaniwai Park & Heritage Gardens. If the weather's not great for seeing marine life in the ocean, see it at the excellent Maui Ocean Center in Mā'alaea on the South Shore, where all manner of live marine creatures including reef fish, sea turtles, manta rays, and sharks swim behind glass.

Children will enjoy the Hawaiian Islands Humpback Whale National Marine Sanctuary on the South Shore and the free museum at Whalers Village in Kā'anapali on West Maui.

For a moving experience, hop aboard the Sugar Cane Train that chugs between Lahaina and Kā'anapali and features a singing conductor.

After Dark

We think the best lū'au is the Old Lahaina Lū'au, which takes place nightly on the oceanfront at the north end of Lahaina. The show is traditional, lively, and colorful; it will keep the whole family entertained. Book in advance to avoid disappointment; this is extremely popular.

Exploring Maui

WORD OF MOUTH

"I'm from Maui, and I find endless beauty every time I visit Hāna. The drive is filled with gorgeous water-falls, pools, and flowers . . . a feast for the senses."

—pupuplatter

Updated
by Bonnie
Friedman

"MAUI NŌ KA 'OI" IS WHAT LOCALS SAY—it's the best, the most, the top of the heap. To those who know Maui well, there's good reason for the superlatives. The island's miles of perfect-tan beaches, lush green valleys, historic villages, top-notch windsurfing and diving, stellar restaurants and high-end hotels, and variety of art and cultural activities have made it an international favorite.

Maui is more than sandy beaches and palm trees: the natural bounty of this place is impressive. Pu'u Kukui, the 5,788-foot interior of the West Maui Mountains, is one of the earth's wettest spots—annual rainfall of 400 inches has sculpted the land into impassable gorges and razor-sharp ridges. On the opposite side of the island, the blistering lava fields at 'Ahihi-Kīna'u receive scant rain. Just above this desertlike landscape, *paniolo,* Hawaiian cowboys, herd cattle on rolling, fertile ranchlands reminiscent of northern California. On the island's rugged east side is the lush, tropical Hawai'i of travel posters.

Nature isn't all Maui has to offer—it's also home to a rich culture and stunning ethnic diversity. In small towns like Pā'ia and Hāna you can see remnants of the past mingling with modern-day life. Ancient *heiau* (Hawaiian stone platforms once used as places of worship) line busy roadways. Old coral and brick missionary homes now house broadcasting networks. The antique smokestacks of sugar mills tower above communities where the children blend English, Hawaiian, Japanese, Chinese, Portuguese, Filipino, and more into one colorful language. Hawai'i is a melting pot like no other. Visiting an eclectic mom-and-pop shop (like Makawao's Komoda Store & Bakery in Upcountry) can feel like stepping into another country, or back in time. The more you look here, the more you will find.

At 729 square mi, Maui is the second-largest Hawaiian island, but offers more miles of swimmable beaches than any of the other islands. Despite growth over the past few decades, the local population is still fairly small, totaling only 119,000.

GEOLOGY

Maui is made up of two volcanoes, one now extinct and the other dormant, which erupted long ago and joined into one island. The resulting depression between the two is what gives the island its nickname, the Valley Isle. West Maui's 5,788-foot Pu'u Kukui was the first volcano to form, a distinction that gives that area's mountainous topography a more weathered look. Rainbows seem to grow wild over this terrain as gentle mists fill the deeply eroded canyons. The Valley Isle's second volcano is the 10,023-foot Haleakalā, where desertlike terrain butts up against tropical forests.

FLORA & FAUNA

Haleakalā is one of few homes to the rare *'ahinahina* (silversword plant). The plant's brilliant silver leaves are stunning against the red lava rock that blankets the walls of Haleakalā's caldera—particularly during blooming season from July to September. A distant cousin of the sunflower, the silversword blooms just once before it dies—producing a single towering stalk awash in tiny fragrant blossoms. Also calling Haleakalā home are a few hundred *nēnē*—the Hawaiian state bird (related to the Canada goose), currently fighting its way back from near extinction. Maui is one of the better islands for whale-watching, and migrating humpbacks can be seen off the island's coast from December to April, and sometimes into May.

HISTORY

Maui's history is full of firsts—Lahaina was the first capital of Hawai'i and the first destination of the whaling industry (early 1800s), which explains why the town still has that fishing-village vibe. Lahaina was also the first stop for missionaries (1823). Although they suppressed aspects of Hawaiian culture, the missionaries did help invent the Hawaiian alphabet and built a printing press in Lahaina (the first west of the Rockies), which rolled out the news in Hawaiian. Maui also boasts the first sugar plantation in Hawai'i (1849) and the first Hawaiian luxury resort (Hotel Hāna-Maui, 1946).

ON MAUI TODAY

In the mid-1970s, savvy marketers saw a way to improve Maui's economy by promoting the Valley Isle to golfers and luxury travelers. The ploy worked all too well; Maui's visitor count continues to swell. Impatient traffic now threatens to overtake the ubiquitous aloha spirit, development encroaches on agricultural lands, and county planners struggle to meet the needs of a burgeoning population. But Maui is still carpeted with an eyeful of green, and for every tailgater, there's a carefree local on "Maui time" who stops for each pedestrian, whale spout, and sunset.

WEST MAUI

Separated from the remainder of the island by steep *pali* (cliffs), West Maui has a reputation for attitude and action. Once upon a time, this was the haunt of whalers, missionaries, and the kings and queens of Hawai'i. Today it's one of Maui's main resort areas. Crowds stroll bustling Front Street in Lahaina, beating the heat with ice cream or shave ice, while pleasure-seekers indulge in golf, shopping, and white-sand beaches in the Kā'anapali and Kapalua resort areas.

LAHAINA

Today Lahaina may best be described as either charming or tacky, depending on your point of view—and opinions do differ. Ethnic mom-and-pops have been supplanted by too many T-shirt shops, but there are some excellent restaurants and interesting galleries. At dusk, when the lights first come on, the town looks vaguely like a Disney theme park. Sunset cruises and other excursions depart from Lahaina Harbor. Happily, at the far south end of town an important ancient site—Moku'ula—is being restored. ■ TIP→ **If you arrange to spend a Friday afternoon exploring Front Street, you can dine in town and hang around for Art Night, when the galleries stay open into the evening and entertainment fills the streets.**

The town has been welcoming visitors for more than 200 years. In 1798, after waging war to unite the Hawaiian Islands, Kamehameha the Great chose Lahaina, then called *Lele,* as the seat of his monarchy. Warriors from Kamehameha's 800 canoes that were stretched along the coast from Olowalu to Honokōwai, turned inland and filled the lush valleys with networks of stream-fed *loi* or taro patches. For nearly 50 years, Lahaina remained the capital of the Hawaiian Kingdom. During this period, the scent of Hawaiian sandalwood brought Chinese traders to these waters. European whaling ships followed, chasing sperm whales from Japan to the Arctic. Lahaina became known around the world for its rough-and-tumble ways, typical of most ports of that time. Despite the efforts of several determined missionaries, smallpox and venereal disease took a terrible toll on the native population.

Then, almost as quickly as it had come, the tide of foreign trade receded. The Hawaiian capital was moved to Honolulu in 1845 and by 1860, the sandalwood forests were empty and sperm whales nearly extinct. Luckily, Lahaina

DID YOU KNOW?

A horseback ride on Sliding Sands Trail in Haleakalā National Park takes you down 2,500 feet to explore lava bombs, cinders, and other features of the stark landscape of the crater floor.

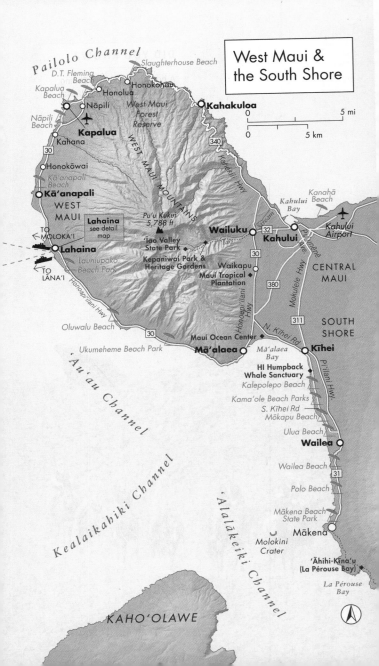

had already grown into an international, sophisticated (if sometimes rowdy) town, laying claim to the first printing press and high school west of the Rockies. Sugar interests kept the town afloat until tourism stepped in.

WALKING TOURS. Lahaina's side streets are best explored on foot. Both the Baldwin Home and the Lahaina Court House offer free self-guided walking tour brochures and maps. The Court House booklet is often recommended and includes more than 50 sites. The Baldwin Home brochure is less well-known but, in our opinion, easier to follow. It details a short but enjoyable loop tour of the town.

MAIN ATTRACTIONS

5 **Baldwin Home Museum.** Begun in 1834 and completed the ★ following year, the coral and stone house was originally home to missionary and doctor Dwight Baldwin and his family. The building has been carefully restored to reflect the period; many of the original furnishings remain. You can view the family's grand piano, the carved four-poster bed, and most interestingly, Dr. Baldwin's dispensary. During a brief tour conducted by Lahaina Restoration Foundation volunteers, you'll be shown the "thunderpot" and told how the doctor single-handedly inoculated 10,000 Maui residents for smallpox. ✉ *696 Front St., Lahaina* ☎ *808/661–3262* ⊕ *www.lahainarestoration.org* 💲 *$3* ⊘ *Daily 10–4.*

NEED A BREAK? The sandwiches have real Gruyère and Emmentaler cheese at **Maui Swiss Cafe** (✉ *640 Front St.*)—expensive ingredients with affordable results. The friendly owner scoops the best and cheapest locally made ice cream in Lahaina. Daily lunch specials are less than $6.

7 **Banyan Tree.** This massive tree was planted in 1873. It's the largest of its kind in the state and provides a welcome retreat for the weary who come to sit under its awesome branches. ■ TIP→The Banyan Tree is a popular and hard-to-miss meeting place if your party splits up for independent exploring. It's also a terrific spot to be when the sun sets—mynah birds settle in here for a screeching symphony, which can be an event in itself. ✉ *Front St., between Hotel and Canal Sts., Lahaina.*

8 **Hale Pa'ahao (Old Prison).** Lahaina's jailhouse dates to rowdy whaling days. Its name literally means "stuck-in-irons

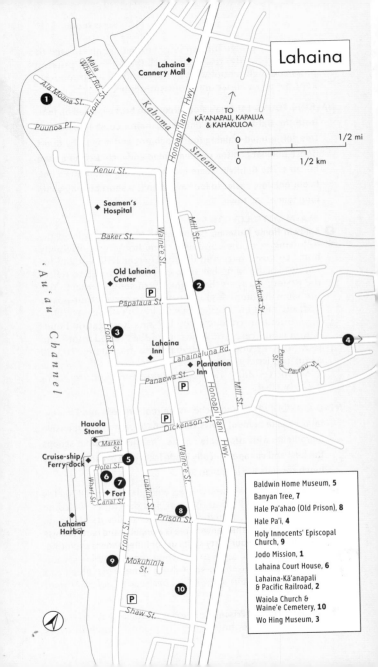

Lahaina

TO KĀ'ANAPALI, KAPALUA & KAHAKULOA

0   1/2 mi

0   1/2 km

1 Jodo Mission

Lahaina Cannery Mall

Mala Wharf Rd.

Ala Moana St.

Front St.

Puunoa Pl.

Kahoma Stream

Honoapi'ilani Hwy.

Kenui St.

Seamen's Hospital

Baker St.

Waine'e St.

Mill St.

Old Lahaina Center

P

Papalaua St.

2

Kukua St.

'Au'au Channel

3

Front St.

Lahaina Inn

Lahainaluna Rd.

Plantation Inn

Panaewa St.

P

Honoapi'ilani Hwy.

Mill St.

Pauoa St.

Paunau St.

4 →

P

Hauola Stone

Dickenson St.

Waine'e St.

Cruise-ship Ferry-dock

Market St.

Hotel St.

5

6 **7**

Fort

Wharf St.

Luakini St.

Canal St.

8

Prison St.

Lahaina Harbor

9

Mokuhinia St.

10

P

Shaw St.

Baldwin Home Museum, **5**

Banyan Tree, **7**

Hale Pa'ahao (Old Prison), **8**

Hale Pa'i, **4**

Holy Innocents' Episcopal Church, **9**

Jodo Mission, **1**

Lahaina Court House, **6**

Lahaina-Kā'anapali & Pacific Railroad, **2**

Waiola Church & Waine'e Cemetery, **10**

Wo Hing Museum, **3**

house," referring to the wall shackles and ball-and-chain restraints. The compound was built in the 1850s by convict laborers out of blocks of coral that had been salvaged from the demolished waterfront Fort. Most prisoners were sent here for desertion, drunkenness, or reckless horse riding. Today, a wax figure representing an imprisoned old sailor tells his recorded tale of woe. ⊠ *Waine'e and Prison Sts., Lahaina* ⊜*Free* ☉ *Weekdays 10–4.*

❾ Holy Innocents' Episcopal Church. Built in 1927, this beautiful open-air church is decorated with paintings depicting Hawaiian versions of Christian symbols, including a Hawaiian Madonna and child, rare or extinct birds, and native plants. The congregation is beautiful, typically dressed in traditional clothing from Samoa and Tonga. Anyone is welcome to slip into one of the pews, carved from native woods. Queen Liliu'okalani, Hawai'i's last reigning monarch, lived in a large grass house on this site as a child. ⊠*South end of Front St. near Mokuhina St., Lahaina.*

❻ Lahaina Court House. The Lahaina Town Action Committee and Lahaina Heritage Museum occupy this charming old government building in the center of town. Pump the knowledgeable staff for interesting trivia and ask for their walking-tour brochure, a comprehensive map to historic Lahaina sites. Erected in 1859 and restored in 1999, the building has served as a customs and court house, governor's office, post office, vault and collector's office, and police court. On August 12, 1898, its postmaster witnessed the lowering of the Hawaiian flag when Hawai'i became a U.S. territory. The flag now hangs above the stairway. You'll find terrific museum displays, the active Lahaina Arts Society, and an art gallery. ■TIP➜**There's also a public restroom.** ⊠*649 Wharf St., Lahaina* ☎*808/661–0111* ⊜*Free* ☉*Daily 9–5.*

★ Fodor'sChoice Waiola Church and Waine'e Cemetery. Better
❿ known as Waine'e Church and immortalized in James Michener's *Hawai'i*, the original building from the early 1800s was destroyed once by fire and twice by fierce windstorms. Repositioned and rebuilt in 1951, it was renamed Waiola ("water of life") and has been standing proudly every since. The adjacent cemetery was the first Christian cemetery in the Islands and is the final resting place of many of Hawai'i's most important monarchs, including Kamehameha the Great's sacred wife, Queen Keōpūolani. ⊠*535 Waine'e St., Lahaina* ☎*808/661–4349.*

Old Lahaina Lūʻau: "A beautiful picture while waiting for the best lūʻau in Hawaiʻi."
—Tammy Davis, Fodors.com photo contest participant.

❸ Wo Hing Museum. Smack-dab in the center of Front Street,
★ this eye-catching Chinese temple reflects the importance
of early Chinese immigrants to Lahaina. Built by the Wo
Hing Society in 1912, the museum now contains beautiful artifacts, historic photos of old Lahaina, and a Taoist
altar. Don't miss the films playing in the rustic theater next
door—some of Thomas Edison's first films, shot in Hawaiʻi
circa 1898, show Hawaiian wranglers herding steer onto
ships. Ask the docent for some star fruit from the tree outside, for the altar or for yourself. ⊠ *858 Front St., Lahaina*
☎ *808/661–5553* 💲 *$1* ⊙ *Daily 10–4.*

ALSO WORTH SEEING

❹ Hale Paʻi. Protestant missionaries established Lahainaluna
Seminary as a center of learning and enlightenment in 1831.
Six years later, they built this printing shop. Here at the
press, they and their young Hawaiian scholars created a
written Hawaiian language and used it to produce a Bible,
history texts, and a newspaper. An exhibit displays a replica of the original Rampage press and facsimiles of early
printing. The oldest U.S. educational institution west of the
Rockies, the seminary now serves as Lahaina's public high
school. ⊠ *980 Lahainaluna Rd., Lahaina* ☎ *808/661–3262*
💲 *Donations accepted* ⊙ *Weekdays 10–4.*

❶ Jodo Mission. This mission, established at the turn of the
century by Japanese contract workers, is one of Lahaina's
most popular sites, thanks to its idyllic setting and spec-

tacular views across the channel. Although the buildings are not open to the public, you can stroll all of the grounds and enjoy glimpses of the 90-foot-high pagoda, as well as a great, 3.5-ton copper and bronze statue of the Amida Buddha. It's a relaxing and contemplative spot just outside the tumult of Lahaina Town. If you're nearby at 8 any evening, listen for the temple bell to toll 11 times; each peal has a specific significance. ✉*12 Ala Moana St., just before Lahaina Cannery Mall, Lahaina* ☎*808/661–4304* ⊕*www. lahainajodomission.org* ✆*Free.*

❷ **Lahaina–Kā'anapali & Pacific Railroad.** Affectionately called the Sugarcane Train, this is Maui's only passenger train. It's an 1890s-vintage railway that once shuttled sugar but now moves sightseers between Kā'anapali and Lahaina. This quaint little attraction with its singing conductor is a big deal for Hawai'i but probably not much of a thrill for those more accustomed to trains (though children like it no matter where they grew up). A barbecue dinner with entertainment is offered on Thursday at 5 PM. ✉*1½ blocks north of Lahainaluna Rd. stoplight, at Hinau St., on Honoapi'ilani Hwy., Lahaina* ☎*808/667–6851 or 800/499–2307* ✆*Round-trip $20.95, dinner train $79* ☉*Daily 10:15–4.*

NORTH OF LAHAINA

As you drive north from Lahaina, the first resort community you come to is Kā'anapali, a cluster of high-rise hotels framing a beautiful white-sand beach. A little farther up the road lie the condo-filled beach towns of Honokōwai, Kahana, and Nāpili, followed by the stunning resort area, Kapalua. At the very end of the Honoapi'ilani Highway you'll find the remote village of Kahakuloa.

KĀ'ANAPALI

In ancient times, this area was known for its bountiful fishing (especially lobster) and its seaside cliffs. Pu'u Keka'a, today incorrectly referred to as "Black Rock," was a *lele*, a place in ancient Hawai'i from which souls leaped into the afterlife. But times changed and the sleepy fishing village was washed away by the wave of Hawai'i's new economy: tourism. Clever marketers built this sunny shoreline into a playground for the world's vacationers. The theatrical look of Hawai'i tourism—planned resort communities where luxury homes mix with high-rise hotels, fantasy swimming pools, and a theme-park landscape—all began right here in the 1960s. Three miles of uninterrupted white-sand beach and placid water form the front yard for this artificial utopia, with its 40 tennis courts and two championship golf courses. The six major hotels here are all worth visiting just for a look around, especially the Hyatt Regency Maui, which has a multimillion-dollar art collection and plenty of exotic birds in the lobby.

Whalers Village. While the kids hit Honolua Surf Company, mom can peruse Versace, Prada, Coach, and several fine jewelry stores at this casual, classy mall fronting Kāʻanapali Beach. Pizza and Häagen-Dazs ice cream are available in the center courtyard. At the beach entrance, you'll find a wonderful restaurant, Hula Grill. ✉2435 Kāʻanapali Pkwy. ☎808/661–4567 ⊕www.whalersvillage.com.

⟲ **Whalers Village Museum.** A giant bony whale greets shoppers to Whalers Village. The massive skeleton is the herald of the Whale Center of the Pacific museum on the second floor where you'll hear stories of the 19th-century *Moby-Dick* era. Baleen, ambergris, and other mysterious artifacts are on display. A short film features Hawaiian turtles and the folklore surrounding them. ✉2435 Kāʻanapali Pkwy., Suite H16 ☎808/661–5992 ☞Free ⊙Daily 9:30 AM–10 PM.

KAPALUA

Beautiful and secluded, Kapalua is West Maui's northernmost resort community. The area got its first big boost in 1978, when the Maui Land & Pineapple Company (ML&P) built the luxurious Kapalua Bay Hotel. ML&P owns the entire area known as "Kapalua Resort," which includes the Ritz-Carlton, three golf courses, and the surrounding fields of Maui Gold pineapple. The quaint Kapalua Bay Hotel has been replaced by extremely upscale residences with a spa and a golf club. The area's shopping and freestanding restaurants cater to dedicated golfers, celebrities who want to be left alone, and some of the world's richest folks. Mists regularly envelop Kapalua, which is cooler and quieter than its southern neighbors. The landscape of tall Cook pines and rolling fairways is reminiscent of Lānaʻi, and the beaches and dining are among Maui's finest.

CHEAP EATS. In contrast to Kapalua's high-end glitz, the old Honolua Store, just above the Ritz-Carlton, still plies the groceries, fish nets, and household wares it did in plantation times. Hefty plate lunches, served at the deli until 2:30 PM, are popular with locals, and very 'ono (delicious). ⊠ *504 Office Rd., Kapalua* ☎*808/669–6128* ⊙ *Daily 6 AM–8 PM.*

THE SOUTH SHORE

Blessed by more than its fair share of sun, the southern shore of Haleakalā was an undeveloped wilderness until the 1970s. Then the sun-worshippers found it; now restaurants, condos, and luxury resorts line the coast from the world-class aquarium at Māʻalaea Harbor, through working-class Kīhei, to lovely Wailea, a resort community rivaling those on West Maui. Farther south, the road disappears and unspoiled wilderness still has its way.

Because the South Shore includes so many fine beach choices, a trip here (if you're staying elsewhere on the island) is an all-day excursion—especially if you include a visit to the aquarium. Get active in the morning with exploring and snorkeling, then shower in a beach park, dress up a little, and enjoy the cool luxury of the Wailea resorts. At sunset, settle in for dinner at one of the area's many fine restaurants.

MĀʻALAEA

Māʻalaea, pronounced Mah-*ah*-lye-*ah,* is not much more than a few condos, an aquarium, and a wind-blasted harbor—but that's more than enough for some visitors. Humpback whales seem to think Māʻalaea is tops for meeting mates. Green sea turtles treat it like their own personal spa, regularly seeking appointments with cleaner wrasses in the harbor. Surfers revere this spot for "freight train," reportedly the world's fastest wave.

A small Shinto shrine stands at the shore here, dedicated to the fishing god Ebisu Sama. Across the street, a giant hook often swings heavy with the sea's bounty, proving the worth of the shrine. Down Hauʻoli Street (Hawaiian for *happy*) the Waterfront restaurant has benefited from its close proximity to the harbor. At the end of Hauʻoli Street (the town's single road), a small community garden is sometimes privy to traditional Hawaiian ceremonies. That's all; there's not much else. But the few residents here like it that way.

Māʻalaea Small Boat Harbor. With only 89 slips and so many good reasons to take people out on the water, this active

DID YOU KNOW?

Snorkel cruises are popular on Maui, but you can find great snorkeling on your own. Try the rocky borders of beaches on the South Shore in places such as Kīhei (shown here) or Wailea.

little harbor needs to be expanded. The Army Corps of Engineers has a plan to do so, but harbor users are fighting it—particularly the surfers, who say the plan would destroy their surf breaks. In fact, the surf here is world-renowned. The elusive spot to the left of the harbor called "freight train" rarely breaks, but when it does, it's said to be the fastest anywhere. ✉*Off Honoapiʻilani Hwy., Rte. 30.*

★ **Fodor's**Choice **Maui Ocean Center.** You'll feel as though you're walking from the seashore down to the bottom of the reef, and then through an acrylic tunnel in the middle of the sea at this aquarium, which focuses on Hawaiʻi and the Pacific. Special tanks get you up close with turtles, rays, sharks, and the unusual creatures of the tide pools. The center is part of a complex of retail shops and restaurants overlooking the harbor. ✉*Enter from Honoapiʻilani Hwy., Rte. 30, as it curves past Māʻalaea Harbor, Māʻalaea* ☎*808/270–7000* ⊕*www.mauioceancenter.com* ☜*$23* ☉*Daily 9–5.*

KĪHEI

Thirty years ago, Kīhei was a dusty, dry nondestination. Now about one-third of the Maui population lives here in one of the fastest-growing towns in America. Development is still under way: a greenway for bikers and pedestrians is under construction, as is a multitude of new homes and properties.

Traffic lights and minimalls may not fit your notion of paradise, but Kīhei offers dependably warm sun, excellent beaches, and a front-row seat to marine life of all sorts. The county beach parks such as Kamaʻole I, II, and III have lawns, showers, and picnic tables. ■TIP→**Remember: beach park or no beach park, the public has a right to the entire coastal strand but not to cross private property to get to it.** Besides all the sun and sand, the town's relatively inexpensive condos and excellent restaurants make this a home base for many Maui visitors.

★ **Hawaiian Island Humpback Whale National Marine Sanctuary.** The sanctuary itself includes virtually all the waters surrounding the archipelago; the Education Center is located beside a restored ancient Hawaiian fishpond, in prime humpback-viewing territory. Whether the whales are here or not, the center is a great stop for youngsters curious to know how things work underwater. Interactive displays and informative naturalists will explain it all. Throughout the year, the center hosts intriguing activities, ranging from moonlight tidal-pool explorations to "Two Ton Talks." ⊠726 S. Kīhei Rd., Kīhei ☎808/879–2818 or 800/831–4888 ⊕www.hawaiihumpbackwhale.noaa.gov ⊠Free ⊙Daily 10–3.

★ **Keālia Pond National Wildlife Reserve.** Long-legged stilts casu-
🕐 ally dip their beaks in the shallow waters of this Wildlife Reserve as traffic shuttles by. If you take time to read the interpretive signs on the new boardwalk, you'll learn that endangered hawksbill turtles return to the sandy dunes here year after year. Sharp-eyed birders may catch sight of occasional migratory visitors, such as a falcon or osprey. ⊠N. Kīhei Rd., Kīhei ⊠Free.

WAILEA & FARTHER SOUTH

Wailea, the South Shore's resort community, is slightly qui-eter and drier than its West Maui sister, Kā'anapali. Many visitors cannot pick a favorite, so they stay at both. The first two resorts were built here in the late 1970s. Soon a cluster of upscale properties sprung up, including the Four Seasons and the Fairmont Kea Lani. Check out the Grand Wailea Resort's chapel, which tells a Hawaiian love story in stained glass. The luxury of the resorts (edging on the excessive) and the simple grandeur of the coastal views make the otherwise stark landscape an outstanding desti-nation. A handful of perfect little beaches, all with public access, front the resorts.

★ **Coastal Nature Trail.** A paved beach walk allows you to stroll among Wailea's prettiest properties, restaurants, and rocky coves. The trail teems with joggers in the morning hours. The *makai,* or ocean, side is landscaped with exceptionally rare native plants. Look for the silvery *hinahina,* named after the Hawaiian moon goddess because of its color. In winter this is a great place to watch whales. ⊠Accessible from Polo or Wailea Beach parks.

The Shops at Wailea. Louis Vuitton, Tiffany & Co., and the sumptuous Cos Bar lure shoppers to this elegant mall. Honolulu Coffee brews perfect shots of espresso to fuel those "shop-'til-you-drop" types. The kids can buy logo shirts in Pacific Sun while mom and dad ponder vacation ownership upstairs. Tommy Bahama's, Ruth's Chris, and Longhi's are all good dining options. ⊠3750 Wailea Alanui Dr. ☎808/891–6770 ⊕www.shopsatwailea.com.

★ **Fodor'sChoice Mākena Beach State Park.** Although it's commonly known as "Big Beach," its correct name is Oneloa ("long sand"), and that's exactly what it is—a huge stretch of heavenly golden sand without a house or hotel in sight. More than a decade ago, Maui citizens campaigned successfully to preserve this beloved beach from development. It's still wild, lacking in modern amenities (such as plumbing) but frequented by dolphins and turtles; sunsets are glorious. At the end of the beach farthest from Wailea, skim-boarders catch air. On the opposite end rises the beautiful hill called Pu'u Ōla'i, a perfect cinder cone. A climb over the steep rocks at this end leads to "Little Beach," which, although technically it's illegal, is clothing-optional. On Sunday, it's a mecca for drummers and island gypsies. On any day of the week watch out for the mean shore break—those crisp, aquamarine waves are responsible for more than one broken arm.

'Ahihi-Kīna'u (La Pérouse Bay). Beyond Mākena Beach, the road fades away into a vast territory of black-lava flows, the result of Haleakalā's last eruption. Also known as La Pérouse Bay, this is where Maui received its first official visit by a European explorer—the French admiral Jean-François de Galaup, Comte de La Pérouse, in 1786. Before it ends, the road passes through the 'Ahihi-Kīna'u Marine Preserve, an excellent place for morning snorkel adventures *(see chapter 4, Water Sports & Tours)*. This is also the start of the Hoapili Trail, or "the King's Trail," where you can hike through the remains of one of Maui's ancient villages. ■TIP➔**Bring water and a hat, as there is little shade and no public facilities, and tread carefully over this culturally important landscape.**

CENTRAL MAUI

Kahului, where you most likely landed when you arrived on Maui, is the industrial and commercial center of the island. The area was developed in the early 1950s to meet the housing needs of the large sugarcane interests here, specifically those of Alexander & Baldwin. The company was tired of playing landlord to its many plantation workers and sold land to a developer who promised to create affordable housing. The scheme worked, and "Dream City," the first planned city in Hawai'i, was born.

West of Kahului is Wailuku. The county seat since 1950, it is the most charming town in Central Maui—though it

wasn't always so. Its name means "Water of Destruction," after the fateful battle in 'Iao Valley that pitted King Kamehameha the Great against Maui warriors. Wailuku was a politically important town until the sugar industry began to decline in the 1960s and tourism took hold. Businesses left the cradle of the West Maui Mountains and followed the new market to the shore, where tourists arrived by the boatload. Wailuku still houses the county government, but has the feel of a town that's been asleep for several decades. The shops and offices now inhabiting Main Street's plantation-style buildings serve as reminders of a bygone era, and continued attempts at "gentrification," at the very least, open the way for unique eateries, shops, and galleries.

You can explore Central Maui comfortably in little more than a half day. These are good sights to squeeze in on the way to the airport, or if you want to combine sightseeing with shopping. Hikers may want to expand their outing to a full day to explore 'Iao Valley State Park.

KAHULUI & WAILUKU

MAIN ATTRACTIONS

★ Fodor'sChoice **Bailey House.** This repository of the largest and
❸ best collection of Hawaiian artifacts on Maui—including objects from the sacred island of Kaho'olawe—was first the Wailuku Seminary for Girls and then the home of missionary teachers Edward and Caroline Bailey. Built in 1833 on the site of the compound of Kahekili (the last ruling chief of Maui), the building was occupied by the Bailey family until 1888. Edward Bailey was something of a renaissance man: beyond being a missionary, he was also a surveyor, a naturalist, and an excellent artist. In addition to the fantastic Hawaiian collection, the museum displays a number of Bailey's landscape paintings, which provide a snapshot of the island during his time. There is missionary-period furniture, and the grounds include gardens with native Hawaiian plants and a fine example of a traditional canoe. The gift shop is one of the best sources on Maui for items that are actually made in Hawai'i. ⊠2375A Main St., Wailuku ☎808/244–3326 ⊕www.mauimuseum.org ⊠$5 ⊗Mon.–Sat. 10–4.

★ Fodor'sChoice **'Iao Valley State Park.** When Mark Twain saw
❷ this park, he dubbed it the Yosemite of the Pacific. Yosemite it's not, but it is a lovely deep valley with the curious 'Iao Needle, a spire that rises more than 2,000 feet from the

valley floor. You can take one of several easy hikes from the parking lot across ʻĪao Stream and explore the thick, junglelike topography. This park has a beautiful network of well-maintained walks, where you can stop and meditate by the edge of a stream or marvel at the native plants and flowers *(see chapter 5, Golf, Hiking & Outdoor Activities)*. Locals come to jump from the rocks or bridge into the stream—this isn't recommended. Mist often rises if there has been a rain, which makes being here even more magical. ✉*Western end of Rte. 32* 🎟*Free* ⊙*Daily 7–7.*

❶ Kepaniwai Park & Heritage Gardens. This county park is a memorial to Maui's cultural roots, with picnic facilities and ethnic displays dotting the landscape. Among the displays are an early-Hawaiian hale (meetinghouse), a New England–style saltbox, a Portuguese-style villa with gardens, and dwellings from such other cultures as China and the Philippines. Next door, the Hawaiʻi Nature Center has excellent interactive exhibits and hikes easy enough for children.

The peacefulness here belies the history of the area. During his quest for domination, King Kamehameha the Great brought his troops from the Big Island of Hawaiʻi to the Valley Isle in 1790 and waged a successful and particularly bloody battle against the son of Maui's chief, Kahekili, near Kepaniwai Park. An earlier battle at the site had pitted Kahekili himself against an older Big Island chief, Kalaniʻōpuʻu. Kahekili prevailed, but the carnage was so great that the nearby stream became known as Wailuku (water of destruction) and the place where fallen warriors choked the stream's flow was called Kepaniwai (the water dam). ✉*ʻĪao Valley Rd., Wailuku* 🎟*Free* ⊙*Daily 7–7.*

❹ Market Street. An idiosyncratic assortment of shops makes Wailuku's Market Street (affectionately known as "Antiques Row") a delightful place for a stroll. Brown-Kobayashi and the Bird of Paradise Unique Antiques are the best for carrying interesting collectibles and furnishings; Sig Zane is arguably Hawaiʻi's best fabric/clothing designer. Cafe Marc Aurel started out as a great espresso spot and has expanded to become a popular gathering place serving food and offering an extraordinary wine list. ✉*Wailuku.*

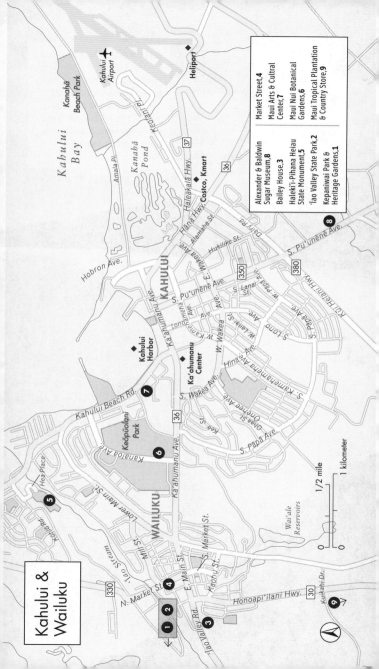

Kahului & Wailuku

Kahului Bay

Kanahā Beach Park

Kanahā Pond

Kahului Airport

Heliport

Amala Pl.

Keolani Pl.

37

36

Haleakalā Hwy.

Costco, Kmart

Hobron Ave.

Dairy Rd.

Hukilike St.

Alamaha St.

Wakea Ave. E.

Hāna Hwy.

KAHULUI

Ka'ahumanu Ave.

S. Pu'unene Ave.

8

350

380

S. Lanai St.

W. Papa Ave.

S. Papa Ave.

Kūihelani Hwy.

Lonohāna Ave.

Kamehameha Ave.

Onomea Ave.

S. Lono Ave.

Kahului Harbor

Ka'ahumanu Center

7

Kahului Beach Rd.

Keōpū'olani Park

6

Kanaloa Ave.

36

S. Wakea Ave.

W. Wakea Ave.

Kea St.

Onehee Ave.

Hina Ave.

S. Kane St.

W. Lani St.

S. Kamehameha Ave.

Ōna St.

S. Papa Ave.

Hea Place

5

Iao Valley Rd.

Lower Main St.

WAILUKU

Mill St.

S. Market St.

Market St.

330

N. Market St.

E. Main St.

Kaohu St.

1 2

4

3

Honoapiʻilani Hwy.

30

Kūihelani Dr.

9

Waiʻale Reservoirs

1/2 mile

1 kilometer

Alexander & Baldwin	Market Street, 4
Sugar Museum, 8	Maui Arts & Cultral
Bailey House, 3	Center, 7
Halekiʻi-Pihana Heiau	Maui Nui Botanical
State Monument, 5	Gardens, 6
ʻIao Valley State Park, 2	Maui Tropical Plantation
Kepaniwai Park &	& Country Store, 9
Heritage Gardens, 1	

DID YOU KNOW?

Maui's South Shore beaches, generally white and sandy, get better as you go south. Wailea's beaches have great views. For wilder landscapes, keep heading south to Mākena.

MAUI SIGHTSEEING TOURS

Maui is really too big to see all in one day, so tour companies offer specialized tours, visiting either Haleakalā or Hāna and its environs. A half-day excursion typically starts at $60 and can go up to as much as $120 depending on the size of the group and length of the tour. Haleakalā sunrise tours may pick you up as early as 2:30 AM.

When booking a tour, remember that some tour companies use air-conditioned buses, whereas others prefer small vans. The key is to ask how many stops you get and how many other passengers will be on board—otherwise you could end up on a packed bus, sightseeing through a window. Guides expect a tip ($1 per person at least), but they're just as cordial without one.

Maui Pineapple Plantation Tour. Explore one of Maui's pineapple plantations on this tour that takes you right into the fields in a company van. The 2¼-hour, $39.95 trip gives you first-hand experience of the operation and its history, some incredible views of the island, and the chance to pick a fresh pineapple for yourself. Tours depart weekday mornings and afternoons from the Kapalua Logo Shop. Reservations are required. ⌧*Maui Gold, Kapalua* ☏808/665–5491.

Polynesian Adventure Tours. This company uses large buses with floor-to-ceiling windows. The drivers are fun and really know the island. ☏808/877–4242 or 800/622–3011 ⊕www.polyad.com.

Roberts Hawai'i Tours. This is one of the state's largest tour companies, and its staff can arrange tours with bilingual guides if asked ahead of time. Eleven-hour trips venture out to Kaupo, the wild area past Hāna. ☏808/871–6226 or 866/898–2519 ⊕ www.robertshawaii.com.

Temptation Tours. Temptation Tours has targeted members of the affluent older crowd (though almost anyone would enjoy these tours) who don't want to be herded onto a crowded bus. Tours in plush six-passenger limo-vans explore Haleakalā and Hāna, and range from $110 to $249 per person. The "Hāna Sky-Trek" includes a return trip via helicopter—perfect for those leery of spending the entire day in a van. ☏808/877–8888 or 800/817–1234 ⊕www.temptationtours.com.

ALSO WORTH SEEING

❽ Alexander & Baldwin Sugar Museum. ★ "A&B," Maui's largest landowner, was one of the "Big Five" companies that spearheaded the planting, harvesting, and processing of sugarcane. Although Hawaiian cane sugar is now being supplanted by cheaper foreign versions—as well as by sugar derived from inexpensive sugar beets—the crop was for many years the mainstay of the Hawaiian economy. You can find the museum in a small, restored plantation manager's house next to the post office and the still-operating sugar refinery (black smoke billows up when cane is burning). Historic photos, artifacts, and documents explain the introduction of sugarcane to Hawai'i and how plantation managers brought in laborers from other countries, thereby changing the Islands' ethnic mix. Exhibits also describe the sugar-making process. ✉ *3957 Hansen Rd., Pu'unēnē* ☎ *808/871–8058* ⊕ *www.sugarmuseum.com* ☜ *$5* ⊙ *Mon.–Sat. 9:30–4:30; last admission at 4.*

❺ Haleki'i-Pihana Heiau State Monument. Stand here at either of the two *heiau* (ancient Hawaiian stone platforms once used as places of worship) and imagine the king of Maui surveying his domain. That's what Kahekili, Maui's last fierce king, did, and so did Kamehameha the Great after he defeated Kahekili's soldiers. Today the view is most instructive. Below, the once-powerful 'Iao Stream has been sucked dry and boxed in by concrete. Before you is the urban heart of the island. The suburban community behind you is all Hawaiian Homelands—property owned solely by native Hawaiians. ✉ *End of Hea Pl., off Kuhio Pl. from Waiehu Beach Rd., Rte. 340, Kahului* ☜ *Free* ⊙ *Daily 7–7.*

❼ Maui Arts & Cultural Center. An epic fund drive by the citizens of Maui led to the creation of this $32 million facility. The top-of-the-line Castle Theater seats 1,200 people on orchestra, mezzanine, and balcony levels; rock stars play the A&B Amphitheater. The MACC (as it's called) also includes a small black-box theater, an art gallery with interesting exhibits, and classrooms. The building itself is worth a visit: it incorporates work by Maui artists, and its signature lava-rock wall pays tribute to the skills of the Hawaiians. But the real draw is the Schaeffer International Gallery, which houses superb rotating exhibits. ✉ *Above harbor on Kahului Beach Rd.* ☎ *808/242–2787, 808/242–7469 box office* ⊕ *www.mauiarts.org* ⊙ *Weekdays 9–5.*

❻ Maui Nui Botanical Gardens. The fascinating plants grown on these 7 acres are representative of precontact Hawai'i. Both native and Polynesian-introduced species are cultivated—including ice-cream bananas, varieties of sweet potatoes and sugarcane, native poppies, hibiscus, and *anapanapa,* a plant that makes a natural shampoo when rubbed between your hands. Ethnobotany tours and presentations are offered on occasion. ⊠*150 Kanaloa Ave.* ☎*808/249–2798* ⊑*Free* ⊕*www.mnbg.org* ⊙*Mon.–Sat. 8–4.*

❾ **Maui Tropical Plantation & Country Store.** When Maui's once-
ℭ paramount crop declined in importance, a group of vision-aries decided to open an agricultural theme park on the site of this former sugarcane field. The 60-acre preserve, on Route 30 just outside Wailuku, offers a 30-minute tram ride through its fields with an informative narration covering growing processes and plant types. Children will probably enjoy the historical-characters exhibit as well as fruit-tast-ing, coconut-husking, and lei-making demonstrations, not to mention some entertaining spider monkeys. There's a restaurant on the property, and a "country store" special-izes in "Made in Maui" products. ⊠*Honoapi'ilani Hwy., Rte. 30, Waikapu* ☎*808/244–7643* ⊑*Free; tram ride with narrated tour $9.50* ⊙*Daily 9–5.*

UPCOUNTRY MAUI

The west-facing upper slopes of Haleakalā are locally called "Upcountry." This region is responsible for much of Hawai'i's produce—lettuce, tomatoes, strawberries, sweet Maui onions, and much, much more. You'll notice cactus thickets mingled with purple jacaranda, wild hibis-cus, and towering eucalyptus trees. Keep an eye out for *pueo,* Hawai'i's native owl, which hunts these fields dur-ing daylight hours.

Upcountry is also fertile ranch land; cowboys still work the fields of the historic 20,000-acre 'Ulupalakua Ranch and the 32,000-acre Haleakalā Ranch. ■TIP→**This is a great area in which to take an agricultural tour and learn more about the island's bounty. Lavender, vegetables, cheese, and wine are among your choices.**

A drive to Upcountry Maui from Wailea (South Shore) or Kā'anapali (West Maui) can be an all-day outing if you take the time to visit Tedeschi Vineyards and the tiny town of Makawao. You may want to cut these side trips short and combine your Upcountry tour with a visit to Haleakalā National Park *(see Haleakalā National Park feature in this chapter).* It's a Maui must-see. If you leave early enough to catch the sunrise from the summit of Haleakalā, you'll have plenty of time to explore the mountain, have lunch in Kula or at 'Ulupalakua Ranch, and end your day with dinner in Makawao.

THE KULA HIGHWAY

Kula . . . most Mauians say it with a hint of a sigh. Why? It's just that much closer to heaven. On the broad shoulder of Haleakalā, this is blessed country. From the Kula Highway most of Central Maui is visible—from the lava-scarred plains of Kenaio to the cruise-ship-lit waters of Kahului Harbor. Beyond the central valley's sugarcane fields, the plunging profile of the West Maui Mountains can be seen in its entirety, wreathed in ethereal mist. If this sounds too prosaic a description, you haven't been here yet. These views, coveted by many, continue to drive real-estate prices further skyward. Luckily, you can still have them for free—just pull over on the roadside and drink them in.

★ **Ali'i Kula Lavender.** Reserve a spot for tea or lunch at this lavender farm with a falcon's view. It's *the* relaxing remedy for those suffering from too much sun, shopping, or golf. Owners Ali'i and Lani lead tours through winding paths of therapeutic lavender varieties, proteas, succulents, and rare Maui wormwood. Their logo, a larger-than-life dragonfly, darts above chefs who are cooking up lavender-infused shrimp appetizers out on the lānai. The gift shop abounds with the farm's own innovative lavender products. ✉*1100 Waipoli Rd., Kula* ☎*808/878–3004* ⊕*www.mauikulalavender.com* ✆*$10 walking tours, $35 tea tours, $70 lunch and wreath-making* ⚗*Reservations essential* ☉*Daily 10–4, walking tours at noon and 2:30.*

Kēōkea. More of a friendly gesture than a town, this tiny outpost is the last bit of civilization before Kula Highway becomes the winding backside road, heading east around to Hāna. A coffee tree pushes through the sunny deck at Grandma's Coffee Shop, the morning watering hole for Maui's cowboys who work at 'Ulupalakua or Kaupō ranch. Kēōkea Gallery next door sells some of the most original artwork on the island. ■**TIP→The only restroom for miles is across the street at the public park, and the view makes stretching your legs worth it.**

☪ **Surfing Goat Dairy.** It takes goats to make goat cheese and they've got plenty of both at this 42-acre farm. Tours range from "casual" to "grand" and particularly delight children. If you have the time, both the two-hour grand tour (twice a

2

month) and the "Evening Chores & Milking Tour" are educational and fun. The owners make more than two dozen kinds of goat cheese, from the plain, creamy "Udderly Delicious" to more exotic cheeses that include other, sometimes tropical, ingredients. All varieties are available for purchase in the dairy store, along with gift baskets and even goat milk soaps. ⊠*3651 Ōmaʻopio Rd., Kula* ☎*808/878–2870* ⊕*www.surfinggoatdairy.com* ⊴*$5–$25* ⊙*Mon.–Sat. 10–5, Sun. 10–2; check ahead for tour schedule*

Tedeschi Vineyards and Winery. You can tour the winery and its historic grounds, the former Rose Ranch, and sample the island's only wines: a pleasant Maui Blush, Maui Champagne, and Tedeschi's annual Maui Nouveau. The top-seller, naturally, is the pineapple wine. The tasting room is a cottage built in the late 1800s for the frequent visits of King Kalākaua. The cottage also contains the '**Ulupalakua Ranch History Room,** which tells colorful stories of the ranch's owners, the *paniolo* (Hawaiian cowboy) tradition that developed here, and Maui's polo teams. The old General Store may look like a museum, but in fact it's an excellent pit stop. ⊠*Kula Hwy., ʻUlupalakua Ranch* ☎*808/878–6058* ⊕*www.mauiwine.com* ⊴*Free* ⊙*Daily 9–5, tours at 10:30 and 1:30.*

MAKAWAO

This once-tiny town, at the intersection of Baldwin and Makawao avenues, has managed to hang on to its country charm (and eccentricity) as it has grown in popularity. The district was originally settled by Portuguese and Japanese immigrants who came to Maui to work the sugar plantations and then moved Upcountry to establish small farms, ranches, and stores. Descendants now work the neighboring Haleakalā and ʻUlupalakua ranches. Every July 4 the *paniolo* (Hawaiian cowboy) set comes out in force for the Makawao Rodeo. The crossroads of town—lined with chic shops and down-home eateries—reflects a growing population of people who came here just because they liked it. For those seeking lush greenery rather than beachside accommodations, there are great, secluded little bed-and-breakfasts in and around the town.

Hui Noʻeau Visual Arts Center. The main house of this nonprofit cultural center on the old Baldwin estate, just outside the town of Makawao, is an elegant two-story Mediterranean-style villa designed in the 1920s by the defining Hawaiʻi architect C. W. Dickey. "The Hui" is the grande dame of Maui's well-known arts scene. The exhibits are always satisfying, and the grounds might as well be a botanical garden. The Hui also offers classes and maintains artists' studios. ⊠*2841 Baldwin Ave., Makawao* ☎*808/572–6560* ⊠*Free* ⊙*Daily 10–4.*

NEED A BREAK? One of Makawao's most famous landmarks is Komoda Store & Bakery (⊠*3674 Baldwin Ave.* ☎*808/572–7261*), a classic mom-and-pop store that has changed little in three-quarters of a century, where you can get a delicious cream puff if you arrive early enough. They make hundreds but sell out each day.

HALEAKALĀ NATIONAL PARK

★ **Fodor's**Choice Haleakalā Crater is the centerpiece of this 27,284-acre national park, established in 1916. The crater is actually an erosional valley, flushed out by water pouring from the summit through two enormous gaps. The small hills within the crater are volcanic cinder cones (called *pu'u* in Hawaiian), each with a small crater at its top, and each the site of a former eruption. The mountain has terrific camping and hiking, including a trail that loops through the crater.

Before you head up Haleakalā, call for the latest **park weather conditions.** Extreme gusty winds, heavy rain, and even snow in winter are not uncommon. Because of the high altitude, the mountaintop temperature is often as much as 30 degrees cooler than that at sea level. Be sure to bring a jacket.

You can learn something of the volcano's origins and eruption history at the **Park Headquarters/Visitor Center,** at a 7,000-foot elevation on Haleakalā Highway. Hikers and campers should check-in here before heading up the mountain. Maps, posters, and other memorabilia are available at the gift shop.

Leleiwi Overlook, at about an 8,800-foot elevation on Haleakalā, is one of several lookout areas in the park. A short walk to the end of the parking lot reveals your first awe-inspiring view of the crater. The small hills in the basin are volcanic cinder cones (called *pu'u* in Hawaiian), each with a small crater at its top, and each the site of a former eruption. If you're here in the late afternoon, it's possible

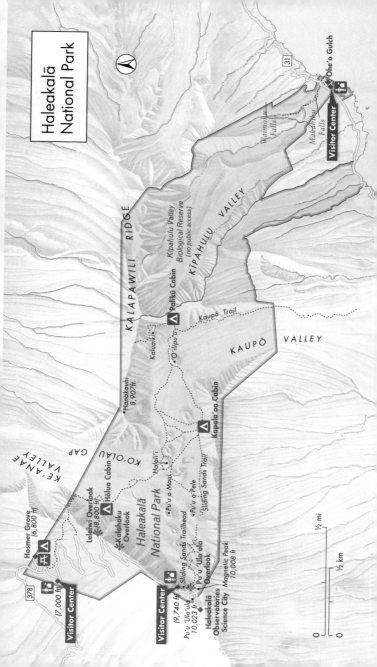

Haleakalā National Park

Haleakalā at sunrise: "All of us were freezing, but in such breathless awe...."
—Homie Holly, Fodors.com photo contest participant.

you'll experience a phenomenon called the Brocken Specter. Named after a similar occurrence in East Germany's
Harz Mountains, the "specter" allows you to see yourself
reflected on the clouds and encircled by a rainbow. Don't
wait all day for this, because it's not a daily occurrence.

The famous silversword plant grows amid the desert like
surroundings at **Kalahaku Overlook,** at the 9,000-foot
level on Haleakalā. This odd, endangered beauty grows
only here at this summit of this mountain, and at the same
elevation on the Big Island's two peaks. It begins life as a
silver, spiny-leaf rosette and is the sole home of a variety
of native insects (it's the only shelter around). The silversword reaches maturity between 7 and 17 years, when it
sends forth a 3- to 8-foot-tall stalk with several hundred
tiny sunflowers. It blooms once, then dies.

The **Haleakalā Visitor Center,** at an elevation of 9,740 feet,
has exhibits inside, and a trail from here leads to White
Hill—a short, easy walk that will give you an even better
view of the valley. Hosmer Grove, just off the highway
before you get to the visitor center, has campsites and interpretive trails. Park rangers maintain a changing schedule of
talks and hikes both here and at the top of the mountain,
including an hour-long loop trail into the Waikamoi Cloud
Forest that will give you insight into Hawai'i's fragile ecol-
ogy. Call the park for current schedules.

Just before the summit, the **Crater Observatory** offers warmth and shelter, informative displays, and an eye-popping view of the cinder-cone-studded, 7-mi-by-3-mi crater. The highest point on Maui is the **Puʻu ʻUlaʻula Overlook,** at the 10,023-foot summit. Here you'll find a glass-enclosed lookout with a 360-degree view. The building is open 24 hours a day, and this is where visitors gather for the best sunrise view. Dawn begins between 5:45 and 7, depending on the time of year. On a clear day you can see the islands of Molokaʻi, Lānaʻi, Kahoʻolawe, and Hawaiʻi (the Big Island). On a *really* clear day you can even spot Oʻahu glimmering in the distance.

The air is very thin at 10,000 feet. Don't be surprised if you feel a little breathless while walking around the summit. Take it easy and drink lots of water. Anyone who has been scuba diving within the last 24 hours should not make the trip up Haleakalā.

On a small hill nearby, you'll see **Science City,** an off-limits research and communications center straight out of an espionage thriller. The University of Hawaiʻi maintains an observatory here, and the Department of Defense tracks satellites. ⊠*Haleakalā Crater Rd. (Rte. 378), Makawao* ☎*808/572–4400, 808/877–5111 for weather conditions* ⊕*www.nps.gov/hale* ☜*$10 per car, good for three days* ☉*Park Headquarters/Visitor Center daily 8–4, Haleakalā Visitor Center daily sunrise–3:30.*

THE NORTH SHORE

Blasted by winter swells and wind, Maui's North Shore draws water-sports thrill-seekers from around the world. But there's much more to this area of Maui than coastline. Inland, a lush, waterfall-fed garden of Eden beckons. In forested pockets, wealthy hermits have carved out a little piece of paradise for themselves.

North Shore action centers around the colorful town of Pāʻia and the windsurfing mecca, Hoʻokipa Beach. It's a far cry from the more developed resort areas of West Maui and the South Shore. Pāʻia is also a starting point for the one of the most popular excursions in Maui, the Road to Hāna (*see Road to Hāna feature in this chapter*). Waterfalls, phenomenal views of the coast and ocean, and lush rain forest are all part of the spectacular 55-mi drive into East Maui.

PĀ'IA

★ This little town on Maui's north shore (at the intersection of Hāna Highway [Highway 36] and Baldwin Avenue) was once a sugarcane enclave, with a mill, plantation camps, and shops. The town boomed during World War II when the marines set up camp in nearby Ha'ikū. The old HC&S sugar mill finally closed and no sign of the military remains, but the town continues to thrive. In the 1970s, Pā'ia became a hippie town as dropouts headed for Maui to open boutiques, galleries, and unusual eateries. In the 1980s windsurfers—many of them European—discovered nearby Ho'okipa Beach and brought an international flavor to Pā'ia.

At the intersection of Hāna Highway and Baldwin Avenue, eclectic boutiques supply everything from high fashion to hemp-oil candles. Some of Maui's best shops for surf trunks, Brazilian bikinis, and other beachwear are here. The restaurants provide excellent people-watching and an array of dining options. A French-Caribbean bistro with a sushi bar in back, a French-Indian creperie, a neo-Mexican gourmet restaurant, and a fish market all compete for your patronage. This abundance is helpful because Pā'ia is the last place to snack before the pilgrimage to Hāna and the first stop for the famished on the return trip.

★ FodorśChoice **Ho'okipa Beach.** There's no better place on this or any other island to watch the world's finest windsurfers in action. The surfers know the five different surf breaks here by name. Unless it's a rare day without wind or waves, you're sure to get a show. ■TIP→**It's not safe to park on the shoulder. Use the ample parking lot at the county park entrance.** ✉ *2 mi past Pā'ia on Rte. 36.*

NEED A BREAK? **Anthony's Coffee** (✉ *90 Hāna Hwy.* ☎ *808/579-8340*) roasts its own beans, sells Maui's own Roselani ice cream and picnic lunches, and is a great place to eavesdrop on the windsurfing crowd. **Mana Foods** (✉ *49 Baldwin Ave.* ☎ *808/579-8078*), the North Shore's natural-foods store, has an inspired deli with wholesome hot and cold items.

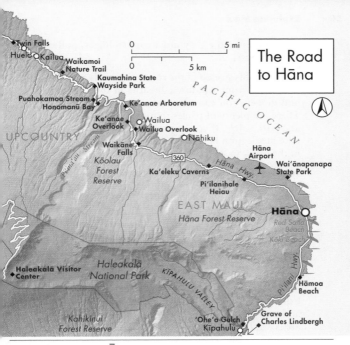

The Road
to Hāna

Twin Falls
Huelo • Kaïlua
Waikamoi
Nature Trail
Kaumahina State
Wayside Park
Puahokamoa Stream • Ke'anae Arboretum
Honomanū Bay
Ke'anae • Wailua
Overlook • Wailua Overlook
Nāhiku
Waikāne
Falls
Kōolau
Forest
Reserve
Ka'eleku Caverns
Pi'ilanihale
Heiau
Hāna
Airport
Wai'ānapanapa
State Park
EAST MAUI
Hāna Forest Reserve
Hāna
Red Sand
Beach
Kōki Beach
Haleakalā Visitor
Center
Haleakalā
National Park
KIPAHULU VALLEY
Kahikinui
Forest Reserve
'Ohe'o Gulch
Kipahulu
Grave of
Charles Lindbergh
Hāmoa
Beach
PACIFIC OCEAN
UPCOUNTRY
360
Hāna Hwy
Pi'ilani Hwy
0   5 mi
0   5 km

THE ROAD TO HĀNA

★ **Fodor's Choice** As you round the impossibly tight turn, a one-lane bridge comes into view. Beneath its worn surface, a lush forested gulch plummets towards the coast. The sound of rushing water fills the air, compelling you to search the overgrown hillside for waterfalls. This is the Road to Hāna, a 55-mi journey into the unspoiled heart of Maui. Tracing a centuries-old path, the road begins as a well-paved highway in Kahului and ends in the tiny town of Hāna on the island's rain-gouged windward side.

Begin your journey in Pā'ia, the little town on Maui's North Shore. Be sure to fill up your gas tank here. There are no gas stations along Hāna Highway, and the station in Hāna closes by 6 PM. You should also pick up a picnic lunch. Lunch and snack choices along the way are limited to rustic fruit stands.

About 10 mi pas Pā'ia, at the bottom of Kaupakalua Road, the roadside mileposts begin measuring the 36 mi to Hāna town. The road's trademark noodling starts about 3 mi after that. Once the road gets twisty, remember that many residents make this trip frequently. They've seen this so many times before they don't care to linger; pull over to let them pass.

All along this stretch of the road, waterfalls are abundant. Roll down your windows. Breathe in the scent of guava and ginger. You can almost hear the bamboo growing. There are plenty of places to pull completely off the road and park safely. If you're prone to carsickness, be sure to take medication before this drive. Sights are listed in here in the order in which you will pass them.

Twin Falls. Keep an eye out for the fruit stand just after mile marker 2. Stop here and treat yourself to some fresh sugarcane juice. If you're feeling adventurous, follow the path beyond the stand to the paradisiacal waterfalls known as Twin Falls. Once a rough trail plastered with "no trespassing" signs, this treasured spot is now easily accessible. Several deep, emerald pools sparkle beneath waterfalls and offer excellent swimming and photo opportunities. While it's still private property, the "no trespassing" signs have been replaced by colorfully painted arrows pointing away from residences and toward the falls. Swim at your own risk and beware: flash floods here and in all East Maui stream areas can be sudden and deadly. Check the weather before you go. ⊠*Hāna Hwy., past mile marker 2.*

Huelo and Kailua. This little farm town of Huelo has two quaint churches. If you linger awhile, you could meet local residents and learn about a rural lifestyle you might not have expected to find on the Islands. The same can be said for nearby Kailua (mile marker 6), home to Alexander & Baldwin's irrigation employees. ⊠*Hāna Hwy. near mile marker 5.*

Waikamoi Nature Trail. Between mile markers 9 and 10, the Waikamoi Nature Trail sign beckons you to stretch your car-weary limbs. A short (if muddy) trail leads through tall eucalyptus trees to a coastal vantage point with a picnic table and barbecue. Signage reminds visitors QUIET, TREES AT WORK and BAMBOO PICKING PERMIT REQUIRED. Awapuhi, or Hawaiian shampoo ginger, sends up fragrant shoots along the trail. ⊠*Hāna Hwy., between mile markers 9 and 10.*

Puahokamoa Stream. The bridge over Puahokamoa Stream is one of many you'll cross en route from Pā'ia to Hāna. It spans pools and waterfalls. Picnic tables are available, so many people favor this as a stopping point, but there are no restrooms. ⊠*Hāna Hwy. near mile marker 11.*

Kaumahina State Wayside Park. This park has a picnic area, restrooms, and a lovely overlook to the Ke'anae Peninsula. ⊠*Hāna Hwy., mile marker 12, Kailua* ☎*808/984–8109* 🖅*Free* ⊙ *Weekdays 8–4.*

Ke'anae Arboretum. Here's a place to learn the names of the many plants and trees now considered native to Hawai'i. The meandering Pi'ina'au Stream adds a graceful touch to the arboretum and provides a swimming pond. You can take a fairly rigorous hike from the arboretum if you can find the trail at one side of the large taro patch. Be careful not to lose the trail once you're on it. A lovely forest waits at the end of the 25-minute hike. ⊠*Hāna Hwy., mile marker 17, Ke'anae* 🖅*Free* ⊙*Daily 24 hrs.*

Ke'anae Overlook. From this observation point, you can take in the quilt-like effect the taro patches create below. The people of Ke'anae are working hard to revive this Hawaiian agricultural art and the traditional cultural values that the crop represents. The ocean provides a dramatic backdrop for the patches. In the other direction there are awesome views of Haleakalā through the foliage. This is a great spot for photos. ⊠*Hāna Hwy. near mile marker 17, Ke'anae.*

Wailua Overlook. From the parking lot you can see Wailua Canyon, but you'll have to walk up steps to get a view of Wailua Village. The landmark in Wailua Village is a church made of coral, built in 1860. Once called St. Gabriel's Catholic Church, the current Our Lady of Fatima Shrine has an interesting legend surrounding it. As the story goes, a storm washed just enough coral up onto the shore to build the church but then took any extra coral back to sea. ⊠*Hāna Hwy. near mile marker 21, Wailua.*

Waikāne Falls. Though not necessarily bigger or taller than the other falls, these are the most dramatic—some say the best—falls you'll find on the road to Hāna. That's partly because the water is not diverted for sugar irrigation. The taro farmers in Wailua need all the runoff. This is a particularly good spot for photos. ⊠*Hāna Hwy. past mile marker 21, Wailua.*

Nāhiku. In ancient times this was a busy settlement with hundreds of residents. Now only about 80 people live in Nāhiku, mostly native Hawaiians and some back-to-the-land types. A rubber grower planted trees here in the early 1900s, but the experiment didn't work out, so Nāhiku was essentially abandoned. The road ends at the sea in a pretty

On the Road to Hāna, a 55-mi journey into the unspoiled heart of Maui.

landing. This is the rainiest, densest part of the East Maui rain forest. ⊠ *Makai side of Hāna Hwy., mile marker 25.*

Ka'eleku Caverns. If you're interested in exploring underground, turn left onto 'Ula'ino Road, just after mile marker 31, and follow the signs to Ka'eleku Caverns. Maui Cave Adventures leads amateur spelunkers into a system of gigantic lava tubes, accentuated by colorful underworld formations. Monday through Saturday, from 10:30 to 3:30, you can take a self-guided, 30- to 45-minute tour for $11.95 per person. Flashlights are provided. Children under five are free with a paying adult. Call ahead to reserve a spot on the guided tour. ⊠ *1¼ mi down 'Ula'ino Rd., off Hāna Hwy.* ☎ *808/248–7308* ⊕ *www.mauicave.com.*

Pi'ilanihale Heiau. The largest prehistoric monument in Hawai'i, this temple platform was built for a great 16th-century Maui king named Pi'ilani and his heirs. This king also supervised the construction of a 10-foot-wide road that completely encircled the island. (That's why his name is part of most of Maui's highway titles.) Hawaiian families continue to maintain and protect this sacred site as they have for centuries, and they have not been eager to turn it into a tourist attraction. However, they now offer a brochure so you can tour the property yourself. Parties of four or more can reserve a guided tour by calling 48 hours in advance. Tours include the 122-acre **Kahanu Garden,** a federally funded research center focusing on the ethnobotany of the Pacific. ⊠*Left on ʻUlaʻino Rd. at mile marker 31 of Hāna Hwy.; the road turns to gravel; continue 1½ mi* ☎*808/248–8912* ≦*Self-guided tours $5, guided tours $10* ☉ *Weekdays 10–2.*

Hāna Airport. Think of Amelia Earhart. Think of Waldo Pepper. If these picket-fence runways don't turn your thoughts to the derring-do of barnstorming pilots, you haven't seen enough old movies. Only the smallest planes can land and depart here, and when none of them happen to be around, the lonely wind sock is the only evidence that this is a working airfield. ⊠*Hāna Hwy. past mile marker 30* ☎*808/248–8208.*

Waiʻānapanapa State Park. The park is right on the ocean, and it's a lovely spot to picnic, hike, or swim. An ancient burial site is nearby, as well as a heiau. Waiʻānapanapa also has one of Maui's only black-sand beaches and some freshwater caves for adventurous swimmers to explore. The water in the tide pools here turns red several times a year. Scientists say it's explained by the arrival of small shrimp, but locals claim the color represents the blood of Popoalaea, who legend says was murdered in one of the caves by her husband, Chief Kaakea. In either case, the dramatic contrast between the rain-forest green of the cliffs and the black volcanic rock is not to be missed. With a permit you can stay in state-run cabins here for less than $30 a night—the price varies depending on the number of people—but reserve early. They often book up a year in advance. ⊠*Hāna Hwy. near mile marker 32, Hāna* ☎*808/984–8109* ≦*Free.*

Hāna. The town centers on its lovely circular bay, dominated on the right-hand shore by a puʻu called Kaʻuiki. A short trail here leads to a cave, the birthplace of Queen Kāʻahumanu. Two miles beyond town another puʻu presides over a loop road that passes Hāna's two best beaches—Koki and Hāmoa. The hill is called Ka Iwi O Pele (Pele's Bone). This area is rich in Hawaiian history and legend. Offshore here, at tiny ʻĀlau Island, the demigod Maui supposedly fished up the Hawaiian islands.

Although sugar was once the mainstay of Hāna's economy, the last plantation shut down in the '40s. In 1946 rancher Paul Fagan built the **Hotel Hāna-Maui** (⊠*5031 Hāna Hwy.* ☎*808/248–8211 or 800/321–4262* ⊕*www.hotelhanamaui. com*) and stocked the surrounding pastureland with cattle. Suddenly, it was the ranch and its hotel that were putting food on most tables. The cross you'll see on the hill above the hotel was put there in memory of Fagan.

For many years, the Hotel Hāna-Maui was the only attraction for diners and shoppers determined to spend some time and money in Hāna after their long drive. Now, the **Hāna Cultural Center Museum** (✉*Ukea St.* ☎*808/248–8622*) also helps to meet that need. Besides operating a well-stocked gift shop, it displays artifacts, quilts, a replica of an authentic *kauhale* (an ancient Hawaiian living complex, with thatch huts and food gardens), and other Hawaiiana. The knowledgeable staff can explain it all to you.

★ **Hāmoa Beach.** Indulge in swimming or bodysurfing at this beautiful salt-and-pepper beach. Picnic tables, restrooms, and showers beneath the idyllic shade of coconut trees offer a more than comfortable rest stop. The road leading to Hāmoa also takes you to **Koki Beach,** where you can watch the Hāna surfers mastering the swells and strong currents, and the seabirds darting over '**Ālau,** the palm-fringed islet off the coast. The swimming is safer at Hāmoa. ✉*Haneo'o Loop Rd., 2 mi east of Hāna town.*

'Ohe'o Gulch. One branch of Haleakalā National Park runs down the mountain from the crater and reaches the sea here, where a basalt-lined stream cascades from one pool to the next. Some tour guides still call this area "Seven Sacred Pools," but in truth there are more than seven, and they've never been considered sacred. You can park here and walk to the lowest pools for a cool swim. The place gets crowded, though, since most people who drive the Hāna Highway make this their last stop. ✉*Pi'ilani Hwy., 10 mi south of Hāna.*

Grave of Charles Lindbergh. The world-renowned aviator chose to be buried here because he and his wife, writer Anne Morrow Lindbergh, spent a lot of time living in the area in a home they'd built. He was buried here in 1974, next to Palapala Ho'omau Congregational Church. Next to the churchyard on the ocean side is a small county park, a good place for a peaceful picnic. ✉*Palapala Ho'omau Congregational Church, Pi'ilani Hwy., Kīpahulu.*

Beaches & Outdoor Activities

WORD OF MOUTH

"I agree with the thought of Wailea for wonderful, uncrowded beaches and great resorts. In the nearby South Kīhei area, the beaches are just as great. The Kama'ole beaches I, II, and III are my favorites. . . ."
—Barbara5353

Updated
by Eliza
Escaño,
Bonnie
Friedman
& Heidi
Pool

OF ALL THE BEACHES ON the Hawaiian Islands, Maui's are some of the most diverse. You'll find the pristine, palm-lined shores you expect with clear and inviting waters the color of sea-green glass, but you'll also discover rich red- and black-sand beaches, craggy cliffs with surging whitecaps, and year-round sunsets that quiet the soul.

Getting into (or onto) the water will be the highlight of your Maui trip. At Lahaina and Māʻalaea harbors, you can board boats for snorkeling, scuba diving, deep-sea fishing, whale-watching, parasailing, and sunset cocktail adventures.

You may come to Maui to sprawl out on the sand, but you'll soon realize there's much more here than the beach. The rain forests, lush valleys, waterfalls, and mountains of the island's large interior provide many options for action and adventure.

BEACHES

As on the other islands, all Maui's beaches are public—but that doesn't mean it's not possible to find a secluded cove where you can truly get away from the world.

The island's leeward shores (the South Shore and West Maui) have the calmest, sunniest beaches. Hit the beach early, when the aquamarine waters are as accommodating as bathwater. In summer, afternoon winds can be a sand-blasting force, which can chase even the most dedicated sun worshippers away. From November through May, the South and West beaches are also great spots to watch the humpback whales that spend the winter and early spring in Maui's waters.

Windward shores (the North Shore and East Maui) offer more adventurous beach-going. Beaches face the open ocean (rather than other islands) and tend to be rockier and more prone to powerful swells. This is particularly true in winter, when the North Shore becomes a playground for experienced big-wave riders and windsurfers. Don't let this keep you away completely, however; some of the island's best beaches are those remote slivers of volcanic sand found on the wild windward shore.

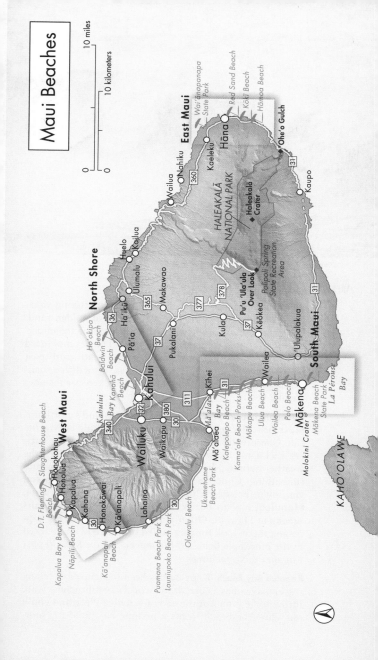
Maui Beaches

Catching a wave close to shore can give you an exciting ride.

WEST MAUI

West Maui beaches are legendary for their glittering aquamarine waters banked by long stretches of golden sand. Reef fronts much of the western shore, making the underwater panorama something to behold. The beaches listed here start in the north at Kapalua and head south past Kā'anapali and Lahaina. Note that there are a dozen roadside beaches to choose from on Route 30; here are the ones we like best.

"Slaughterhouse" (Mokulē'ia) Beach. The island's northernmost beach is part of the Honolua-Mokulē'ia Marine Life Conservation District. "Slaughterhouse" is the surfers' nickname for what is officially Mokulē'ia. When the weather permits, this is a great place for bodysurfing and sunbathing. Concrete steps and a green railing help you get down the sheer cliff to the sand. The next bay over, Honolua, has no beach but offers one of the best surf breaks in Hawai'i. Often you can see competitions happening there; look for cars pulled off the road and parked in the pineapple field. ⊠*Mile marker 32 on Rte. 30 past Kapalua* ⟟*No facilities.*

Kapalua Bay Beach. Kapalua has been recognized by many travel magazines as one of the world's best beaches. Walk through the tunnel at the end of Kapalua Place and you'll see why—the beach fronts a pristine bay good for snor-

keling, swimming, and general lazing. Located just north of Nāpili Bay, this lovely, sheltered shore often remains calm late into the afternoon, although there may be strong currents offshore. Snorkeling is easy here and there are lots of colorful reef fish to see. This area is quite popular and is bordered by the Kapalua Resort, so don't expect to have the beach to yourself. ⊠*From Rte. 30, turn onto Kapalua Pl., walk through tunnel* ⚬*Toilets, showers, parking lot.*

BEACHES KEY	
👫	Restroom
🚿	Showers
🏄	Surfing
🤿	Snorkel/Scuba
👫	Good for kids
🅿	Parking

★ **Fodor'sChoice** **Nāpili Beach.** Surrounded by sleepy condos, ☺ this round bay is a turtle-filled pool lined with a sparkling white crescent of sand. Sunbathers love this beach, which is also a terrific sunset spot. The shore break is steep but gentle, so it's great for boogie boarding and bodysurfing. It's easy to keep an eye on kids here as the entire bay is visible from any point in the water. The beach is right outside the Nāpili Kai Beach Club, a popular little resort for honeymooners, only a few miles south of Kapalua. ⊠*5900 Lower Honoapi'ilani Hwy., look for Nāpili Pl. or Hui Dr.* ⚬*Showers, parking lot.*

☺ **Kā'anapali Beach.** Stretching from the Sheraton Maui at its ★ northernmost end to the Hyatt Regency Maui at its southern tip, Kā'anapali Beach is lined with resorts, condominiums, restaurants, and shops. If you're looking for quiet and seclusion, this is not the beach for you. But if you want lots of action, lay out your towel here. The center section in front of Whalers Village is also called "Dig Me Beach," and it is one of Maui's best people-watching spots: catamarans, windsurfers, and parasailers head out from here while the beautiful people take in the scenery. A cement pathway weaves along the length of this 3-mi-long beach, leading from one astounding resort to the next.

The drop-off from Kāʻanapali's soft, sugary sand is steep, but waves hit the shore with barely a rippling slap. The area at the northernmost end (in front of the Sheraton Maui), known as Kekaʻa, was, in ancient Hawaiʻi, a lele, or jumping-off place for spirits. It's easy to get into the water from the beach to enjoy the prime snorkeling among the lava rock outcroppings. ✉ *Follow any of 3 Kāʻanapali exits from Honoapiʻilani Hwy. and park at any hotel* ♿ *Toilets, showers, parking lot.*

MAUI BEACHES ARE FREE. All of the island's beaches are free and open to the public—even those that grace the front yards of fancy hotels—so you can make yourself at home on any one of them. Some of the prettiest beaches are often hidden by buildings; look for the blue BEACH ACCESS signs that indicate public rights-of-way through condominiums, resorts, and other private properties.

THE SOUTH SHORE

Sandy beach fronts nearly the entire southern coastline of Maui, from Kīhei at the northern end to Mākena at the southern tip. The farther south you go, the better the beaches get. Kīhei has excellent beach parks right in town, with white sand, showers, restrooms, picnic tables, and barbecues. Good snorkeling can be found along the beaches' rocky borders. As good as Kīhei is, Wailea is even better. Wailea's beaches are cleaner, facilities tidier, and views even more impressive. ⚠ **Note that break-ins have been reported at many of these beach parking lots.** As you head out to Mākena, the terrain gets wilder. Bring lunch, water, and sunscreen with you.

The following South Shore beaches are listed from north Kīhei southeast to Mākena.

Kamaʻole I, II, and III. Three steps from South Kīhei Road, you can find three golden stretches of sand separated by outcroppings of dark, jagged lava rocks. You can walk the length of all three beaches if you're willing to get your feet wet. The northernmost of the trio, Kamaʻole I (across from the ABC Store, in case you forgot your sunscreen), offers perfect swimming with a sandy bottom a long way out and an active volleyball court. If you're one of those people who like your beach sans sand, there's also a great lawn for you to spread out on at the south end of the beach.

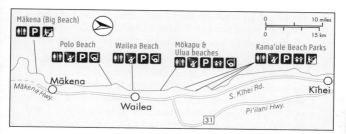

Kama'ole II is nearly identical minus the lawn. The last beach, the one with all the people on it, is Kama'ole III, perfect for throwing a disk or throwing down a blanket. This is a great family beach, complete with a playground, volleyball net, barbecues, kite flying, and frequently, rented inflatable castles—a birthday-party must for every cool kid living on the island.

Locally—and quite disrespectfully, according to native Hawaiians—known as "Kam" I, II, and III, all three beaches have great swimming and lifeguards. In the morning the water can be as still as a lap pool. Kama'ole III offers terrific breaks for beginning bodysurfers. ■ TIP→The public restrooms have seen better days; decent facilities are found at convenience stores and eateries across the street. ⊠ *S. Kīhei Rd., between Ke Ali'i Alanui Rd. and Keonekai Rd.* ⌂ *Lifeguard, toilets, showers, picnic tables, grills/firepits, playground, parking lot.*

☺ **Mōkapu & Ulua.** Look for a little road and public parking lot next to the Wailea Marriott. This gets you to Mōkapu and Ulua beaches. Though there are no lifeguards, families love this place. Reef formations create tons of tide pools for kids to explore and the beaches are protected from major swells. Snorkeling is excellent at Ulua, the beach to the left of the entrance. Mōkapu, to the right, tends to be less crowded. The Renaissance Wailea used to front this beach but the hotel has been demolished and construction of a new resort property is planned. ⊠ *Wailea Alanui Dr., north of Wailea Marriott resort* ⌂ *Toilets, showers, parking lot.*

Wailea Beach. A road just after the Grand Wailea Resort takes you to Wailea Beach, a wide, sandy stretch with snorkeling, swimming, and, if you're a guest of the Four Seasons Resort, Evian spritzes! If you're not a guest at the Grand Wailea or Four Seasons, the private cabanas and chaise longues can be a little annoying, but any complaint is more than made up for by the calm, unclouded waters and soft, white sand. ⊠ *Wailea Alanui Dr., south of Grand Wailea Resort entrance* ☆ *Toilets, showers, parking lot.*

Polo Beach. From Wailea Beach you can walk to this small, uncrowded crescent fronting the Fairmont Kea Lani resort. Swimming and snorkeling are great here and it's a good place to whale-watch. As at Wailea Beach, private cabanas occupy prime sandy real estate, but there's plenty of room for you and your towel, and even a nice grass picnic area. The pathway connecting the two beaches is a great spot to jog or leisurely take in awesome views of nearby Molokini and Kaho'olawe. Rare native plants grow along the ocean, or *makai,* side of the path; the honey-sweet-smelling one is *naio,* or false sandalwood. ⊠ *Wailea Alanui Dr., south of Fairmont Kea Lani resort entrance* ☞ *Toilets, showers, picnic tables, grills/firepits, parking lot.*

★ Fodor'sChoice **Mākena (Big Beach).** Locals successfully fought to give Mākena—one of Hawai'i's most breathtaking beaches—state-park protection. It's often mistakenly referred to as "Big Beach," but natives prefer its Hawaiian name, Oneloa. This stretch of deep-golden sand abutting sparkling aqua water is 3,000-feet-long and 100-feet-wide. It's never crowded, no matter how many cars cram into the lots. The water is fine for swimming, but use caution. △**The shore drop-off is steep and swells can get deceptively big.** Despite the infamous "Mākena cloud," a blanket that rolls in during the early afternoon and obscures the sun, it rarely rains here. For a dramatic view of the beach, climb Pu'u Ōla'i, the steep cinder cone near the first entrance. Continue over the cinder cone's side to discover "Little Beach"—clothing-optional by popular practice, although technically illegal. On Sunday, free spirits of all kinds crowd Little Beach's tiny shoreline for a drumming circle and bonfire. Little Beach has the island's best bodysurfing (no pun intended). Skim-boarders catch air at Mākena's third entrance. Each of the three paved entrances has portable toilets. ⊠ *Off Wailea Alanui Dr.* ☆ *Toilets, parking lot.*

THE NORTH SHORE

Many of the folks you see jaywalking in Pā'ia sold everything they owned to come to Maui and live a beach-bum's life. Beach culture abounds on the North Shore. But these folks aren't sunbathers; they're big-wave riders, windsurfers, or kiteboarders. The North Shore is their challeng-

BEACH SAFETY

Hawai'i's beautiful beaches can be dangerous at times due to large waves and strong currents—so much so that the state rates wave hazards using three signs: a yellow square (caution), a red stop sign (high hazard) and a black diamond (extreme hazard). Signs are posted and updated three times daily or as conditions change.

Visiting beaches with lifeguards is recommended, and you should swim only when there's a normal caution rating. Never swim alone or dive into unknown water or shallow breaking waves. If you're unable to swim out of a rip current, tread water and wave your arms in the air to signal for help.

Even in calm conditions, there are other dangerous things in the water to be aware of, including razor-sharp coral, jellyfish, eels, and sharks. Jellyfish cause the most ocean injuries, and signs are posted along beaches when they're present. Box jellyfish swarm to Hawaii's leeward shores 9 to 10 days after a full moon. Portuguese man-of-wars are usually found when winds blow from the ocean onto land. Reactions to a sting are usually mild (burning sensation, redness, welts); however, in some cases they can be severe (breathing difficulties).

If you are stung by a jellyfish, pick off the tentacles, rinse the affected area with water and apply ice. Seek first-aid from a lifeguard if you experience severe reactions.

According to state sources, the chances of getting bitten by a shark in Hawaiian waters are very low; sharks attack swimmers or surfers three or four times per year. Of the 40 species of sharks found near Hawai'i, tiger sharks are considered the most dangerous. They are recognized by their blunt snouts and vertical bars on their sides. To reduce your shark-attack risk

■ Swim, surf, or dive with others at beaches patrolled by lifeguards.

■ Avoid swimming at dawn, dusk, and night, when some shark species may move inshore to feed.

■ Don't enter the water if you have open wounds or are bleeding.

■ Avoid murky waters, harbor entrances, areas near stream mouths, channels, or steep drop-offs.

■ Don't wear high-contrast swimwear or shiny jewelry.

■ Don't swim near dolphins, which are often prey for large sharks.

■ If you spot a shark, leave the water quickly and calmly.

ing sports arena. Beaches here face the open ocean and tend to be rougher and windier than beaches elsewhere on Maui—but don't let that scare you off. On calm days, the reef-speckled waters are truly beautiful and offer a quieter and less commercial beach-going experience than the leeward shore. Beaches below are listed from Kahului (near the airport) eastward to Ho'okipa.

Kanahā Beach. Windsurfers, kiteboarders, joggers, and picnicking families like this long, golden strip of sand bordered by a wide grassy area with lots of shade. The winds pick up in the early afternoon, making for the best kiteboarding and windsurfing conditions—if you know what you're doing, that is. The best spot for watching kiteboarders is at the far left end of the beach. ⊠*Drive through airport and make right onto car-rental road (Koeheke); turn right onto Amala Pl. and take any left (there are 3 entrances) into Kanahā* ☐*Lifeguard, toilets, showers, picnic tables, grills/firepits, parking lot.*

☼ **Baldwin Beach.** A local favorite, right off the highway and
★ just west of Pā'ia town, Baldwin Beach is a big stretch of comfortable white sand. This is a good place to lie out, jog, or swim, though the waves can sometimes be choppy and the undertow strong. Don't be afraid of those big brown blobs floating beneath the surface; they're just pieces of seaweed awash in the surf. You can find shade along the beach beneath the ironwood trees, or in the large pavilion, a spot regularly overtaken by local parties and community events.

The long, shallow pool at the Kahului end of the beach is known as "Baby Beach." Separated from the surf by a flat reef wall, this is where ocean-loving families bring their kids (and sometimes puppies) to practice a few laps. Take a relaxing stroll along the water's edge from the one end of Baldwin Beach to Baby Beach and enjoy the scenery. The view of the West Maui Mountains is hauntingly beautiful from here. ⊠*Hāna Hwy., 1 mi west of Baldwin Ave.* ⚲*Lifeguard, toilets, showers, picnic tables, grills/firepits, parking lot.*

★ **Ho'okipa Beach.** If you want to see some of the world's finest windsurfers in action, hit this beach along the Hāna Highway. The sport was largely developed right at Ho'okipa and has become an art and a career to some. This beach is also one of Maui's hottest surfing spots, with waves that can be as high as 20 feet. This is not a good swimming beach, nor the place to learn windsurfing, but it's great for hanging out and watching the pros. Bust out your telephoto lens at the cliffside lookout to capture the aerial acrobatics of board-sailors and kiteboarders. ⊠*2 mi past Pā'ia on Rte. 36* ⚲*Lifeguard, toilets, showers, picnic tables, grills/firepits, parking lot.*

GEAR UP! Forget your beach gear? No need to fear, Maui is the land-of-plenty when it comes to stores just waiting to pawn off their boogie boards and beach mats. Look for Long's Drugs (in Kīhei and Kahului) or the ABC Stores (in Kā'napali, Lahaina, Kīhei, and more) for extra sunscreen, shades, towels, and umbrellas. If you want better deals and don't mind the drive into town, look for Kmart (424 Dairy Rd.) or Wal-Mart (101 Pakaula St.) in Kahului. For more extensive gear, check out Sports Authority (270 Dairy Rd.) in Kahului. Equipment rentals are available at shops and resorts, too.

EAST MAUI & HĀNA

Hāna's beaches will literally stop you in your tracks—they're that beautiful. Black-and-red sands stand out against pewter skies and lush tropical foliage creating picture-perfect scenes, which seem too breathtaking to be real. Rough conditions often preclude swimming, but that doesn't mean you can't explore the shoreline. Beaches below are listed in order from the west end of Hāna town eastward.

★ **Fodor's**Choice **Wai'ānapanapa State Park.** Small but rarely crowded, this beach will remain in your memory long after visiting. Fingers of white foam rush onto a black volcanic-pebble beach fringed with green beach vines and palms. Swimming here is both relaxing and invigorating: strong currents bump smooth stones up against your ankles while seabirds flit above a black, jagged sea arch draped with

DID YOU KNOW?

You won't find plumbing at stunning Mākena Beach State Park on the South Shore, but the undeveloped, golden-sand, 3,000-foot-long "Big Beach" is home to dolphins and turtles. Sunsets here are glorious.

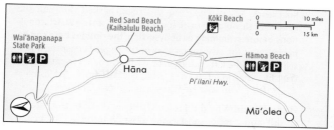

vines. At the edge of the parking lot, a sign tells you the sad story of a doomed Hawaiian princess. Stairs lead through a tunnel of interlocking Polynesian *hau* branches to an icy cave pool—the secret hiding place of the ancient princess. ⚠ **You can swim in this pool, but be wary of mosquitoes!** In the other direction, a 3-mi, dramatic coastal path continues beyond the campground, past sea arches, blowholes, and cultural sites all the way to Hāna town. Grassy tent sites and rustic cabins that accommodate up to six people are available by reservation only; call ahead for information. ✉ *Hāna Hwy. near mile marker 32* ☎ *808/984–8109* ⚴ *Toilets, showers, picnic tables, grills/firepits, parking lot.*

★ **Red Sand Beach (Kaihalulu Beach).** Kaihalulu Beach, better known as Red Sand Beach, is unmatched in its raw and remote beauty. It's not simple to find, but when you round the last corner of the trail and are confronted with the sight of it, your jaw is bound to drop. Earthy red cliffs tower above the deep maroon–sand beach and swimmers bob about in a turquoise blue lagoon formed by volcanic boulders just offshore (it's like floating around in a giant natural bathtub). It's worth spending a night in Hāna just to make sure you can get here early and have some time to enjoy it before anyone else shows up.

Keep in mind that getting here is not easy and you have to pass through private property along the way—do so at your own risk. You need to tread carefully up and around Kaʻuiki (the red-cinder hill); the cliff-side cinder path is slippery and constantly eroding. Hiking is not recommended in shoes without traction, or in bad weather. By popular practice, clothing on the beach is optional. ✉ *At end of Uākea Rd. past baseball field. Park near community center, walk through grass lot to trail below cemetery* ⚴ *No facilities.*

Kōkī Beach. You can tell from the trucks parked alongside the road that this is a favorite local surf spot. ■TIP→**Watch conditions before swimming or bodysurfing; the riptides here can be mean.** Look for awesome views of the rugged coastline and a sea arch on the left end. *Iwa,* or white-throated frigate birds, dart like pterodactyls over ʻAlau islet offshore. ✉*Haneoʻo Loop Rd., 2 mi east of Hāna town* ♿*No facilities.*

Hāmoa Beach. Why did James Michener describe this stretch of salt-and-pepper sand as the most "South Pacific" beach he'd come across, even though it's located in the North Pacific? Maybe it was the perfect half-moon shape, speckled with the shade of palm trees. Perhaps he was intrigued by the jutting black coastline, often outlined by rain showers out at sea, or the pervasive lack of hurry he felt once settled in here. Whatever it was, many still feel the lure. The beach can be crowded but nonetheless relaxing. Expect to see a few chaise longues and a guest-only picnic area set up by the Hotel Hāna-Maui. Early mornings and late afternoons are best for swimming. At times, the churning surf might intimidate beginning swimmers, but bodysurfing can be great here. ✉*½ mi past Kōkī Beach on Haneoʻo Loop Rd., 2 mi east of Hāna town* ♿*Toilets, showers, picnic tables, parking lot.*

On Maui, you can learn to surf, catch a ferry to Lānaʻi, or grab a seat on a fast inflatable. Along the leeward coastline, from Kāʻanapali on the West Shore all the way down to the tip of ʻĀhihi-Kīnaʻu on the South Shore, you can discover great snorkeling and swimming. If you're a thrill-seeker, head out to the North Shore and Hoʻokipa, where surfers, kiteboarders, and windsurfers catch big waves and big air. For easy reference, activities are listed in alphabetical order.

DEEP-SEA FISHING

If fishing is your sport, Maui is your island. In these waters you'll find ʻahi, *aku* (skipjack tuna), barracuda, bonefish, *kawakawa* (bonito), mahimahi, Pacific blue marlin, ono, and *ulua* (jack crevalle). You can fish year-round and you don't need a license. ■TIP→**Because boats fill up fast during busy seasons (Christmas, spring break, tournament weeks), consider making reservations before coming to Maui.**

Plenty of fishing boats run out of Lahaina and Māʻalaea harbors. If you charter a private boat, expect to spend in the neighborhood of $700 to $1,000 for a thrilling half-day in the swivel seat. You can share a boat for much less if you don't mind close quarters with a stranger who may get seasick, drunk, or worse . . . lucky! Before you sign up, you should know that some boats keep the catch. They will, however, fillet a nice piece for you to take home. And if you catch a real beauty, you might even be able to have it professionally mounted.

■TIP→**Don't go out with a boater who charges for the fish you catch—that's harbor robbery.** You're expected to bring your own lunch and non-glass beverages. (Shop the night before; it's hard to find snacks at 6 AM.) Boats supply coolers, ice, and bait. A 10% to 20% tip is suggested.

BOATS & CHARTERS

★ **Finest Kind Inc.** A record 1,118-pound Blue Marlin was reeled in by the crew aboard *Finest Kind,* a lovely 37-foot Merritt kept so clean you'd never guess the action it's seen. Ask Captain Dave about his pet frigate bird—he's been around these waters long enough to befriend other expert fishers. This family-run company operates four boats and special-izes in live bait. Shared charters start at $150 for four hours and up to $189 for a full day. All-day private trips go from $700 to $1,000. Add 7% for tax and harbor fees. Check for any specials before booking. ⊠*Lahaina Harbor, Slip 7* ☎*808/661–0338* ⊕*www.finestkindsportfishing.com.*

Kai Palena Sportfishing. Captain Fuzzy Alboro runs a seri-ous and highly recommended operation on the 32-foot Die Hard. Check-in is at 3 AM, and he takes a maximum of six people per trip. The cost is from $200 for a shared boat to $1,100 for a private charter; add 7% tax. The catch is split evenly on a shared boat, while private groups keep as much as they can consume. ⊠*511 Pikanele St., Lahaina Harbor, Slip 10* ☎*808/878–2362.*

Strike Zone. This is one of the few charters to offer morn-ing bottom-fishing trips (for smaller fish such as snap-per), as well as deep-sea trips (for the big ones—ono, 'ahi, mahimahi, and marlin). *Strike Zone* is a 43-foot Delta that offers plenty of room (16-person max). Lunch and soft drinks are included. The catch is shared with the entire boat. The cost is $168 per adult and $148 per child for a pole; spectators can ride for $78, plus 7% tax. There is also an afternoon bottom-fishing trip available on *Strike Zone,* which lasts four hours and costs $128 plus tax per person. The six- and four-hour bottom-fish-ing trips run Monday, Wednesday, Friday, and Saturday;

the six-hour deep-sea trips run Tuesday, Thursday, and Sunday, all weather-permitting. All trips leave at 6:30 AM. ✉*Māʻalaea Harbor, Slip 64, Māʻalaea* ☎*808/879–4485* ⊕*www.strikezonemaui.com.*

KAYAKING

Kayaking is a fantastic way to experience Maui's coast up close. Floating aboard a "plastic popsicle stick" is easier than you might think, and allows you to cruise out to vibrant, living coral reefs and waters where dolphins and even whales roam. Kayaking can be a leisurely paddle or a challenge of heroic proportions, depending on your ability, the location, and the weather. ■TIP➔**Though you can rent kayaks independently, we recommend taking a guide.** An apparently calm surface can hide extremely strong ocean currents—and you don't *really* want to take an unplanned trip to Tahiti. Most guides are naturalists who will steer you away from surging surf, lead you to pristine reefs, and point out camouflaged fish, like the stalking hawkfish. Not having to schlep your gear on top of your rental car is a bonus. A half-day tour runs around $75. Custom tours can be arranged.

If you decide to strike out on your own, tour companies will rent kayaks for the day with paddles, life vests, and roof racks, and many will meet you near your chosen location. Ask for a map of good entries and plan to avoid paddling back to shore against the wind (schedule extra time for the return trip regardless). Read weather conditions, bring binoculars and take a careful look from the bay before heading in. For beginners, get there early before the trade wind kicks in, and try sticking close to the shore. When you're ready to snorkel, secure your belongings in a dry pack on board and drag your boat by its bowline behind you. (This isn't as bad as it sounds.) ■TIP➔**The ʻĀhihi-Kīnaʻu Natural Area Reserve at the southernmost point of South Maui is closed to commercial traffic and you may not take rented kayaks into the reserve.**

BEST SPOTS

In West Maui, past the steep cliffs on the Honoapiʻilani Highway and before you hit Lahaina, there's a long stretch of inviting coastline, including **Ukumehame** (✉*Between mile markers 12 and 14 on Rte. 30*) and Olowalu beaches. This is a good spot for beginners; entry is easy and there's much to see in every direction. If you want to snorkel, the

The sandy crescent of Nāpili Beach on West Maui is a lovely place to wait for sunset.

best visibility is farther out at Olowalu, at about 25 feet depth. ⚠ **Watch for sharp kiawe thorns buried in the sand on the way into the water.**

Mākena Landing (✉ *Off Mākena Rd.*) is an excellent taking-off point for a South Shore adventure. Enter from the paved parking lot or the small sandy beach a little south. The bay itself is virtually empty, but the right edge is flanked with brilliant coral heads and juvenile turtles. If you round the point on the right, you come across Five Caves, a system of enticing underwater arches. In the morning you may see dolphins, and the arches are havens for lobsters, eels, and spectacularly hued butterfly fish. Check out the million-dollar mansions lining the shoreline and guess which celebrity lives where.

EQUIPMENT, LESSONS & TOURS
Maui Sea Kayaking. Since 1988, this company has been guiding small groups (four-person trips) to secret spots along Maui's coast. They take great care in customizing their outings. For example, the guides accommodate kayakers with disabilities as well as senior kayakers, and they offer kid-size gear. For paddlers looking to try something new, they also offer kayak surfing. Trips start at $85 and leave from various locations, depending upon the weather. ☎ *808/572–6299* ⊕ *www.maui.net/~kayaking.*

★ Fodor'sChoice **South Pacific Kayaks.** These guys pioneered recreational kayaking on Maui—they know their stuff. Guides are friendly, informative, and eager to help you get the most out of your experience; we're talking true, fun-loving, kayak geeks. Some activity companies show a strange lack of care for the marine environment; South Pacific stands out as adventurous *and* responsible. They offer a variety of trips leaving from both West Maui and South Shore locations, including an advanced four-hour "Molokini Challenge." Trips range from $54 to $149. ☎800/776–2326 or 808/875–4848 ⊕ www.southpacifickayaks.com.

KITEBOARDING

Catapulting up to 40 feet in the air above the breaking surf, kiteboarders hardly seem of this world. Silken kites hold the athletes aloft for precious seconds—long enough for the execution of mind-boggling tricks—then deposit them back in the sea. This new sport is not for the weak-kneed. No matter what people might tell you, it's harder to learn than windsurfing. The unskilled (or unlucky) can be caught in an upwind and carried far out in the ocean, or worse—dropped smack on the shore. Because of insurance (or the lack thereof), companies are not allowed to rent equipment. Beginners must take lessons, and then purchase their own gear. Devotees swear that after your first few lessons, committing to buying your kite is easy.

LESSONS

Aqua Sports Maui. "To air is human," or so they say at Aqua Sports, which calls itself the local favorite of kiteboarding schools. They've got a great location right near Kite Beach, at the west (left) end of Kanahā Beach, and offer basic through advanced kiteboarding lessons. Rates start at $210 for a three-hour basics course taught by certified instructors. ✉ Amala Pl., near Kite Beach, Kahului ☎808/242–8015 ⊕ www.mauikiteboardinglessons.com.

Hawaiian Sailboarding Techniques. Pro kiteboarder and legendary windsurfer Alan Cadiz will have you safely ripping in no time at lower Kanahā Beach Park. A "Learn to Kitesurf" package starts at $225 for a three-hour private lesson, which includes all equipment. As opposed to observing from the shore, instructors paddle after students on a chaseboard to give immediate feedback. HST is in the highly regarded Hi Tech Surf & Sports store, located in the Triangle Square shopping center. ⊠*425 Koloa St., Kahului* ☎*808/871–5423 or 800/968–5423* ⊕*www.hstwindsurfing.com.*

PARASAILING

Parasailing is an easy, exhilarating way to earn your wings: just strap on a harness attached to a parachute, and a powerboat pulls you up and over the ocean from a launching dock or a boat's platform. ■TIP→**Parasailing is limited to West Maui, and "thrill craft"—including parasails—are prohibited in Maui waters during humpback whale–calving season, December 15 to May 15.**

West Maui Parasail. Launch 400 feet above the ocean for a bird's-eye view of Lahaina, or be daring at 800 feet for smoother rides and better views. The captain will be glad to let you experience a "toe dip" or "freefall" if you request it. For safety reasons, passengers weighing less than 100 pounds must be strapped together in tandem. Hourlong trips departing from Lahaina Harbor, Slip #15, and Kāʻanapali Beach include eight- to 10-minute flights and run from $62 for the 400-foot ride to $70 for the 800-foot ride. Observers must pay $30 each. ☎*808/661–4060* ⊕*www.westmauiparasail.com.*

RAFTING

The high-speed, inflatable rafts you find on Maui are nothing like the raft that Huck Finn used to drift down the Mississippi. While passengers grip straps, these rafts fly, skimming and bouncing across the sea. Because they're so maneuverable, they go where the big boats can't—secret coves, sea caves, and remote beaches. Two-hour trips run around $50, half-day trips upward of $100. ■TIP→**Although safe, these trips are not for the faint of heart. If you have back or neck problems or are pregnant, you should reconsider this activity.**

TOURS

Blue Water Rafting. One of the few ways to get to the stunning Kanaio Coast (the roadless southern coastline beyond ʻĀhihi-Kīnaʻu), this rafting tour begins trips conveniently at the Kīhei boat ramp. Dolphins, turtles, and other marine life are the highlight of this adventure, along with sea caves, lava arches, and views of Haleakalā. Two-hour trips start at $49 plus tax; longer trips cost $90 to $115 and include a deli lunch. ⊠*2777 South Kīhei Rd., Kīhei* ☎*808/879–7238* ⊕*www.bluewaterrafting.com.*

Ocean Riders. This West Maui tour crosses the ʻAuʻAu channel to Lānaʻi's Shipwreck Beach, then circles the island for 70 mi of remote coast. For snorkeling, the "back side" of Lānaʻi is one of Hawaiʻi's unsung marvels. Tours—$129 plus tax per person—depart from Mala Wharf, at the northern end of Front Street and include snorkel gear, a fruit breakfast, and a deli lunch. ⊠*Lahaina* ☎*808/661–3586* ⊕*www.mauioceanriders.com.*

SAILING

With the islands of Molokaʻi, Lānaʻi, Kahoʻolawe, and Molokini a stone's throw away, Maui waters offer visually arresting backdrops for sailing adventures. Sailing conditions can be fickle, so some operations throw in snorkeling or whale-watching, and others offer sunset cruises. *(For more sunset cruises, see chapter 7, Entertainment & Nightlife.)* Winds are consistent in summer, but variable in winter, and afternoons are generally windier all throughout the year. Prices range from around $40 for two-hour trips to $80 for half-day excursions. ■ TIP→ **You won't be sheltered from the elements on the trim racing boats, so be sure to bring a hat (one that won't blow away), a light jacket or cover-up, sunglasses, and extra sunscreen.**

BOATS & CHARTERS

America II. This one-time America's Cup contender offers an exciting, intimate alternative to crowded catamarans. For fast action, try a morning trade-wind sail. Sunset sails are generally calmer—a good choice if you don't want to spend two hours fully exposed to the sun. Plan to bring a change of clothes, because you will get wet. Snack and beverages are provided. No one under five years old is permitted. ⊠*Lahaina Harbor Slip 6* ☎*808/667–2195* ⊕*www.sailingonmaui.com.*

Paragon. If you want to snorkel and sail, this is your boat. Many snorkel cruises claim to sail but actually motor most of the way; Paragon is an exception. Both Paragon vessels (one catamaran in Lahaina, the other in Māʻalaea) are ship-shape, and crews are competent and friendly. Their mooring in Molokini Crater is particularly good, and they often stay after the masses have left. The Lānaʻi trip includes a picnic lunch on the beach, snorkeling, and an afternoon blue water swim. Extras on their trips to Lānaʻi include mai tais and sodas, hot and cold *pūpū* (Hawaiian tapas), and champagne. ⊠*Lahaina and Māʻalaea Harbors* ☎808/244–2087 or 800/441–2087 ⊕*www.sailmaui.com.*

Trilogy Excursions. With more than 35 years of sailing tradition, not to mention a commitment to Hawaiiana and the ecosystem, Trilogy remains a favorite of locals and visitors alike. It is one of only two companies that sail to Molokini. A two-hour sail starts at $59. Alcohol is not provided. Book online for a 10% discount. ⊠*Māʻalaea Harbor, Slip 99, Lahaina Harbor, or by the* Kāʻanapali Beach Hotel ☎808/661–4743 or 888/225–6284 ⊕*www. sailtrilogy.com.*

SCUBA DIVING

Maui, just as scenic underwater as it is on dry land, has been rated one of the top 10 dive spots in North America. A big advantage here is that divers see more large animals than they would in areas such as the Caribbean. It's common on any dive to see huge sea turtles, eagle rays, and small reef sharks, not to mention many varieties of angelfish, parrotfish, eels, and octopi. Most of the species are unique to this area, which is unlike other popular dive destinations. For example, of Maui's 450 species of reef fish, 25% are endemic to the island. In addition, the terrain itself is different from other dive spots. Here you'll find ancient and intricate lava flows full of nooks where marine life hide and breed. Although the water tends to be a bit rougher—not to mention colder—here, divers are given a great thrill during humpback-whale season, when you can actually hear whales singing underwater.

Some of the finest diving spots in all of Hawaiʻi lie along the Valley Isle's western and southwestern shores. Dives are best in the morning, when visibility can hold a steady 100 feet. If you're a certified diver, you can rent gear at any Maui dive shop simply by showing your PADI or NAUI card. Unless you're familiar with the area, however, it's probably best to hook up with a dive shop for an underwater tour. Tours include tanks and weights and start around $130. Wet suits and BCs are rented separately, for an additional $15 to $30. Shops also offer introductory dives ($100 to $160) for those who aren't certified. ■TIP→**Before signing on with any of these outfitters, it's a good idea to ask a few pointed questions about your guide's experience, the weather outlook, and the condition of the equipment.**

Diving 101

If you've always wanted gills, Hawai'i is a good place to get them. Although the bulky, heavy equipment seems freakish on shore, underwater it allows you to move about freely, almost weightlessly. As you descend into another world, you slowly grow used to the sound of your own breathing and the strangeness of being able to do so 30-plus feet down.

Most resorts offer introductory dive lessons in their pools, which allow you to acclimate to the awkward breathing apparatus before venturing out into the great blue. If you aren't starting from a resort pool, no worries. Most intro dives take off from calm, sandy beaches, such as Ulua or Kā'anapali. If you're bitten by the deep-sea bug and want to continue diving, you should get certified. Only certified divers can rent equipment or go on more adventurous dives, such as night dives, open-ocean dives, and cave dives.

There are several certification companies, including PADI, NAUI, and SSI. PADI, the largest, is the most comprehensive. A child must be at least 10 to be certified. Once you begin your certification process, stick with the same company. The dives you log will not apply to another company's certification. (Dives with a PADI instructor, for instance, will not count toward SSI certification.) Remember that you will not be able to fly or go to the airy summit of Haleakalā within 24 hours of diving. Open-water certification will take three to four days and cost around $350. From that point on, the sky . . . or rather, the sea's the limit!

Before you head out on your dive, be sure to check conditions. If you have access to the Internet, check the Glenn James weather site, ⊕*www.hawaiiweathertoday.com*, for a breakdown on the weather, wind, and visibility conditions.

BEST SPOTS

Honolua Bay (✉*Between mile markers 32 and 33 on Rte. 30, look for narrow dirt road to left*) has beach entry. This West Maui marine preserve is alive with many varieties of coral and tame tropical fish, including large *ulua*, *kāhala*, barracuda, and manta rays. With depths of 20 to 50 feet, this is a popular summer dive spot, good for all levels. ■TIP→**High surf often prohibits winter dives.**

Only 3 mi offshore from Wailea on the South Shore, **Molokini Crater** is world renowned for its deep, crystal clear, fish-filled waters. A crescent-shaped islet formed by the eroding top of a volcano, the crater is a marine preserve ranging 10 to 80 feet in depth. The numerous tame fish and brilliant coral dwelling within the crater make it a popular introductory dive site. On calm days, the back side of Molokini (called Back Wall) can be a dramatic sight for advanced divers—giving them visibility of up to 150 feet. The enormous drop-off into the ʻAlalākeiki Channel (to 350 feet) offers awesome seascapes, black coral, and chance sightings of larger pelagic fish and sharks.

On the South Shore, a popular dive spot is **Mākena Landing**, also called Five Graves or Five Caves. About 1/5 mi down Mākena Road, you'll feast on underwater delights—caves, ledges, coral heads, and an outer reef home to a large green-sea-turtle colony (called "Turtle Town"). △**Entry is rocky lava, so be careful where you step.** This area is for the more experienced diver. Rookies can enter farther down Mākena Road at Mākena Landing, and dive to the right.

EQUIPMENT, LESSONS & TOURS

★ **Ed Robinson's Diving Adventures.** Ed wrote the book, literally, on Molokini. Because he knows so much, he includes a "Biology 101" talk with every dive. An expert marine photographer, he offers diving instruction and boat charters to South Maui, the backside of Molokini, and Lānaʻi. Weekly night dives are available, and there's a 10% discount if you book three or more days. Check out the Web site for good info and links on scuba sites, weather, and sea conditions. Dives start at $135. ⊠ Box 616, Kīhei ☎808/879–3584 or 800/635–1273 ⊕www.mauiscuba.com.

Maui Dive Shop. With six locations island-wide, Maui Dive Shop offers scuba charters, diving instruction, and equipment rental. Excursions, offering awe-inspiring beach and boat dives, go to Molokini Back Wall (most advanced dive), Shipwreck Beach on Lānaʻi, and more. Night dives and customized trips are available, as are full SSI and PADI certificate programs. ⊠1455 S. Kīhei Rd., Kīhei ☎808/879–3388 or 800/542–3483 ⊕www.mauidiveshop.com.

Shaka Divers. Shaka provides personalized dives including a great four-hour intro dive ($89), a refresher course ($79), scuba certification ($375), and shore dives ($59) to Mākena, Ulua, Five Graves (at Mākena Landing), Turtle Town, Bubble Cave, Black Sand Beach, and more. Typical

DID YOU KNOW?

Did You Know? The water quality in Hawai'i is typically outstanding; many sites afford 30-foot-plus visibility. On snorkel cruises, you can often stare from the boat rail right down to the bottom.

dives last about an hour, with 30 to 100 feet visibility. Dives can be booked on short notice, with afternoon tours available (hard to find on Maui). Shaka also offers night dives, torpedo scooter dives, and "bug hunt" expeditions (lobster hunts). Look for the Scuba Bus, blowing bubbles as it drives down the road. ⊠*24 Hakoi Pl., Kīhei* ☎*808/250–1234* ⊕*www.shakadivers.com.*

SNORKELING

3

No one should leave Maui without ducking underwater to meet a sea turtle, moray eel, or humuhumunukunukuāpua'a—the state fish. ■TIP→**Visibility is best in the morning, before the wind picks up.**

There are two ways to approach snorkeling—by land or by sea. Daily around 7 AM, a parade of boats heads out to Lāna'i or Molokini Crater, that ancient cone of volcanic cinder off the coast of Wailea. Boat trips offer some advantages—deeper water, seasonal whale-watching, crew assistance, lunch, and gear. But you don't need a boat; much of Maui's best snorkeling is found just steps from the road. Nearly the entire leeward coastline from Kapalua south to 'Āhihi-Kīna'u offers prime opportunities to ogle fish and turtles. If you're patient and sharp-eyed, you may glimpse eels, octopi, lobsters, eagle rays, and even a rare shark or monk seal.

WORD OF MOUTH. **"You should plan on all snorkeling activities for first thing in the morning, as the wind is lower and the water less choppy. Most every day, wind will come up before noon and make snorkeling difficult. Sometimes the wind is actually too much to sit on the beach with, and you end up lazing by the pool."—Ag3046**

BEST SPOTS

Snorkel sites here are listed from north to south, starting at the northwest corner of the island.

On the west side of the island, just north of Kapalua, **Honolua Bay** (⊠*Between mile markers 32 and 33 on Rte. 30, dirt road to left*) Marine Life Conservation District has a superb reef for snorkeling. When conditions are calm, it's one of the island's best spots with tons of fish and colorful corals to observe. ■TIP→**Make sure to bring a fish key with you, as you're sure to see many species of triggerfish, filefish, and wrasses.** The coral formations on the right side of the bay are particularly dramatic and feature pink, aqua, and orange varieties. Take care entering the water; there's no beach and the rocks and concrete ramp can be slippery.

The northeast corner of this windward-facing bay periodically gets hammered by big waves in winter, and high-profile surf contests are held here. Avoid the bay then, and after a heavy rain (you'll know because Honolua stream will be running across the access path).

Just minutes south of Honolua, dependable **Kapalua Bay** (⊠*From Rte. 30, turn onto Kapalua Pl., and walk through tunnel*) beckons. As beautiful above the water as it is below, Kapalua is exceptionally calm, even when other spots get testy. Needle and butterfly fish dart just past the sandy beach, which is why it's sometimes crowded. ⚠**Sand can be particularly hot here; watch your toes!**

★ **Fodor's Choice** We think **Black Rock** (⊠*In front of Kā'anapali Sheraton Maui, Kā'anapali Pkwy.*), at the northernmost tip of Kā'anapali Beach on West Maui, is tops for snorkelers of any skill level. The entry couldn't be easier—dump your towel on the sand in front of the Sheraton Maui resort and in you go. Beginners can stick close to shore and still see lots of action. Advanced snorkelers can swim beyond the sand to the tip of Black Rock, or Keka'a Point, to see larger fish and eagle rays. One of the underwater residents, a turtle named "Volkswagen" for its hefty size, can be found here. He sits very still; you must look closely. Equipment can be rented on-site. Parking, in a small lot adjoining the hotel, is the only hassle.

Along Honoapi'ilani Highway (Route 30) there are several favorite snorkel sites including the area just out from the cemetery at **Hanakao'o Beach Park** (⊠*Near mile marker 23 on Rte. 30*). At depths of 5 and 10 feet, you can see a variety of corals, especially as you head south toward Waihikuli Wayside Park. Farther down the highway, the shallow coral reef at **Olowalu** (⊠*South of Olowalu General Store on Rte. 30, at mile marker 14*) is good for a quick underwater tour, though the best spot is a ways out, at depths of 25 feet or more. Closer to shore, the visibility can be hit or miss, but if you're willing to venture out about 50 yards, you'll have easy access to an expansive coral reef with abundant fish life—no boat required. Swim offshore toward the pole sticking out of the reef. Except for during a south swell, this area is calm and good for families with small children; turtles are plentiful. Boats sometimes stop nearby (they refer to this site as "Coral Gardens") on their return trip from Molokini.

Excellent snorkeling is found down the coastline between Kīhei and Mākena on the South Shore. The best spots are along the rocky fringes of Wailea's beaches, Mōkapu, Ulua, Wailea, and Polo, off Wailea Alanui Drive. Find one of the public parking lots sandwiched between Wailea's luxury resorts, and enjoy these beaches' sandy entries, calm waters with relatively good visibility, and variety of fish species. Of the four beaches, Ulua has the best reef. You can glimpse a box-shape puffer fish here, and listen to snapping shrimp and parrot fish nibbling on coral.

At the very southernmost tip of paved road in South Maui lies **'Āhihi-Kīna'u** (⊠ *Just before end of Mākena Alanui Rd., follow marked trails through trees*) Natural Area Reserve, also referred to as La Pérouse Bay. Despite its barren, lava-scorched landscape, the area recently gained such popularity with adventurers and activity purveyors that it had to be closed to commercial traffic. A ranger is stationed at the parking lot to assist visitors. It's difficult terrain and sometimes crowded, but if you make use of the rangers' suggestions (stay on marked paths, wear sturdy shoes to hike in and out), you can experience some of the reserve's outstanding treasures, such as the sheltered cove known as the "Fish Bowl." ■ TIP➔**Be sure to bring water: this is a hot and unforgiving wilderness.**

EQUIPMENT

Most hotels and vacation rentals offer free use of snorkel gear. Beachside stands fronting the major resort areas rent equipment by the hour or day. ■ TIP➔**Don't shy away from asking for instructions; a snug fit makes all the difference in the world. A mask fits if it sticks to your face when you inhale deeply through your nose. Fins should cover your entire foot (unlike diving fins, which strap around your heel).** If you're squeamish about using someone else's gear (or need a prescription lens), pick up your own at any discount shop. Costco and Long's Drugs have better prices than ABC stores; dive shops have superior equipment.

Maui Dive Shop. You can rent pro gear (including optical masks, boogie boards, and wet suits) from six locations island-wide. Pump these guys for weather info before heading out—they'll know better than last night's news forecaster, and they'll give you the real deal on condi-

tions. ✉*1455 S. Kīhei Rd., Kīhei* ☎*808/873–3388* ⊕*www.
mauidiveshop.com.*

Snorkel Bob's. If you need gear, Snorkel Bob's will rent you
a mask, fins, and a snorkel, and throw in a carrying bag,
map, and snorkel tips for as little as $9 per week. Avoid the
circle masks and go for the split-level ($22 per week); it's
worth the extra cash. ✉*Nāpili Village Hotel, 5425 Lower
Honoapi'ilani Hwy., Nāpili* ☎*808/669–9603* ✉*Dickenson
Square, Dickenson St., Lahaina* ☎*808/662–0104* ✉*1279
S. Kīhei Rd., #310, Kīhei* ☎*808/875–6188* ✉*Kamaole
Beach Center, 2411 S. Kīhei Rd., Kīhei* ☎*808/879–7449*
⊕*www.snorkelbob.com.*

TOURS

The same boats that offer whale-watching, sailing, and diving also offer snorkeling excursions. Trips usually include
visits to two locales, lunch, gear, instruction, and possible
whale or dolphin sightings. Some captains troll for fish
along the way, and, if they're lucky, will occasionally catch
big game fish such as a marlin or mahimahi.

Molokini Crater, a moon-shaped crescent about 3 mi off
the shore of Wailea, is the most popular snorkel cruise
destination. You can spend half a day floating above the
fish-filled crater for about $80. Some say it's not as good
as it's made out to be, and that it's too crowded, but others
consider it to be one of the best spots in Hawai'i. Visibility
is generally outstanding and fish are incredibly tame. Your
second stop will be somewhere along the leeward coast,
either "Turtle Town" near Mākena or "Coral Gardens"
toward Lahaina. ■TIP→**Be aware that on blustery mornings,
there's a good chance the waters will be too rough to moor in
Molokini and you'll end up snorkeling some place off the shore,
which you could have driven to for free.** For the safety of everyone on the boat, it's the captain's prerogative to choose the
best spot for the day.

If you've tried snorkeling and are tentatively thinking about
scuba, you may want to try *snuba,* a cross between the two.
With snuba, you dive down 20 feet below the surface, only
you're attached to an air hose from the boat. Many of the
boats now offer snuba as well as snorkeling; expect to pay
between $45 and $65 in addition to the regular cost of a
snorkel cruise.

Snorkel cruises vary slightly—some serve mai tais and
steaks whereas others offer beer and cold cuts. You might

prefer a large ferry boat to a smaller sailboat, or vice versa. Whatever trip you choose, be sure you know where to go to board your vessel; getting lost in the harbor at 6 AM is a lousy start to a good day. ■TIP→**Bring sunscreen, an underwater camera (they're double the price on board), a towel, and a cover-up for the windy return trip.** Even tropical waters get chilly after hours of swimming, so consider wearing a rash guard. Wet suits can usually be rented for a fee. Hats without straps will blow away, and valuables should be left at home.

★ **Ann Fielding's Snorkel Maui.** For a personal introduction to Maui's undersea universe, this guided tour is the undisputable authority. A marine biologist, Fielding—formerly with the University of Hawai'i, Waikīkī Aquarium, and the Bishop Museum, and the author of several guides to island sea life—is the Carl Sagan of Hawai'i's reef cosmos. She'll not only show you fish, but she'll also introduce you to *individual* fish. This is a good first experience for dry-behind-the-ears types. Snorkel trips cost $90 per adult, and include a snack and equipment. Groups travel to snorkel sites by car, not boat. ☎808/572–8437 ⊕www. maui.net/~annf.

Maui Classic Charters. This company offers two top-rate snorkel trips at a good value. Hop aboard the *Four Winds II*, a 55-foot, glass-bottom catamaran, for one of the most dependable snorkel trips around. You'll spend more time than the other charter boats do at Molokini and enjoy turtle-watching on the way home. The trip includes optional snuba ($49 extra), Continental breakfast, and a deluxe barbecue lunch, beer, wine, and soda. For a faster ride, try the *Maui Magic,* Mā'alaea's fastest power cat. This boat takes fewer people (45 max) than some of the larger vessels, and as an added bonus, they offer snuba and play Hawaiian music on the ride. This one's good for kids. Trips range from $98 to $109; book online at least seven days in advance for a 15% discount. ⊠*Mā'alaea Harbor, Slips 55 and 80* ☎808/879–8188 *or* 800/736–5740 ⊕www. mauicharters.com.

Paragon. With this company, you get to snorkel and sail— they have some of the fastest vessels in the state. As long as conditions are good, you'll hit prime snorkel spots in Molokini, Lāna'i, and occasionally, Coral Gardens. The Lāna'i trip includes a Continental breakfast, a picnic lunch on the beach, snacks, open bar, a snorkel lesson, and plenty of time in the water. The friendly crew takes good care of you, making sure you get the most value and enjoyment from your trip. ⊠ *Māʻalaea Harbor Slip 72, or Lahaina Harbor* ☎ *808/244–2087* ⊕ *www.sailmaui.com.*

↻ ★ **Trilogy Excursions.** The longest-running operation on Maui is the Coon family's Trilogy Excursions. In terms of comprehensive offerings, this company's got it: six beautiful multihulled sailing vessels (though they usually only sail for a brief portion of the trip) at three departure sites. All excursions are manned by energetic crews who will keep you well-fed and entertained with stories of the islands and plenty of corny jokes. A full-day catamaran cruise to Lānaʻi includes Continental breakfast and barbecue lunch on board, a guided van tour of the island, a "Snorkeling 101" class, and time to snorkel in the waters of Lānaʻi's Hulopoʻe Marine Preserve (Trilogy has exclusive commercial access). There is a barbecue dinner on Lānaʻi and an optional dolphin safari. The company also offers a Molokini and Honolua Bay snorkel cruise that is top-notch. Many people consider a Trilogy excursion the highlight of their trip. ⊠ *Māʻalaea Harbor, Slip 99, Lahaina Harbor, or by Kāʻanapali Beach Hotel resort* ☎ *808/661–4743 or 888/225–6284* ⊕ *www.sailtrilogy.com.*

SURFING

Maui's diverse coastline has surf for every level of waterman or—woman. Waves on leeward-facing shores (West and South Maui) tend to break in gentle sets all summer long. Surf instructors in Kīhei and Lahaina can rent you boards, give you onshore instruction, and then lead you out through the channel, where it's safe to enter the surf. They'll shout encouragement while you paddle like mad for the thrill of standing on water—some will even give you a helpful shove. These areas are great for beginners; the only danger is whacking a stranger with your board or stubbing your toe against the reef.

The North Shore is another story. Winter waves pound the windward coast, attracting water champions from every corner of the world. Adrenaline addicts are towed in by Jet Ski to a legendary, deep-sea break called Jaws. Waves here periodically tower upward of 40 feet, dwarfing the helicopters seeking to capture unbelievable photos. The only spot for viewing this phenomenon (which happens just a few times a year) is on private property. So, if you hear the surfers next to you crowing about Jaws "going off," cozy up and get them to take you with them.

Whatever your skill, there's a board, a break, and even a surf guru to accommodate you. A two-hour lesson is a good intro to surf culture. Surf camps are becoming increasingly popular, especially with women. One- or two-week camps offer a terrific way to build muscle and self-esteem simultaneously. **Maui Surfer Girls** (⊕*www.mauisurfergirls. com*) immerses adventurous young ladies in wave-riding wisdom during overnight, one- and two-week camps. Coed camps are sponsored by **Action Sports Maui** (⊕*www. actionsportsmaui.com*).

BEST SPOTS

Beginners can hang 10 at Kīhei's **Cove Park** (✉*S. Kīhei Rd., Kīhei*), on the South Shore, a sometimes crowded but reliable 1- to 2-foot break. Boards can easily be rented across the street, or in neighboring Kalama Park parking lot. The only bummer is having to balance the 9-plus-foot board on your head while crossing busy South Kīhei Road. But hey, that wouldn't stop world-famous longboarder Eddie Aikau, now would it?

Long- or shortboarders can paddle out anywhere along Lahaina's coastline. One option is at **Launiupoko State Wayside** (✉*Honoapi'ilani Hwy. near mile marker 18*). The east end of the park has an easy break, good for beginners. Even better is **Ukumehame** (✉*Honoapi'ilani Hwy. near mile marker 12*), also called "Thousand Peaks." You'll soon see how the spot got its name—the waves here break again and again in wide and consistent rows, giving lots of room for beginning and intermediate surfers.

For advanced wave riders, **Ho'okipa Beach Park** (✉*2 mi past Pā'ia on Ha'na Hwy.*) boasts several well-loved breaks, including "Pavilions," "Lanes," "the Point," and "Middles." Surfers have priority until 11 AM, when windsurfers move in on the action. ■TIP→ **Competition is stiff here, and the attitudes can be "agro." If you don't know what you're doing, consider watching from the shore.**

You can get the wave report each day by checking page 2 of the *Maui News,* logging onto the Glenn James weather site at ⊕*www.hawaiiweathertoday.com*, or calling ☎808/871–5054 (for the weather forecast) or ☎808/877–3611 (for the surf report).

EQUIPMENT & LESSONS

Big Kahuna Adventures. Rent surfboards (soft-top longboards) here for $20 for two hours, or $30 for the day. The shop also offers surf lessons, and rents kayaks and snorkel gear. Located across from Cove Park. ✉ *1913-C S. Kīhei Rd., Kīhei* ☎*808/875–6395* ⊕*www.bigkahunaadventures.com.*

★ **Goofy Foot.** Surfing "goofy foot" means putting your right foot forward. They might be goofy, but we like the right-footed gurus here. Their safari shop is just plain cool and only steps away from "Breakwall," a great beginner's spot in Lahaina. Two-hour classes with five or fewer students are $65, and six-hour classes with lunch and an ocean-safety course are $300. They promise you'll be standing within a two-hour lesson—or it's free. ✉*505 Front St, Suite 123, Lahaina* ☎*808/244–9283* ⊕*www.goofyfootsurfschool.com.*

Hāna Highway Surf. If you're heading out to the North Shore surf, you can pick up boards ranging from beginner's soft-tops to high-performance shortboards here for $20 per day. ✉*149 Hāna Hwy., Pā'ia* ☎*808/579–8999.*

Hi Tech Maui. Locals hold Hi Tech in the highest regard. They have some of the best boards, advice, and attitudes around. Rent surfboards for $20 per day (or soft boards for $14); $112 for the week. They rent even their best models—choose from longboards, shortboards, and hybrids. All rentals come with board bags, roof racks, and oh yeah, wax. ✉*425 Koloa St., Kahului* ☎*808/877–2111* ⊕*www. htmaui.com.*

Nancy Emerson School of Surfing. Nancy's motto is "If my dog can surf, so can you." Instructors here will get even the most shaky novice riding with their "Learn to Surf in One Lesson" program. A two-hour group lesson (six students max) is $75. Surf clinics with Nancy herself—a pro surf champion and occasional Hollywood stunt double—are offered occasionally; lessons with her equally qualified instructors are $165–$200 for two hours. Multiple-day sessions start at $350. They provide the boards and rash guards. ✉*505 Front St., Suite 224B, Lahaina* ☎*808/244–7873* ⊕*www. mauisurfclinics.com.*

WHALE-WATCHING

From November through May, whale-watching becomes one of the most popular activities on Maui. During the season, all outfitters offer whale-watching in addition to their regular activities, and most do an excellent job. Boats leave the wharves at Lahaina and Māʻalaea in search of humpbacks, allowing you to enjoy the awe-inspiring size of these creatures in closer proximity.

As it's almost impossible *not* to see whales in winter on Maui, you'll want to prioritize: is adventure or comfort your aim? If close encounters with the giants of the deep are your desire, pick a smaller boat that promises sightings. Those who think "green" usually prefer the smaller, quieter vessels that produce the least amount of negative impact to the whales' natural environment. If an impromptu marine-biology lesson sounds fun, go with the Pacific Whale Foundation. Two-hour forays into the whales' world are around $30. For those wanting to sip mai tais as whales cruise calmly by, stick with a sunset cruise on a boat with an open bar and *pūpū* ($40 and up). ■TIP→ **Afternoon trips are generally rougher because the wind picks up, but some say this is when the most surface action occurs.**

Every captain aims to please during whale season, getting as close as legally possible (100 yards). Crew members know when a whale is about to dive (after several waves of its heart-shaped tail) but rarely can predict breaches (when the whale hurls itself up and almost entirely out of the water). Prime-viewing space (on the upper and lower decks, around the railings) is limited, so boats can feel crowded even when half full. If you don't want to squeeze in beside strangers, opt for a smaller boat with fewer bookings. Don't forget to bring sunscreen, sunglasses, light long sleeves, and a hat you can secure. Winter weather is less predictable and at times can be extreme, especially as the wind picks up. Arrive early to find parking.

BEST SPOTS

From December 15 to May 1 the Pacific Whale Foundation has naturalists stationed in two places—on the rooftop of their headquarters and at the scenic viewpoint at **McGregor Point Lookout** (⊠*Between mile markers 7 and 8 on Honoapiʻilani Hwy., Rte. 30*). Just like the commuting traffic, whales cruise along the *pali,* or cliff-side, of West Maui's Honoapiʻilani Highway all day long. △ **Make sure to park safely before craning your neck out to see them.**

CLOSE UP

The Humpback's Winter Home

The humpback whales' attraction to Maui is legendary. More than half the Pacific's humpback population winters in Hawai'i, especially in the waters around the Valley Isle, where mothers can be seen just a few hundred feet offshore training their young calves in the fine points of whale etiquette. Watching from shore it's easy to catch sight of whales spouting, or even breaching—when they leap almost entirely out of the sea, slapping back onto the water with a huge splash.

At one time there were thousands of the huge mammals, but a history of overhunting and marine pollution dwindled the world population to about 1,500. In 1966 humpbacks were put on the endangered species list. Hunting or harassing whales is illegal in the waters of most nations, and in the United States, boats and airplanes are restricted from getting too close. The jury is still out, however, on the effects military sonar testing has on the marine mammals.

Marine biologists believe the humpbacks (much like the humans) keep returning to Hawai'i because of its warmth. Having fattened themselves in subarctic waters all summer, the whales migrate south in the winter to breed, and a rebounding population of thousands cruise Maui waters. Winter is calving time, and the young whales, born with little blubber, probably couldn't survive in the frigid Alaskan waters. No one has ever seen a whale give birth here, but experts know that calving is their main winter activity, since the 1- and 2-ton youngsters suddenly appear while the whales are in residence.

The first sighting of a humpback whale spout each season is exciting and reassuring for locals on Maui. A collective sigh of relief can be heard, "Ah, they've returned." In the not-so-far distance, flukes and flippers can be seen rising above the ocean's surface. It's hard not to anthropomorphize the tail-waving; it looks like such an amiable, human gesture. Each fluke is uniquely patterned, like a human's fingerprint, and is used to identify the giants as they travel halfway around the globe and back.

3

The northern end of **Keawakapu Beach** (⊠*S. Kīhei Rd. near Kilohana Dr.*) seems to be a whale magnet. Situate yourself on the sand or at the nearby restaurant, and you're bound to see a mama whale patiently teaching her calf the exact technique of flipper-waving.

Humpback whale calves are plentiful in winter; this one is breaching off West Maui.

BOATS & CHARTERS

Marine Charters. Two-hour cruises narrated by a naturalist are offered aboard *Pride of Maui*, a 65-foot power catamaran (140 passengers max). There's a main cabin, upper sundeck, and swim platform—and you can listen to the whales sing. Trips start at $26 per adult, and include *pūpū* and an open bar. ✉*Mā'alaea Harbor, Slip 70, Mā'alaea* ☎*877/867–7433 or 808/242–0955* ⊕*www.prideofmaui.com.*

⟲ **Pacific Whale Foundation.** This nonprofit organization pio-
★ neered whale-watching back in 1979 and now runs four boats, with 15 trips daily. As the most recognizable name in whale-watching, the crew (with a certified marine biologist on board) offers insights into whale behavior (do they *really* know what those tail flicks mean?) and suggests ways for you to help save marine life worldwide. The best part about these trips is the underwater hydrophone that allows you to actually listen to the whales sing. Trips meet at the Foundation's store, where you can buy whale paraphernalia, snacks, and coffee—a real bonus for 8 AM trips. Passengers are then herded much like migrating whales down to the harbor. These trips are more affordable than others, but you'll be sharing the boat with about 100 people in stadium seating. Once you catch sight of the wildlife up-close, however, you can't help but be thrilled. ✉*Mā'alaea and Lahaina harbors* ☎*800/942–5311 or 808/249–8811* ⊕*www.pacificwhale.org.*

Trilogy Excursions. Trilogy whale-watching trips consist of smaller crowds of about 20 to 30 passengers, and include beverages and snacks, an onboard marine naturalist, and hydrophones (microphones that detect underwater sound waves). Trips are $39 plus tax. Book online for a discount. ⊠*Loading at* Kāʻanapali Beach Hotel ☎*808/661–4743 or 888/225–6284* ⊕*www.sailtrilogy.com.*

WINDSURFING

Something about Maui's wind and water stirs the spirit of innovation. Windsurfing, invented in the 1950s, found its true home at Hoʻokipa on Maui's North Shore in 1980. Seemingly overnight, windsurfing pros from around the world flooded the area. Equipment evolved, amazing film footage was captured, and a new sport was born.

If you're new to the action, you can get lessons from the experts island-wide. For a beginner, the best thing about windsurfing is (unlike surfing) you don't have to paddle. Instead, you have to hold on like heck to a flapping sail, as it whisks you into the wind. Needless to say, you're going to need a little coordination and balance to pull this off. Instructors start you out on a beach at Kanahā, where the big boys go. Lessons range from two-hour introductory classes to five-day advanced "flight school." If you're an old salt, pick up tips and equipment from the companies below.

ON THE SIDELINES. Few places lay claim to as many windsurfing tournaments as Maui. In March the PWA Hawaiian Pro-Am Windsurfing competition gets under way at Hoʻokipa Beach. In June the Da Kine Windsurfing Classic lures top windsurfers to Kanahā Beach, and in November the Aloha Classic World Wave Sailing Championships takes place at Hoʻokipa. For competitions featuring amateurs as well as professionals, check out the Maui Race Series (☎808/877–2111), six events held at Kanahā Beach in Kahului in summer.

BEST SPOTS

After **Hoʻokipa Bay** (⊠*2 mi past Pāʻia on Hāna Hwy.*) was discovered by windsurfers three decades ago, this windy beach 10 mi east of Kahului gained an international reputation. The spot is blessed with optimal wave-sailing wind and sea conditions, and can offer the ultimate aerial experience.

In summer the windsurfing crowd heads south to **Kalepolepo Beach** (⊠*S. Kīhei Rd. near Ohukai St.*) on the South Shore. Trade winds build in strength and by afternoon a swarm of dragonfly-sails can be seen skimming the whitecaps, with the West Maui Mountains as a backdrop.

A great site for speed, **Kanahā Beach Park** (⊠*Behind Kahului Airport*) is dedicated to beginners in the morning hours, before the waves and wind really get roaring. After 11 AM, the professionals choose from their quiver of sails the size and shape best suited for the day's demands. This beach tends to have smaller waves and forceful winds—sometimes sending sailors flying at 40 knots. ■TIP→**If you aren't ready to go pro, this is a great place for a picnic while you watch from the beach.**

EQUIPMENT & LESSONS

Action Sports Maui. The quirky, friendly professionals here will meet you at Kanahā on the North Shore, outfit you with your sail and board, and guide you through your first "jibe" or turn. They promise your learning time will be cut in half. Don't be afraid to ask lots of questions. Lessons are held at 9 AM every morning except Sunday at Kanahā, and start at $69 for a two-hour class. Three- and five-day courses cost $225 and $375. ⊠*6 E. Waipuilani Rd., Kīhei* ☎*808/871–5857* ⊕*www.actionsportsmaui.com.*

Hi Tech Surf & Sports. Known locally as Maui's finest windsurfing school, Hawaiian Sailboarding Techniques (HST, located in Hi Tech) brings you quality instruction by skilled sailors. Founded by Alan Cadiz, an accomplished World Cup Pro, the school sets high standards for a safe, quality windsurfing experience. Hi Tech itself offers excellent equipment rentals; $50 gets you a board, two sails, a mast, and roof racks for 24 hours. ⊠*425 Koloa St., Kahului* ☎*808/877–2111* ⊕*www.htmaui.com.*

Second Wind. Located in Kahului, this company rents boards with two sails for $46 per day. Boards with three sails go for $49 per day. Intro classes start at $79. ⊠*11 Hāna Hwy., Kahului* ☎*808/877–7467* ⊕*www.secondwindmaui.com.*

Whether you're riding horseback or back-roading it on an ATV, there's plenty to keep you busy. This chapter will get your toes out of the sand and into your hiking boots or golf shoes. For easy reference, activities are listed in alphabetical order.

AERIAL TOURS

Helicopter flight-seeing excursions can take you over the West Maui Mountains, Hāna, Haleakalā Crater, even the Big Island lava flow, or the islands of Lānaʻi and Molokaʻi. This is a beautiful, exciting way to see the island, and the *only* way to see some of its most dramatic areas and waterfalls. Tour prices usually include a DVD of your trip so you can relive the experience at home. Prices run from about $159 for a half-hour rain-forest tour to more than $400 for a 90-minute mega-experience that includes a champagne toast on landing. Generally the 45- to 50-minute flights are the best value, and if you're willing to chance it, considerable discounts may be available if you call last minute or book online.

It takes about 90 minutes to travel inside the volcano, then down to the village of Hāna. Some companies stop in secluded areas for refreshments. Helicopter-tour operators throughout the state come under sharp scrutiny for passenger safety and equipment maintenance. Don't be shy; ask about a company's safety record, flight paths, age of equipment, and level of operator experience. Generally, though, if they're still in business they're doing something right.

Blue Hawaiian Helicopters. This company has provided aerial adventures in Hawaiʻi since 1985, and has been integral in some of the filming Hollywood has done on Maui. Its EcoStar helicopters are air-conditioned and have noise-blocking headsets for all passengers. Flights are 30 to 70 minutes and cost $159 to $371. They also offer a fly–drive special to Hāna with Temptation Tours limo vans. Charter flights are also available. ⊠*Kahului Heliport, Hangar 105, Kahului* ☎*808/871–8844* ⊕*www.bluehawaiian.com.*

Sunshine Helicopters. Sunshine offers tours of Maui, Lānaʻi, and Molokaʻi, as well as the Big Island, in its *Black Beauty* AStar or WhisperStar aircraft. A pilot-narrated DVD of your actual flight is available for purchase. Prices start at $175 for 30 to 90 minutes. First-class seating is available for an additional fee. ⊠*Kahului Heliport, Hangar 107, Kahului* ☎*808/871–0722 or 800/544–2520* ⊕*www. sunshinehelicopters.com.*

ATV TOURS

Haleakalā ATV Tours. Haleakalā ATV Tours explore the mountainside in their own way: propelled through the forest on 420 cc, four-wheel-drive, Honda Rancher all-terrain vehicles. Their two-hour tour of Haleakalā Ranch costs $105. On the three-hour adventure ($145), you begin at Haleakalā Ranch and rev right up to the pristine Waikamoi rain-forest preserve. Riders must be at least 16 years old, and there is limited passenger availability. Private tours are available for $205 per person. Discounts may be obtained by booking online. Haleakalā ATV Tours is now offering combination ATV and Zipline tours with Skyline Eco Adventures on Sunday for $187. ☎ *808/661–0288 or 877/661–0288* ⊕ *www.atvmaui.com.*

BIKING

Maui County biking is safer and more convenient than in the past, but long distances and mountainous terrain keep it from being a practical mode of travel. Still, painted bike lanes enable cyclists to travel all the way from Mākena to Kapalua, and you'll see hardy souls battling the trade winds under the hot Maui sun.

Several companies offer guided bike tours down Haleakalā. This activity is a great way to enjoy an easy, gravity-induced bike ride, but isn't for those not confident in their ability to handle a bike. The ride is inherently dangerous due to the slope, sharp turns, and the fact that you're riding down an actual road with cars on it. That said, the guided bike companies do take every safety precaution. A few companies are now offering unguided (or as they like to say "self-guided") tours where they provide you with the bike and transportation to the mountain and then you're free to descend at your own pace. Most companies offer discounts for Internet bookings. Sunrise is downright cold at the summit, so dress in layers.

⚠ **At this writing officials at Haleakalā National Park have suspended bike tours within the park boundaries.** Some companies have made arrangements to provide a van tour of the summit prior to beginning the downhill bike ride outside park boundaries. Check with the individual companies for updates, tour routes, and amenities.

BEST SPOTS

Though it's changing, at present there are few truly good spots to ride on Maui. Street bikers will want to head out to scenic **Thompson Road** (⊠ *Off Rte. 37, Kula Hwy., Keokea*). It's quiet, gently curvy, and flanked by gorgeous views on both sides. Plus, because it's at a higher elevation, the air temperature is cooler and the wind lighter. The coast back down toward Kahului on the Kula Highway is worth the ride up. Mountain bikers have favored the remote **Polipoli Forest** (⊠ *Off Rte. 377, end of Waipoli Rd.*) for its bumpy trail through an unlikely forest of conifers.

EQUIPMENT & TOURS

Haleakalā Bike Company. If you're thinking about an unguided Haleakalā bike trip, consider one of the trips offered by this company. Meet at the Old Haʻikū Cannery and take their van shuttle to the summit. Along the way you'll learn about the history of the island, the volcano, and other Hawaiiana. Unlike the guided trips, food is not included although there are several spots along the way down to stop, rest, and eat. The simple, mostly downhill route takes you right back to the cannery where you started. HBC offers bike sales, rentals, and services. Prices range from $69 to $115. ⊠ *810 Haʻikū Rd., Suite 120, Haʻikū* ☎ *808/575–9575 or 888/922–2453* ⊕ *www.bikemaui.com.*

Island Biker. This is the premier bike shop on Maui when it comes to rental, sales, and service. They offer 2005 Specialized standard front-shock bikes, road bikes, and full-suspension mountain bikes. Daily or weekly rates range $40 to $150, and include a helmet, pump, water bottle, and flat-repair kit. They can suggest routes appropriate for mountain or road biking, or you can join a biweekly group ride. ⊠ *415 Dairy Rd., Kahului* ☎ *808/877–7744* ⊕ *www. islandbikermaui.com.*

Maui Downhill. If biking down the side of Haleakalā sounds like fun, several companies are ready to book you a tour. Maui Downhill vans will pick you up at your resort, shuttle you to the mountain, help you onto a bike, and follow you as you coast down through clouds and gorgeous scenery into the town of Pukalani. Their Super Sunrise and Super Day safaris include a van tour of the summit. There is also a combination bike and winery tour that gives you an opportunity to visit Maui's Winery (also known as Tedeschi Vineyards). Treks cost $125 to $175, and include a continental breakfast at the company's base. ⊠ *199 Dairy*

Rd., Kahului ☎*808/871–2155 or 800/535–2453* ⊕*www.
mauidownhill.com.*

West Maui Cycles. Servicing the west side of the island, WMC
offers an assortment of cycles including cruisers for $15
per day ($60 per week); hybrids for $30 per day ($120
per week); and Cannondale road bikes and front-suspen-
sion Giantbikes for $50 per day ($200 per week). Sales
and service are available. ⊠*1087 Limahana St., Lahaina*
☎*808/661–9005* ⊕*www.westmauicycles.com.*

GOLF

Maui's natural beauty and surroundings offer some of the
most jaw-dropping vistas imaginable on a golf course.
Holes run across small bays, past craggy lava outcrops,
and up into cool, forested mountains. Most courses have
mesmerizing ocean views, some close enough to feel the
salt in the air. And although many of the courses are affili-
ated with resorts (and therefore a little pricier), the gen-
eral-public courses are no less impressive. You might even
consider a ferry ride to the neighbor island of Lāna'i for
a round on either of its two championship courses *(see
chapter 8, Lāna'i).*

Green Fees: Green fees listed here are the highest course rates
per round on weekdays and weekends for U.S. residents.
(Some courses charge non–U.S. residents higher prices.)
Discounts are often available for resort guests and for those
who book tee times on the Web. Rental clubs may or may
not be included with green fees. Twilight fees are usually
offered; call individual courses for information.

■TIP→**Resort courses, in particular, offer more than the usual
three sets of tees, sometimes four or five. So bite off as much or
little challenge as you like.** Tee it up from the tips and you'll
end up playing a few 600-yard par 5s and see a few 250-
yard forced carries.

WEST MAUI

★ **Kā'anapali Golf Resort.** The Royal Kā'anapali (North) Course
(1962) is one of three in Hawai'i designed by Robert Trent
Jones Sr., the godfather of modern golf architecture. The
greens average a whopping 10,000 square feet, necessary
because of the often-severe undulation. The par-4 18th hole
(into the prevailing trade breezes, with out-of-bounds on
the left, and a lake on the right) is notoriously tough. The
Kā'anapali Kai (South) Course (Arthur Jack Snyder, 1976)

shares similar seaside-into-the-hills terrain, but is rated a couple of strokes easier, mostly because putts are less treacherous. ⊠2290 Kā'anapali Pkwy., Lahaina ☎808/661–3691 ⊕www.kaanapali-golf.com ⚑North Course: 18 holes. 6500 yds. Par 71. Slope 126. Green Fee: $225. South Course: 18 holes. 6400 yds. Par 70. Slope 124. Green Fee: $185 ☞Facilities: Driving range, putting green, rental clubs, golf carts, lessons, restaurant, bar.

★ **Fodor's**Choice **Kapalua Resort.** Perhaps Hawai'i's best-known golf resort and the crown jewel of golf on Maui, Kapalua hosts the PGA Tour's first event each January: the Mercedes Championships at the Plantation Course at Kapalua. Ben Crenshaw and Bill Coore (1991) tried to incorporate traditional shot values in a very nontraditional site, taking into account slope, gravity, and the prevailing trade winds. The par-5 18th, for instance, plays 663 yards from the back tees (600 yards from the resort tees). The hole drops 170 feet in elevation, narrowing as it goes to a partially guarded green, and plays downwind and down-grain. Despite the longer-than-usual distance, the slope is great enough and the wind at your back usually brisk enough to reach the green with two well-struck shots—a truly unbelievable finish to a course that will challenge, frustrate, and reward the patient golfer.

The Bay Course (Arnold Palmer and Francis Duane, 1975) is the more traditional of Kapalua's courses, with gentle rolling fairways and generous greens. The most memorable hole is the par-3 fifth, with a tee shot that must carry a turquoise finger of Onelua Bay. The Kapalua Golf Academy (⊠1000 Office Rd. ☎808/669–6500) offers 23 acres of practice turf and 11 teeing areas, a special golf fitness gym, and an instructional bay with video analysis. Each of the courses has a separate clubhouse. The Bay Course: ⊠300 Kapalua Dr., Kapalua ☎808/669–8820 ⊕www.kapaluamaui.com/golf ⚑18 holes. 6600 yds. Par 72. Slope 133. Green Fee: $215 ☞Facilities: Driving range, putting green, rental clubs, pro shop, lessons, restaurant, bar. The Plantation Course: ⊠2000 Plantation Club Dr., Kapalua ☎808/669–8877 ⊕www.kapaluamaui.com/golf ⚑18 holes. 7411 yds. Par 73. Slope 135. Green Fee: $295 ☞Facilities: Driving range, putting green, golf carts, pull carts, rental clubs, pro shop, golf academy/lessons, restaurant, bar.

THE SOUTH SHORE

★ **Fodors**Choice **Mākena Resort.** Robert Trent Jones Jr. and Don Knotts (not the actor) built the first course at Mākena in 1981. A decade later Jones was asked to create 18 totally new holes and blend them with the existing course to form the North and South courses, which opened in 1994. Both courses—sculpted from the lava flows on the western flank of Haleakalā—offer quick greens with lots of breaks, and plenty of scenic distractions. On the North Course, the fourth is one of the most picturesque inland par 3s in Hawai'i, with the green guarded on the right by a pond. The sixth is an excellent example of option golf: the fairway is sliced up the middle by a gaping ravine, which must sooner or later be crossed to reach the green. Although trees frame most holes on the North Course, the South Course is more open. This means it plays somewhat easier off the tee, but the greens are trickier. The view from the elevated tee of the par-5 10th is lovely with the lake in the foreground mirroring the ocean in the distance. The par-4 16th is another sight to see, with the Pacific running along the left side. ⊠*5415 Mākena Alanui, Mākena* ☎*808/879–3344* ⊕*www. princeresortshawaii.com/maui-golf.php* ⌦*North Course: 18 holes. 6567 yds. Par 72. Slope 135. Green Fee: $190. South Course: 18 holes. 6630 yds. Par 72. Slope 133. Green Fee: $190* ☞*Facilities: Driving range, putting green, golf carts, rental clubs, pro shop, golf academy/lessons, restaurant, bar.*

★ **Fodors**Choice **Wailea.** Wailea is the only Hawai'i resort to offer three different courses: Gold, Emerald, and Old Blue. Designed by Robert Trent Jones Jr., these courses share similar terrain, carved into the leeward slopes of Haleakalā. Although the ocean does not come into play, its beauty is visible on almost every hole. ■TIP➔**Remember, putts break dramatically toward the ocean.**

Jones refers to the Gold Course at Wailea (1993) as the "masculine" course. Host to the Championship Senior Skins Game in February, it's all trees and lava and regarded as the hardest of the three courses. The trick here is to note even subtle changes in elevation. The par-3 eighth, for example, plays from an elevated tee across a lava ravine to a large, well-bunkered green framed by palm trees, the blue sea, and tiny Molokini. The course has been labeled a "thinking player's" course because it demands strategy and careful club selection. The Emerald Course at Wailea (1994) is the "feminine" layout with lots of flowers and bunkering away from greens. This by no means suggests that it plays easy. Although this may seem to render the bunker benign, the opposite is true. A bunker well in front of a green disguises the distance to the hole. Likewise, the Emerald's extensive flower beds are designed to be dangerous distractions because of their beauty. The Gold and Emerald share a clubhouse, practice facility, and 19th hole. Judging elevation change is also key at Wailea's first course, the Old Blue Course (Arthur Jack Snyder, 1971). Fairways and greens tend to be wider and more forgiving than on the Gold or Emerald, and run through colorful flora that includes hibiscus, wiliwili, bougainvillea, and plumeria. Old Blue Course: ✉120 Kaukahi St., Wailea ☎808/875–5155 or 888/328–6284 ⊕www.waileagolf. com ⚑18 holes. 6765 yds. Par 72. Slope 129. Green Fee: $185 ☞Facilities: Driving range, putting green, golf carts, rental clubs, pro shop, golf academy/lessons, restaurant, bar. Gold and Emerald Courses: ✉100 Wailea Golf Club Dr., Wailea ☎808/875–7450 or 888/328–6284 ⊕www. waileagolf.com ⚑Gold Course: 18 holes. 6653 yds. Par 72. Slope 132. Green Fee: $200. Emerald Course: 18 holes. 6,407 yds. Par 72. Slope 130. Green Fee: $200 ☞Facilities: Driving range, putting green, golf carts, rental clubs, pro shop, golf academy/lessons, restaurant, bar.

CENTRAL MAUI

★ FodorśChoice **The Dunes at Maui Lani.** This is Robin Nelson (1999) at his minimalist best, a bit of British links in the middle of the Pacific. Holes run through ancient, lightly wooded sand dunes, 5 mi inland from Kahului Harbor. Thanks to the natural humps and slopes of the dunes, Nelson had to move very little dirt and created a natural beauty. During the design phase he visited Ireland, and not so coincidentally the par-3 third looks a lot like the Dell at Lahinch: a white dune on the right sloping down into a deep bunker and partially obscuring the right side of the green—just one of several blind to semi-blind shots here. Popular with residents, this course has won several awards including "Best 35 New Courses in America" by *Golf Magazine* and "Five Best Kept Secret Golf Courses in America" by *Golf Digest.* ✉380 Kuihelani Hwy., Kahului ☎808/873–0422 ⊕www.dunesatmauilani.com ⚑18 holes. 6841 yds. Par 72. Slope 136. Green Fee: $99 ☞Facilities: Driving range, putting green, golf carts, rental clubs, pro shop, golf academy/lessons, restaurant, bar.

UPCOUNTRY

Pukalani Golf Course. At 1,110 feet above sea level, Pukalani (Bob E. and Robert L. Baldock, 1970) provides one of the finest vistas in all Hawai'i. Holes run up, down, and across the slopes of Haleakalā. The trade winds tend to come up in the late morning and afternoon. This—combined with frequent elevation change—makes club selection a test. The fairways tend to be wide, but greens are undulating and quick. ⊠ *360 Pukalani St., Pukalani* ☎ *808/572–1314* ⊕ *www.pukalanigolf.com* ↥ *18 holes. 6962 yds. Par 72. Slope 127. Green Fee: $78* ☞ *Facilities: Driving range, putting green, rental clubs, golf carts, pro shop.*

3

HANG GLIDING & PARAGLIDING

Hang Gliding Maui. Armin Engert will take you on an instructional powered hang-gliding trip out of Hāna Airport in East Maui. With more than 7,500 hours in flight and a perfect safety record, Armin flies you 1,000 feet over Maui's most beautiful coast. A 30-minute flight lesson costs $130, and a 60-minute lesson is $220. This is easily one of the coolest things you can do in Hāna. Snapshots of your flight from a wing-mounted camera cost an additional $30, and a 34-minute DVD of the flight is available for $70. Reservations are required. ⊠ *Hāna Airport, Hāna* ☎ *808/572–6557* ⊕ *www.hangglidingmaui.com.*

Proflyght Paragliding. Proflyght is the only paragliding outfit on Maui to offer solo, tandem, and instruction at Polipoli State Park. The leeward slope of Haleakalā lends itself perfectly to paragliding with breathtaking scenery and upcountry air currents that increase and rise throughout the day. Polipoli creates tremendous thermals that allow one to peacefully descend 3,000 feet to the landing zone. Owner–pilot Dexter Clearwater boasts a perfect safety record with tandems and student pilots since taking over the company in 2002. Ask and Dexter will bring along his flying duck Chuckie or his paragliding puppy Daisy. Prices start at $175, with full certification available. ⊠ *Polipoli State Park, Kula* ☎ *808/874–5433* ⊕ *www.paraglidehawaii.com.*

HIKING

Hikes on Maui include treks along coastal seashore, verdant rain forest, and alpine desert. Orchids, hibiscus, ginger, heliconia, and anthuriums grow wild on many trails, and exotic fruits like mountain apple, lilikoi (passion fruit), thimbleberry, and strawberry guava provide refreshing snacks for hikers. Ironically, much of what you see in lower altitude forests is alien, brought to Hawai'i at one time or another by someone hoping to improve upon nature. Plants like strawberry guava and ginger may be tasty, but they grow over native forest plants and have become serious, problematic weeds.

The best hikes get you out of the imported landscaping and into the truly exotic wilderness. Hawai'i possesses some of the world's rarest plants, insects, and birds. Pocket field guides are available at most grocery or drug stores and can really illuminate your walk. Before you know it you'll be nudging your companion and pointing out trees that look like something out of a Dr. Seuss book. If you watch the right branches quietly you can spot the same honeycreepers or happy-face spiders scientists have spent their lives studying.

BEST SPOTS

★ **Fodor's**Choice Hiking **Haleakalā Crater** (✉ *Haleakala National Park* ☎*808/572–4400*) is undoubtedly the best hiking on the island. There are 30 mi of trails, two camping areas, and three cabins. If you're in shape, you can do a day hike descending from the summit (along Sliding Sands Trail) to the crater floor. If you're in shape and have time, consider spending several days here amid the cinder cones, lava flows, and all that loud silence. ■TIP➔ **At this writing, the National Park Service planned to close Sliding Sands Trail for rehabilitation work. Check with officials at Haleakala National Park before making plans to hike the trail.**

Going into the crater is like going to a different planet. In the early 1960s NASA actually brought moon-suited astronauts here to practice what it would be like to "walk on the moon." Today, on one of the many hikes—most moderate to strenuous—you'll traverse black sand and wild lava formations, follow the trail of blooming *'ahinahina* (silverswords), watch for *nēnē* (Hawaiian geese) as they fly above you, and witness tremendous views of big sky and burned-red cliffs. Be sure to bring layered clothing—and plenty of warm clothes if you're staying overnight. It may be scorching hot during the day, but it gets mighty chilly after dark. Ask a ranger about water availability before starting your hike. Note that overnight visitors must get a permit at park headquarters before entering the crater; day-use visitors do not need a permit.

A branch of Haleakalā National Park, **'Ohe'o Gulch** (⊠*Route 31, 10 mi past Hāna town,* ☎ *808/572–4400*) is famous for its pools (the area is sometimes called the "Seven Sacred Pools"). Truth is, there are more than seven pools, and there's nothing sacred about them. The owner of the Hotel Hāna started calling the area "Seven Sacred Pools" to attract the masses to sleepy old Hāna. His plan worked and the name stuck, much to the chagrin of most Mauians. The Pools of 'Ohe'o is another name for them. The best time to visit the pools is in the morning, before the crowds and tour buses arrive. Start your day with a vigorous hike. 'Ohe'o has some fantastic trails to choose from, including our favorite, the Pipiwai Trail *(see below)*. When you're done, nothing could be better than going to the pools, lounging on the rocks, and cooling off in the freshwater reserves.

You'll find 'Ohe'o Gulch on. All visitors must pay a $10 national park fee (per car not per person), which is valid for three days and can be used at Haleakalā's summit as well. Important note: The road beyond 'Ohe'o Gulch to Kaupo was closed at this writing because of a 2006 earthquake that caused some instability and falling rocks. ■TIP➔**Check with officials at Haleakalā National Park before traveling beyond 'Ohe'o Gulch.**

WORD OF MOUTH. **"If you do the trip to Hāna, plan on a long day. Take some hiking shoes and hike to the waterfalls at 'Ohe'o Gulch [on the Pipiwai Trail]. It's about an hour hike up but absolutely worth the effort. The bamboo forest is unforgettable and the waterfall is spectacular. Be sure to take plenty of water as no potable water is available at the park."—Spokaneman**

A much neglected hike in southwestern Maui is the 5.5-mi coastal **Hoapili Trail** (⊠*Follow Mākena Alanui to end of paved road at La Pérouse Bay, walk through parking lot along dirt road, follow signs*) beyond the 'Āhihi-Kīna'u Natural Area Reserve. Named after a bygone Hawaiian king, it follows the shoreline, threading through the remains of ancient Hawaiian villages. The once-thriving community was displaced by one of Maui's last lava flows. Later, King Hoapili was responsible for overseeing the creation of an island-wide highway. This remaining section, a wide path of stacked lava rocks, is a marvel to look at and walk on, though it's not the easiest surface for the ankles. (It's rumored to have once been covered in grass.) You can wander over to the Hanamanioa lighthouse, or quietly ponder the rough life of the ancients.

Wear sturdy shoes and bring extra water. This is brutal territory with little shade and no facilities. Beautiful, yes. Accommodating, no.

★ One of Maui's great wonders, **ʻĪao Valley State Park** is the site of a famous battle to unite the Hawaiian Islands. Out of the clouds, the **ʻĪao Needle,** a tall chunk of volcanic rock, stands as a monument to the long-ago lookout for Maui warriors. Today, there's nothing warlike about it: the valley is a peaceful land of lush, tropical plants, clear pools and a running stream, and easy, enjoyable walks. You have a choice of two paved walkways in the park: you can either cross the ʻĪao Stream and explore the junglelike area, or ascend the stairs up to the ʻĪao Needle for spectacular views of Central Maui, or pause in the garden of Hawaiian heritage plants and marvel at the local youngsters hurling themselves from the bridge into the chilly pools below. ✛ *To get to ʻĪao Valley State Park, go through Wailuku and continue to the west end of Route 32. The road dead-ends into the parking lot.* ☎ *808/984–8109* ⊙ *Daily 7 AM to 7 PM* ▣ *Free.*

GOING WITH A GUIDE

★ **Fodor's** Choice **Friends of Haleakalā National Park.** This nonprofit offers day and overnight service trips into the crater, and in the Kipahulu region. The purpose of your trip, the service work itself, isn't too much—mostly removing invasive plants and light cabin maintenance. Chances are you'll make good friends and have more fun than on a hike you'd do on your own. Trip leader Farley, or one of his equally knowledgeable cohorts, will take you to places you'd never otherwise see, and teach you about the native flora and birds along the way. Bring your own water and rain gear; share food in group dinners. Admission is free. ☎ *808/248–7660* ⊕ *www.fhnp.org.*

★ **Fodor's** Choice **Hike Maui.** Hike Maui is the oldest hiking company in the Islands, its rain forest, mountain ridge, crater, coastline, and archaeological-snorkel hikes are led by such knowledgeable folk as ethno-botanists and marine biologists. Prices range from $75 to $150 for hikes of 3 to 10 hours, including lunch (discounts are available for advance, online bookings). Hike Maui supplies waterproof day packs, rain ponchos, first-aid gear, water bottles, lunch and/or snacks for the longer hikes, and transportation to the site. If you're ready for more extreme adventure, ask about Maui Canyon Adventures, a sister company that offered rapelling and more in gorgeous canyons. ☎808/879–5270 ⊕*www.hikemaui.com.*

Maui Eco Adventures. For excursions into remote areas, Maui Eco Adventures is your choice. The ecologically minded company leads hikes into private or otherwise inaccessible areas. Hikes, which can be combined with kayaking, mountain biking, or sailing trips, explore botanically rich valleys in Kahakuloa and East Maui, as well as Hāna, Haleakalā, and more. Guides are botanists, mountaineers, boat captains, and backcountry chefs. Excursions are $80 to $160. ✉*180 Dickenson St., Suite 101, Lahaina* ☎808/661–7720 or 877/661–7720 ⊕*www.ecomaui.com.*

★ **Sierra Club.** A great avenue into the island's untrammeled wilderness is Maui's chapter of the Sierra Club. Rather than venturing out on your own, join one of the club's hikes into pristine forests and Valley Isle watersheds, or along ancient coastal paths. Several hikes a month are led by informative leaders who carry first-aid kits and make arrangements to access private land. Some outings include volunteer service, but most are just for fun. Bring your own food and water, sturdy shoes, and a suggested donation of $5—a true bargain. ✉*Box 791180, Pā'ia* ☎808/573–4147 ⊕*www.hi.sierraclub.org/maui.*

HORSEBACK RIDING

Several companies on Maui offer horseback riding that's far more appealing than the typical hour-long trudge over a dull trail with 50 other horses.

GOING WITH A GUIDE

★ Fodor'sChoice **Maui Stables.** Hawaiian-owned and run, this company provides a trip back in time, to an era when life moved more slowly and reverently—though galloping is allowed, if you're able to handle your horse! Educational tours begin at the stable in remote Kipahulu (near Hāna), and pass through several historic Hawaiian sites. Before heading up into the forest, your guides intone the words to a traditional *oli,* or chant, asking for permission to enter. By the time you reach the mountain pasture overlooking Waimoku Falls, you'll feel lucky to have been a part of the tradition. Both morning and afternoon rides are available at $150 per rider. ⊠*Between mile markers 40 and 41 on Hwy. 37, Hāna* ☎*808/248–7799* ⊕*www.mauistables.com.*

★ **Fodor's Choice Mendes Ranch.** Family-owned and run, Mendes operates out of the beautiful ranchland of Kahakuloa on the windward slopes of the West Maui Mountains. Two-hour morning and afternoon trail rides ($110) are available with an optional barbecue lunch ($20). Cowboys will take you cantering up rolling pastures into the lush rain forest to view some of Maui's biggest waterfalls. Mendes caters to weddings and parties and offers private trail rides on request. Should you need accommodations they have a home and bunk for rent right on the property. ⊠*Hwy. 340, Wailuku* ☎*808/244–7320 or 808/871–8222* ⊕*www. mendesranch.com.*

Pi'iholo Ranch. The local wranglers here will lead you on a rousing ride through family ranchlands—up hillside pastures, beneath a eucalyptus canopy, and past many native trees. Morning picnic rides are 3½ hours and include lunch. Morning and afternoon "country" rides are two hours. Their well-kept horses navigate the challenging terrain easily, but hold on when deer pass by! Prices are $120 to $160. Private rides and lessons are available. ⊠*End of Waiahiwi Rd., Makawao* ☎*808/357–5544* ⊕*www.piiholo.com.*

ZIPLINE TOURS

Skyline Eco Adventures. Skyline Eco Adventures operates in two locations on Maui: the original course on the slope of Haleakalā, and the newer venue at 1,000 feet above Kā'anapali. Good-natured guides give expert instruction and have you "zipping" confidently across deep gulches and canyons on a narrow zipline. A harness keeps you supported for the quick ride. You must be at least 10 years old, weigh between 80 and 260 pounds, and be able to hike a moderate distance over uneven terrain in order to participate. Closed-toe athletic-type shoes are required, and you can expect to get dirty. For the Haleakalā tour ($89), dress in layers, as it can get chilly at the 4,000-plus foot elevation, especially in the morning. The Kā'anapali tour ($149) includes breakfast or lunch. Advance reservations are suggested, especially in the summer, and discounts are available for online bookings. ☎*808/878–8400* ⊕*www.zipline.com.*

4

Shops & Spas

WORD OF MOUTH

"The Hyatt Regency spa in West Maui is beautiful, full of light. . . . It feels very Hawaiian. The Grand Wailea on the South Shore was more ornate. Quite nice, but I preferred the beachy, modern vibe of the Hyatt."

—Gellers

Updated
by Nicole
Crane

WE HOPE YOU'VE SAVED ROOM in your suitcase. With the help of our shopping guide, you'll find the top shops for everything "Maui grown," from lilikoi (passion-fruit) jams and fresh pineapples to Koa wood bowls and swimwear.

But before packing up your plunder, stop by one of the local spas to soak in some of these natural resources and more. Most treatments are infused with ingredients indigenous to the Valley Isle, like kukui nut, coconut, ginger, and eucalyptus. Plus, you're sure to find a spa product or two to bring home. Lavender salt bath, anyone?

SHOPPING

Whether you're searching for a dashboard hula dancer or an original Curtis Wilson Cost painting, you can find it on Front Street in Lahaina or at the Shops at Wailea. Art sales are huge in the resort areas, where artists regularly show up to promote their work. Alongside the flashy galleries are standards like Quicksilver and ABC store, where you can stock up on swim trunks, sunscreen, and flip-flops.

Don't miss the great boutiques lining the streets of small towns like Pā'ia and Makawao. You can purchase boutique fashions and art while strolling through these charming, quieter communities. Notably, several local designers—Tamara Catz, Sig Zane, and Maui Girl—all produce top-quality island fashions. In the neighboring galleries, local artisans turn out gorgeous work in a range of prices. Special souvenirs include rare hardwood bowls and boxes, prints of sea life, Hawaiian quilts, and blown glass.

Specialty food products—pineapples, coconuts, or Maui onions—and "Made in Maui" jams and jellies make great, less-expensive souvenirs. Cook Kwee's Maui Cookies have gained a following, as have Maui Potato Chips. Coffee sellers now offer Maui-grown-and-roasted beans alongside the better-known Kona varieties. Remember that fresh fruit must be inspected by the U.S. Department of Agriculture before it can leave the state, so it's safest to buy a box that has already passed inspection.

Business hours for individual shops on the island are usually 9 to 5, seven days a week. Shops on Front Street and in shopping centers tend to stay open later (until 9 or 10 on weekends).

Spa Grande, Grand Wailea Resort

WEST MAUI

SHOPPING CENTERS

Lahaina Cannery Mall. In a building reminiscent of an old pineapple cannery are 50 shops and an active stage. The mall hosts fabulous free events year-round (like the International Jazz Festival). Recommended stops include Na Hoku, purveyor of striking Hawaiian heirloom jewelry and pearls; Totally Hawaiian Gift Gallery; and Kite Fantasy, one of the best kite shops on Maui. An events schedule is on the Web site (⊕*www.lahainacannerymall.com*). ✉*1221 Honoapiʻilani Hwy., Lahaina* ☎*808/661–5304.*

Lahaina Center. Island department store Hilo Hattie Fashion Center anchors the complex and puts on a free hula show at 2:30 PM every Wednesday and 3:30 PM every Friday. In addition to Hard Rock Cafe, Warren & Annabelle's Magic Show, and a four-screen cinema, you can find a replica of an ancient Hawaiian village complete with three full-size thatch huts built with 10,000 feet of Big Island ʻōhiʻa wood, 20 tons of *pili* grass, and more than 4 mi of handwoven coconut *senit* (twine). There's all that *and* validated parking. ✉*900 Front St., Lahaina* ☎*808/667–9216.*

Whalers Village. Chic Whalers Village has a whaling museum and more than 50 restaurants and shops. Upscale haunts include Louis Vuitton, Coach, and Tiffany & Co. The complex also offers some interesting diversions: Hawaiian artisans display their crafts daily; hula dancers perform on an outdoor stage weeknights from 6:30 to 7:30; and three films spotlighting whales and marine history are shown daily for free at the Whale Center of the Pacific. ⊠ *2435 Kāʻanapali Pkwy., Kāʻanapali* ☎ *808/661–4567.*

BOOKSTORES

★ FodorsChoice **Old Lahaina Book Emporium.** Down a narrow alley you will find this bookstore stacked from floor to ceiling with new and antique finds. Spend a few moments (or hours) browsing the maze of shelves filled with mystery, sci-fi, nature guides, art, military history, and more. Collectors can scoop up rare Hawaiian memorabilia: playing cards, coasters, rare editions, and out-of-print books chronicling Hawaiʻi's colorful past. ⊠ *In alley next door, 834 Front St., Lahaina* ☎ *808/661–1399*

CLOTHING

Hilo Hattie Fashion Center. Hawaiʻi's largest manufacturer of aloha shirts and muʻumuʻu also carries brightly colored blouses, skirts, and children's clothing. ⊠ *Lahaina Center, 900 Front St., Lahaina* ☎ *808/661–8457.*

Honolua Surf Company. If you're not in the mood for a matching aloha shirt and muʻumuʻu ensemble, check out this surf shop—popular with young men and women for surf trunks, casual clothing, and accessories. ⊠ *845 Front St., Lahaina* ☎ *808/661–8848.*

Maggie Coulombe. Maggie Coulombe's cutting-edge fashions have the style of SoHo and the heat of the Islands. The svelte, body-clinging designs are unique and definitely worth a look. ⊠ *505 Front St., Lahaina* ☎ *808/662–0696.*

FOOD

Lahaina Square Shopping Center Foodland. This Foodland serves West Maui and is open daily from 6 AM to midnight. ⊠ *840 Waineʻe St., Lahaina* ☎ *808/661–0975.*

Safeway. Safeway has three stores on the island open 24 hours daily. ⊠ *Lahaina Cannery Mall, 1221 Honoapiʻilani Hwy., Lahaina* ☎ *808/667–4392.*

GALLERIES

Lahaina Galleries. Works of both national and international artists are displayed at the gallery's two locations in West Maui. ⊠ *828 Front St., Lahaina* ☎ *808/661–6284* ⊠ *The Shops at Wailea, 3750 Wailea Alanui Dr., Wailea* ☎ *808/874–8583.*

Lahaina Printsellers Ltd. Hawai'i's largest selection of original antique maps and prints pertaining to Hawai'i and the Pacific is available here. You can also buy museum-quality reproductions and original oil paintings from the Pacific Artists Guild. A second, smaller shop is at 505 Front Street. ✉ *Whalers Village, 2435 Kā'anapali Pkwy., Kā'anapali* ☎ *808/667–7617.*

Martin Lawrence Galleries. Martin Lawrence displays the works of noted mainland artists, including Andy Warhol and Keith Haring, in a bright and friendly gallery. ✉ *Lahaina Market Pl., Front St. and Lahainaluna Rd., Lahaina* ☎ *808/661–1788*

Village Gallery. This gallery, with two locations on the island, showcases the works of such popular local artists as Betty Hay Freeland, Margaret Bedell, George Allan, Joyce Clark, Pamela Andelin, Stephen Burr, and Macario Pascual. ✉ *120 Dickenson St., Lahaina* ☎ *808/661–4402* ✉ *Ritz-Carlton, 1 Ritz-Carlton Dr., Kapalua* ☎ *808/669–1800*

JEWELRY

Jessica's Gems. Jessica's has a good selection of Hawaiian heirloom jewelry, including custom designs by Maui designer David Welty, and its Lahaina store specializes in black pearls. ✉ *Whalers Village, 2435 Kā'anapali Pkwy., Kā'anapali* ☎ *808/661–4223* ✉ *858 Front St., Lahaina* ☎ *808/661–9200.*

Lahaina Scrimshaw. Here you can buy brooches, rings, pendants, cuff links, tie tacks, and collector's items adorned with intricately carved sailors' art. ✉ *845A Front St., Lahaina* ☎ *808/661–8820* ✉ *Whalers Village, 2435 Kā'anapali Pkwy., Kā'anapali* ☎ *808/661–4034.*

Maui Divers. This company has been crafting gold and coral into jewelry for more than 40 years. ✉ *640 Front St., Lahaina* ☎ *808/661–0988.*

CENTRAL MAUI

SHOPPING CENTERS

Maui Marketplace. On the busy stretch of Dairy Road, just outside the Kahului Airport, this behemoth marketplace couldn't be more conveniently located. The 20-acre complex houses several outlet stores and big retailers, such as Pier One Imports, Sports Authority, and Borders Books & Music. Sample local food at the Kau Kau Corner food court. ✉ *270 Dairy Rd., Kahului* ☎ *808/873–0400.*

Made-on-Maui Gifts

If you are looking for a good local souvenir to take home to the family, you don't have to resort to a touristy T-shirt or refrigerator magnet. Several locally owned companies make their products on-island, allowing you to have a fun take-home gift that still supports local businesses and crafts.

■ *Koa* jewelry boxes from **Maui Hands.**

■ Fish-shaped sushi platters and bamboo chopsticks from the **Maui Crafts Guild.**

■ Black pearl pendant from **Maui Divers.**

■ Handmade Hawaiian quilt from **Hāna Coast Gallery.**

■ Jellyfish paperweight from **Hot Island Glass.**

■ Fresh plumeria lei, made by you!

One good source of retro bargains as well as locally made crafts is the **Maui Swap Meet.** This Saturday flea market in Central Maui is the biggest bargain on the island, with crafts, gifts, souvenirs, fruit, flowers, jewelry, antiques, art, shells, and lots more. ⊠*Rte. 3500, off S. Pu'unēnē Ave., Kahului* ☎*808/877-3100* ☎*50¢* ⊙*Sat. 7 AM–noon.*

Queen Ka'ahumanu Center. This is Maui's largest mall with 75 stores, a movie theater, an active stage, and a food court. The mall's interesting rooftop, composed of a series of manta ray–like umbrella shades, is easily spotted. Stop at Camellia Seeds for what the locals call "crack seed," a snack made from dried fruits, nuts, and lots of sugar. Other stops here include mall standards such as Macy's, Pacific Sunwear, and American Eagle Outfitters. ⊠*275 W. Ka'ahumanu Ave., Kahului* ☎*808/877–3369.*

CLOTHING

Hi-Tech. Stop here immediately after deplaning to stock up on surf trunks, windsurfing gear, bikinis, and sundresses. ⊠*425 Koloa St., Kahului* ☎*808/877–2111.*

★ Fodor'sChoice **Sig Zane.** Local clothing designer Sig Zane draws inspiration from island botanical treasures—literally. His sketches of Hawaiian flowers such as *puakenikeni* and *maile* decorate the brightly colored fabrics featured in his shop. The aloha shirts and dresses here are works of art—original and not too flashy. ⊠*53 Market St., Wailuku* ☎*808/249–8997.*

FOOD

Maui Coffee Roasters. This café and roasting house near Kahului Airport is the best stop for Kona and Island coffees. The salespeople give good advice and will ship items. You even get a free cup of joe in a signature to-go cup when you buy a pound of coffee. ✉ *444 Hāna Hwy., Unit B, Kahului* ☎ *808/877–2877*

Safeway. Safeway has three stores on the island open 24 hours daily. ✉ *170 E. Kamehameha Ave., Kahului* ☎ *808/877–3377.*

THE SOUTH SHORE

SHOPPING CENTERS

Azeka Place Shopping Center. Azeka II, on the *mauka* (toward the mountains) side of South Kīhei Road, has the Coffee Store (the place for iced mochas), Who Cut the Cheese (the place for aged gouda), and the Nail Shop (the place for shaping, waxing, and tweezing). Azeka I, the older half on the *makai* (toward the ocean) side of the street, has a decent Vietnamese restaurant and Kīhei's post office. ✉ *1280 S. Kīhei Rd., Kīhei* ☎ *808/879–5000.*

Kīhei Kalama Village Marketplace. This is a fun place to investigate. Shaded outdoor stalls sell everything from printed and hand-painted T-shirts and sundresses to jewelry, pottery, wood carvings, fruit, and gaudily painted coconut husks—some, but not all, made by local craftspeople. ✉ *1941 S. Kīhei Rd., Kīhei* ☎ *808/879–6610.*

Rainbow Mall. This mall is one-stop shopping for condo guests—it offers video rentals, Hawaiian gifts, plate lunches, and a liquor store. ✉ *2439 S. Kīhei Rd., Kīhei.* ☎ *808/879–1145.*

The Shops at Wailea. Stylish, upscale, and close to most of the resorts, this mall brings high fashion to Wailea. Luxury boutiques such as Gucci, Fendi, Cos Bar, and Tiffany & Co. have shops, as do less-expensive chains like Gap, Guess, and Tommy Bahama's. Several good restaurants face the ocean, and regular Wednesday-night events include live entertainment, art exhibits, and fashion shows. ✉ *3750 Wailea Alanui Dr., Wailea* ☎ *808/891–6770.*

CLOTHING

Cruise. This upscale resort boutique has sundresses, swimwear, sandals, bright beach towels, and a few nice pieces of resort wear. ⊠*In Grand Wailea, 3850 Wailea Alanui Dr., Wailea* ☎*808/875–1234.*

Hilo Hattie Fashion Center. Hawai'i's largest manufacturer of aloha shirts and mu'umu'u also carries brightly colored blouses, skirts, and children's clothing. ⊠*297 Pi'ikea Ave., Kīhei* ☎*808/875–4545.*

Honolua Surf Company. If you're in the mood for colorful print tees and sundresses, check out this surf shop. It's popular with young men and women for surf trunks, casual clothing, and accessories. ⊠*2411 S. Kīhei Rd., Kīhei* ☎*808/874–0999.*

Sisters & Company. Opened by four sisters, this little shop has a lot to offer—current brand-name clothing such as True Religion and Da-nang, locally made jewelry, beach sandals, and gifts. Sister No. 3, Rhonda, runs a tiny, ultra-hip hair salon in back while Caroline, Sister No. 2, offers mani-pedis. ⊠*The Shops at Wailea, 3750 Wailea Alanui Dr., Wailea* ☎*808/874–0003.*

Tommy Bahama's. It's hard to find a man on Maui who *isn't* wearing a TB–logo aloha shirt. For better or worse, here's where you can get yours. Make sure to grab a Barbados Brownie on the way out at the restaurant attached to the shop. ⊠*The Shops at Wailea, 3750 Wailea Alanui Dr., Wailea* ☎*808/879–7828.*

FOOD

Foodland. In Kīhei town center, this is the most convenient supermarket for those staying in Wailea. It's open round-the-clock. ⊠*1881 S. Kīhei Rd., Kīhei* ☎*808/879–9350.*

Safeway. Safeway has three stores on the island open 24 hours daily. ⊠*277 Pi'ikea Ave., Kīhei* ☎*808/891–9120.*

UPCOUNTRY, THE NORTH SHORE & HĀNA

CLOTHING

Biasa Rose. This boutique offers hip island styles for the whole family. Unique gifts—pillows, napkins, photo albums—are on display along with comfy cotton Splendid and James Perse tees, airy Calyso wrap dresses, and vintage aloha shirts. ⊠*104 Hāna Hwy., Pā'ia* ☎*808/579–8602.*

Collections. This eclectic boutique is brimming with pretty jewelry, humorous gift cards, housewares, Italian bags and sandals, yoga wear, and Asian print silks. ✉*3677 Baldwin Ave., Makawao* ☎*808/572–0781.*

★ **Fodor'sChoice Maui Girl.** This is *the* place for swimwear, cover-ups, beach hats, and sandals. Maui Girl designs its own suits and imports teenier versions from Brazil as well. Tops and bottoms can be purchased separately, greatly increasing your chances of finding a suit that actually fits. ✉*12 Baldwin Ave., Pā'ia* ☎*808/579–9266.*

Moonbow Tropics. If you're looking for an aloha shirt that won't look out of place on the mainland, make a stop at this little store, which sells the best-quality shirts on the island. ✉*36 Baldwin Ave., Pā'ia* ☎*808/579–8592.*

★ **Fodor'sChoice Tamara Catz.** This Maui designer already has a worldwide following, and her sarongs and super-stylish beachwear have been featured in many fashion magazines. If you're looking for a sequined bikini or a delicately embroidered sundress, this is the place to check out. ✉*83 Hāna Hwy., Pā'ia* ☎*808/579–9184.*

FOOD

Mana Foods. Stock up on local fish and grass-fed beef for your barbecue here. You can find the best selection of organic produce on the island, as well as a great bakery and deli at this typically crowded health-food store. ✉*49 Baldwin Ave., Pā'ia* ☎*808/579–8078.*

GALLERIES

★ **Hāna Coast Gallery.** One of the best places to shop on the island, this 3,000-square-foot gallery has fine art and jewelry on consignment from local artists. ✉*Hotel Hāna-Maui, Hāna Hwy., Hāna* ☎*808/248–8636 or 800/637–0188.*

★ **Fodor'sChoice Maui Crafts Guild.** This is one of the more interesting galleries on Maui. Set in a two-story wooden building alongside the highway, the Guild is crammed with treasures. Resident artists craft everything in the store—from Norfolk-pine bowls to *raku* (Japanese lead-glazed) pottery to original sculpture. The prices are surprisingly low. Upstairs, see original pieces by local artist Randy Groden or watch Groden at work in his on-site studio. ✉*43 Hāna Hwy., Pā'ia* ☎*808/579–9697.*

★ **Maui Hands.** This gallery shows work by dozens of local artists, including *paniolo-* (Hawaiian cowboy) theme lithographs by Sharon Shigekawa, who knows whereof she paints: she rides each year in the Kaupō Roundup. ⊠*3620 Baldwin Ave., Makawao* ☏*808/572–5194*.

JEWELRY

Maui Master Jewelers. The exterior of this shop is as rustic as all the old buildings of Makawao, so there's no way to prepare yourself for the elegance of the handcrafted jewelry displayed within. ⊠*3655 Baldwin Ave., Makawao* ☏*808/573–5400*.

SPAS

Traditional Swedish massage and European facials anchor most spa menus, though you'll also find shiatsu, ayurveda, aromatherapy, and other body treatments drawn from cultures across the globe. *Lomi Lomi,* traditional Hawaiian massage involving powerful strokes down the length of the body, is a regional specialty passed down through generations. Many treatments incorporate local plants and flowers. *Awapuhi,* or Hawaiian ginger, and *noni,* a pungent-smelling fruit, are regularly used for their therapeutic benefits. *Limu,* or seaweed, and even coffee are employed in rousing salt scrubs and soaks. And this is just the beginning.

A BUDGET-FRIENDLY SPA. If hotel spa prices are a little intimidating, Try **Spa Luna** (⊠ *810 Ha'ikū Rd., Ha'ikū* ☏ *808/575–2440* ⊕ *www. spaluna.com*), a day spa, which is also an aesthetician's school. In the former Ha'ikū Cannery, it offers services ranging from massage to microdermabrasion. You can opt for professional services, but the student clinics are the real story here. The students' are subject to rigorous training, and their services are offered at a fraction of the regular cost ($30 for a 50-minute massage).

★ **Heavenly Spa by Westin at the Westin Maui.** An exquisite 80-minute Lavender Body Butter treatment is the star of this spa's menu, thanks to a partnership with a local lavender farm. Other options include cabana massage (for couples, too) and water lily sunburn relief with green tea. The facility is flawless, and it's worth getting a treatment just to sip lavender lemonade in the posh ocean-view waiting room. The open-air yoga studio and the gym offer energizing workouts. Bridal parties can request a private area within the salon. ⊠*Westin Kā'anapali, 2365 Kā'anapali Pkwy., Kā'anapali* ☎*808/661–2588* ⊕*www.westinmaui. com* ☞*$130 50-min massage, $285 day spa packages. Hair salon, hot tub, sauna, steam room. Gym with: cardiovascular machines, free weights, weight-training equipment. Services: aromatherapy, body wraps, facials, hydrotherapy, massage, Vichy shower. Classes and programs: aquaerobics, yoga.*

★ **Fodor's**Choice **Honua Spa at Hotel Hāna-Maui.** A bamboo gate opens into an outdoor sanctuary with a lava-rock basking pool and hot tub; at first glimpse this spa seems to have been organically grown, not built. The decor here can hardly be called decor—it's an abundant, living garden. Taro varieties, orchids, and ferns still wet from Hāna's frequent downpours nourish the spirit as you rest with a cup of jasmine tea, or take an invigorating dip in the plunge pool. Signature aromatherapy treatments utilize *Honua*, the spa's own sumptuous blend of sandalwood, coconut, ginger, and vanilla orchid essences. The Hāna Wellness package is a blissful eight hours of treatments, which can be shared between the family, or enjoyed alone. ⊠*Hotel Hāna-Maui, 5031 Hāna Hwy., Hāna* ☎*808/270–5290* ⊕*www.hotelhanamaui.com* ☞*$140 60-min massage, $395 spa packages. Hair salon, outdoor hot tub, steam room. Gym with: cardiovascular machines, free weights, weighttraining equipment. Services: aromatherapy, body wraps, facials, hydrotherapy, massage. Classes and programs: meditation, Pilates, yoga.*

★ **Fodor's**Choice **The Spa at Four Seasons Resort Maui.** The Four Seasons' hawklike attention to detail is reflected here. Thoughtful gestures like fresh flowers beneath the massage table (to give you something to stare at), organic herbal tea in the "relaxation room," and your choice of music begin to ease your mind and muscles before your treatment even begins. The spa is genuinely stylish and serene, and the therapists are among the best. Thanks to an exclusive partnership, the spa offers treatments created by celebrity skin-care specialist Kate Somerville. The "Ultimate Kate" is 80 minutes of super hydrating, collagen-increasing magic, incorporating light therapy and powerful, tingling products that literally wipe wrinkles away. ⊠*3900 Wailea Alanui Dr., Wailea* ☎*808/874–8000 or 800/334–6284* ⊕*www.fourseasons. com/maui* ☞*$145 50-min massage, $380 3-treatment packages. Hair salon, steam room. Gym with: cardiovascular machines, free weights, weight-training equipment. Ser-*

Honua Spa at Hotel Hāna-Maui

The Spa at the Four Seasons Resort Maui

Spa Grande, Grand Wailea Resort

vices: aromatherapy, body wraps, facials, hydrotherapy, massage. Classes and programs: aquaerobics, meditation, personal training, Pilates, Spinning, tai chi, yoga.

★ **Fodor's**Choice **Spa Grande, Grand Wailea Resort.** Built to satisfy an indulgent Japanese billionaire, this 50,000-square-foot spa makes others seem like well-appointed closets. Slathered in honey and wrapped up in the steam room (if you go for the Ali'i honey steam wrap), you'll feel like royalty. All treatments include a loofah scrub and a trip to the *termé*, a hydrotherapy circuit including a Roman Jacuzzi, furo bath, plunge pool, powerful waterfall and Swiss jet showers, and five therapeutic baths. (Soak for 10 minutes in the moor mud to relieve sunburn or jellyfish stings.) To fully enjoy the baths, plan to arrive an hour before your treatment. Free with treatments, the termé is also available separately for $85 ($115 for nonhotel guests). At times—especially during the holidays—this wonderland can be crowded. ✉ *3850 Wailea Alanui Dr., Wailea* ☎ *808/875–1234 or 800/888–6100* ⊕ *www.grandwailea.com* ☞ *$160 50-min massage, $375 half-day spa packages. Hair salon, hot tub, sauna, steam room. Gym with: cardiovascular machines, free weights, racquetball, weight-training equipment. Services: aromatherapy, body wraps, facials, hydrotherapy, massage, Vichy shower. Classes and programs: aquaerobics, cycling, Pilates, qigong, yoga.*

Spa Kea Lani, Fairmont Kea Lani. This small spa is a little cramped, but nicely appointed: fluffy robes and Italian mints greet you upon arrival. We recommend the excellent *lomi lomi* massage—a series of long, soothing strokes combined with gentle stretching, or the *ili ili* hot stone therapy. Both treatments employ indigenous healing oils: rich *kukui* nut, kava, and *noni*, and tropical fragrances. Poolside massages by the divinely serene adult pool can be reserved on the spot. Not in a lounging mood? Check out the state-of-the-art 1,750-square-foot fitness center. ✉ *4100 Wailea Alanui Dr., Wailea* ☎ *808/875–4100 or 800/659–4100* ⊕ *www.kealani.com* ☞ *$150 50-min massage, $330 spa packages. Hair salon, steam room. Gym with: cardiovascular machines, free weights, weight-training equipment. Services: aromatherapy, body wraps, facials, hydrotherapy, massage. Classes and programs: aquaerobics, body sculpting, personal training, yoga.*

Spa Moana, Hyatt Regency Maui. Spa Moana's oceanfront salon has a million-dollar view; it's a perfect place to beautify before your wedding or special anniversary. An older facility, it's spacious and well-appointed, offering traditional Swedish and Thai massage, reiki, and shiatsu, in addition to numerous innovative treatments such as the invigorating Ka'anapali coffee salt scrub, and the immune-boosting Ali'i Royal Experience, a papaya—pineapple–grapeseed scrub and propolis lotion rub combined with a facial and *kukui* nut oil scalp massage. For body treatments, the oceanfront rooms are a tad too warm—request one in back. ✉*200 Nohea Kai Dr., Lahaina* ☎*808/661–1234 or 800/233–1234* ⊕*www.maui.hyatt.com* ☞*$140 50-min massage, $356 spa packages. Hair salon, hot tub, sauna, steam room. Gym with: cardiovascular machines, free weights, weight-training equipment. Services: aromatherapy, body wraps, facials, massage, Vichy shower. Classes and programs: aquaerobics, Pilates, tai chi, yoga.*

Waihua, Ritz-Carlton, Kapalua. This 14,000-square-foot facility, refurbished in 2008, includes Waihua signature treatments on the menu, such as "Harmony" or "Family Relations," which employ aromatherapy, hot stones, and massage. High-quality, handcrafted products enhance treatments inspired by Hawaiian culture, such as the *lomi lomi* massage with healing plant essences followed by a salt foot scrub. Attention fitness junkies: personal TVs are attached to the state-of-the-art cardiovascular machines in the oceanview fitness center. ✉*1 Ritz-Carlton Dr., Kapalua* ☎*808/669–6200 or 800/262–8440* ⊕*www.ritzcarlton.com* ☞*$140 50-min massage, $425 half-day spa packages. Hair salon, hot tubs (outdoor and indoor), sauna, steam room. Gym with: cardiovascular machines, free weights, weight-training equipment. Services: aromatherapy, body wraps, facials, massage. Classes and programs: aquaerobics, cycling, nutrition, Pilates, yoga.*

Entertainment & Nightlife

WORD OF MOUTH

"Went to the Old Lahaina Lū'au at night. What fun! Food was good, and plenty of it. Friday is Art Night in Lahaina. The shops are open late, and the numerous galleries have special things going on. It was fun to walk around."

—LindaSus

Updated
by Eliza
Escaño

LOOKING FOR WILD ISLAND NIGHTLIFE? We can't promise you'll always find it here—and sometimes you'll just have to be the party. This island has little of Waikīkī's after-hours decadence, and the club scene can be quirky, depending on the season and the day of the week. But sometimes Maui will surprise you with a big-name concert, world-class DJ, outdoor festival, or special event.

Lahaina and Kīhei are your best bets for action. Lahaina tries to uphold its reputation as a party town, and succeeds every Halloween when thousands of masqueraders converge for a Mardi Gras–style party on Front Street. Kīhei is a bit more local and can be something of a rough and rowdy crowd in parts. On the right night, both towns stir with activity, and if you don't like one scene, there's always next door.

Outside of Lahaina and Kīhei, you might be able to hit an "on" night in Pā'ia (North Shore) or Makawao (Upcountry), especially on weekend nights. Your best bet? Pick up the free *MauiTime Weekly,* or Thursday's edition of the *Maui News,* where you'll find a listing of all your after-dark options, island-wide.

★ The **Maui Arts & Cultural Center** (⊠*1 Cameron Way, above harbor on Kahului Beach Rd.* ☎*808/242–2787*) is the hub of all highbrow arts and quality performances. Their events calendar features everything from rock to reggae to Hawaiian slack-key guitar, international dance and circus troupes, political and literary lectures, art films, cult classics—you name it. Each Wednesday (and occasionally Friday) evening, the MACC (as it's locally known) hosts movie selections from the Maui Film Festival. The complex includes the 1,200-seat Castle Theater, a 4,000-seat amphitheater for large outdoor concerts, the 350-seat McCoy Theater for plays and recitals, and a courtyard café offering preshow dining and drinks. For information on current events, check the Events Box Office (☎*808/242–7469* ⊕*www.mauiarts. org*) or *Maui News.*

ENTERTAINMENT

Before 10 PM, there's a lot to offer by way of lū'au shows, dinner cruises, and tiki-lighted cocktail hours. Aside from that, you should at least be able to find some down-home DJ-spinning or the strum of acoustic guitars at your nearest watering hole or restaurant.

MAUI MIDNIGHT. If you want to see any action on Maui, head out early. Otherwise, you might be out past what locals call "Maui Midnight," where as early as 9 PM the restaurants close and the streets empty. What can you expect, though, when most people wake up with the sun? After a long, salty day of sea and surf, you might be ready for some shut-eye yourself.

DINNER CRUISES & SHOWS

There's no better place to see the sun set on the Pacific than from one of Maui's many boat tours. You can find a tour to fit your mood, as you can choose anything from a quiet, sit-down dinner to a festive, beer-swigging booze cruise. Note, however, that many cocktail cruises have recently put a cap on the number of free drinks offered with open bars, instead including a limited number of drinks per ticket.

Tours leave from Mā'alaea or Lahaina harbors. Be sure to arrive at least 15 minutes early (count in the time it will take to park). The dinner cruises typically feature music and are generally packed—which is great if you're feeling social, but you might have to fight for a good seat. You can usually get a much better meal at one of the local restaurants, and opt instead for a different type of tour. Most nondinner cruises offer *pūpū* (appetizers) and sometimes a chocolate and champagne toast.

Winds are consistent in summer, but variable in winter—sometimes making for a rocky ride. If you're worried about sea sickness, you might consider a catamaran, which is much more stable than a monohull. Keep in mind, the boat crews are experienced in dealing with such matters. The best advice? Take Dramamine before the trip, and if you feel sick, sit in the shade (but not inside the cabin), place a cold rag or ice on the back of your neck, and *breathe* as you look at the horizon. In the worst-case scenario, aim downwind—and shoot for distance.

Kaulana Cocktail Cruise. This two-hour sunset cruise prides itself on its live music and festive atmosphere. Accommodating up to 100 people, the cruise generally attracts a younger, more boisterous crowd. *Pūpū*, such as meatballs, smoked salmon, and teriyaki pineapple chicken are served, and there is a full bar (two drinks included). Freshly baked chocolate chip cookies are passed around toward the end of the trip. ⊠*Lahaina Harbor, Slip 3* ☎*800/621–3601* ⊕*www.tombarefoot.com/maui/kaulana_sunset.html* ☎*$49* ⊗*Mon., Wed., and Fri. 4:30–7:30* PM.

Paragon Champagne Sunset Sail. This 47-foot catamaran brings you a performance sail within a personal setting. Limited to groups of 24 (with private charters available), you can spread out on deck and enjoy the gentle trade winds. An easygoing, attentive crew will serve you hot and cold *pūpū,* such as grilled chicken skewers, spring rolls, and a fruit platter, along with beer, wine, mai tais, and champagne at sunset. This is one of the best trips around. ⊠*Loading Dock, Lahaina Harbor* ☎*808/244–2087* ⊕*www.sailmaui.com* ⊠*$51* ⊙*Mon., Wed., Fri. evenings only; call for check-in times.*

Pride Charters. A 65-foot catamaran built specifically for Maui's waters, the *Pride of Maui* has a spacious cabin, dance floor, and large upper deck for unobstructed viewing. Evening cruises include premium, top-shelf cocktails and an impressive spread of baby back ribs, grilled chicken, roasted veggies, artichoke dip, and penne pasta salad. Desserts include tropical cake and assorted tarts. ⊠*Māʻalaea Harbor, Māʻalaea* ☎*877/867–7433* ⊕*www.prideofmaui. com* ⊠*$59.95* ⊙*Tues., Thurs., and Sat. 5–7:30* PM.

Spirit of Lahaina Cocktail or Dinner Cruise. This double-deck, 65-foot catamaran offers you a choice of a full dinner cruise, featuring a salad bar, freshly grilled steak, mahimahi, and shrimp, or a cocktail cruise with appetizers, drinks, and dessert. Both cruises feature contemporary Hawaiian music and hula show. ⊠ *Lahaina Harbor, Slip 4, Lahaina* ☎*808/662–4477* ⊕*www.spiritoflahaina.com* ⊠*$76 dinner cruise, $55 cocktail cruise* ⊙*Daily 5–7:15* PM.

LŪʻAU

A trip to Hawaiʻi isn't complete without a good lūʻau. With the beat of drums and the sway of hula, lūʻau give you a snippet of Hawaiian culture left over from a long-standing tradition. Early Hawaiians celebrated many occasions with lūʻau—weddings, births, battles, and more. The feasts originally brought people together as an offering to the gods, and to practice *hoʻokipa,* the act of welcoming guests. The word *lūʻau* itself refers to the taro root, a staple of the Hawaiian diet, which, when pounded, makes a grey, pudding-like substance called *poi.* You'll find *poi* at all the best feasts, along with platters of salty fish, fresh fruit, and *kālua* (baked underground) pork. *For more information about Hawaiian food and lūau, see the Authentic Taste of Hawaiʻi feature in chapter 6, Where to Eat.*

Lūʻau are still held by locals today to mark milestones or as informal, family-style gatherings. For tourists, they are a major attraction, and for that reason, have become big business. Keep in mind—some are watered-down tourist traps just trying to make a buck, others offer a night you'll never forget. As the saying goes, you get what you pay for.

■ TIP→ **Many of the best lūʻau book weeks, sometimes months, in advance, so reserve early. Plan your lūʻau night early on in your trip to help you get into the Hawaiian spirit.**

★ **The Feast at Lele.** "Lele" is an older, more traditional name for Lahaina. This feast redefines the lūʻau by crossing it with island-style fine dining in an intimate beach setting. Each course of this succulent sit-down meal expresses the spirit of specific island cultures—Hawaiian, Samoan, Tongan, Tahitian—and don't forget dessert. Dramatic Polynesian entertainment accompanies the dinner, along with excellent wine and liquor selections. This is the most expensive lūʻau on the island for a reason: Lele is top-notch. ✉ *505 Front St., Lahaina* ☎ *808/667–5353* ☊ *Reservations essential* ⊕ *www.feastatlele.com* 🖭 *$105 adult, $75 child* ☉ *Nightly at sunset; 5:30 PM in winter, 6 PM in summer.*

★ **Fodor'sChoice Old Lahaina Lūʻau.** Many consider this the best lūʻau on Maui; it's certainly the most traditional. Located right on the water, at the northern end of town, the Old Lahaina Lūʻau is small, personal, and as authentic as it gets. Sitting either at a table or on a *lauhala* mat, you'll dine on all-you-can-eat Hawaiian cuisine: pork *laulau* (wrapped with taro sprouts in *tī* leaves), aʻhi *poke* (pickled raw tuna, tossed with herbs and seasonings), *lomilomi* salmon (rubbed with onions and herbs), Maui-style mahimahi, *haupia* (coconut pudding), and more. At sunset the show begins a historical journey that relays key periods in Hawaiʻi's history, from the arrival of the Polynesians to the influence of the missionaries and, later, tourism. The tanned, talented performers will charm you with their music, chanting, and variety of hula styles (modern and *kahiko*, the ancient way of communicating with the gods). But if it's fire dancers you want to see, you won't find them here, as they aren't considered traditional. Although it's performed nightly, this lūʻau sells out regularly. Make your reservations when planning your trip to Maui. You can cancel up until 10 AM the day of the scheduled show. ✉ *1251 Front St., makai (toward the ocean) of Lahaina Cannery Mall, Lahaina* ☎ *808/667–1998* ☊ *Reservations essential* ⊕ *www.oldlahainaluau.com* 🖭 *$89*

5

adult, $59 child 2–12. Nightly at 5:30 PM in winter, 6 PM in summer.

Wailea Beach Marriott Honua'ula Lū'au. This lū'au offers an open bar, a tasty buffet, and a sunset backdrop that can't be beat. The stage is placed right next to the water, and the show features an *imu* (underground oven) ceremony to start, and Polynesian dancers performing a blend of modern acrobatics (including an impressive fire-knife dance) and traditional hula. ✉*3700 Wailea Alanui Dr.* ☎*808/879–1922* ⊕*www.marriotthawaii.com* ⚓*Reservations essential* 💲*$85 adult ($95 for premium seating), $42 child 6–12 ($52 for premium seating)* ⊙*Mon. and Thurs.–Sat. 5 PM.*

WHAT'S A LAVA FLOW? Can't decide between a piña colada or strawberry daiquiri? Go with a Lava Flow—a mix of light rum, coconut and pineapple juice, and a banana, with a swirl of strawberry puree. Add a wedge of fresh pineapple and a paper umbrella, and mmm . . . good. Try one at Lulu's in Kīhei.

FILM
In the heat of the afternoon, a theater may feel like paradise. There are megaplexes showing first-run movies in Kukui Mall (Kīhei), Lahaina Center, and Maui Mall and Ka'ahumanu Shopping Center (Kahului).

★ **Maui Film Festival.** In this ongoing celebration, the Maui Arts & Cultural Center features art-house films every Wednesday (and sometimes Friday) evening at 5 and 7:30 PM, accompanied by live music, dining, and poetry in the Candlelight Café & Cinema. In the summer, an international weeklong festival attracts big-name celebrities to Maui for cinema under the stars. ☎*808/579–9244 recorded program information* ⊕*www.mauifilmfestival.com.*

THEATER
For live theater, check local papers for events and showtimes.

★ **"'Ulalena" at Maui Theatre.** One of Maui's hottest tickets, ☾ "'Ulalena" is a 75-minute musical extravaganza that is well received by audiences and Hawaiian-culture experts alike. Cirque du Soleil–inspired, the ensemble cast (20 singer-dancers and a 5-musician orchestra) mixes native rhythms and stories with acrobatic performance. High-tech stage wizardry gives an inspiring introduction to island culture. It has auditorium seating, and beer and wine are for sale at the concession stand. There are dinner-theater packages

in conjunction with top Lahaina restaurants. ✉*878 Front St., Lahaina* ☎*808/661–9913 or 877/688–4800* ⊕*www. mauitheatre.com* ⚞*Reservations essential* ✆*$50–$99.50 for a dinner package* ⊘*Mon.–Sat. at 6:30* PM.

Warren & Annabelle's. This is one show not to miss—it's serious comedy with amazing sleight of hand. Magician Warren Gibson entices guests into his swank nightclub with red carpets and a gleaming mahogany bar, and plies them with à la carte appetizers (coconut shrimp, crab cakes), desserts (rum cake, crème brûlée), and "smoking cocktails." Then, he performs tableside magic while his ghostly assistant, Annabelle, tickles the ivories. This is a nightclub, so no one under 21 is allowed. ✉*Lahaina Center, 900 Front St., Lahaina* ☎*808/667–6244* ⊕*www.hawaiimagic.com* ⚞*Reservations essential* ✆*$50 or $86, including food and drinks* ⊘*Mon.–Sat. at 5 and 7:30* PM.

WORD OF MOUTH. "We loved Warren & Annabelle's. Whe thought the food was tasty, and Warren's magic was incredible. We would see it again even if he didn't change the show. The size of the theater (75) makes it an intimate experience."—DebitNM

NIGHTLIFE

Your best bet when it comes to bars on Maui? If you walk by and it sounds like it's happening, go in. If you want to scope out your options in advance, be sure to check the free *MauiTime Weekly,* found at most stores and restaurants, to find out who's playing where. *Maui News* also publishes an entertainment schedule in its Thursday edition of the "Maui Scene." With an open mind (and a little luck), you can usually find a good scene for fun.

WEST MAUI

BARS & RESTAURANTS
Hard Rock Cafe. You've seen one Hard Rock Cafe, you've seen them all. However, Maui's Hard Rock brings you Reggae Monday, featuring beloved local reggae star Marty Dread ($5 cover, 10 PM). ✉*Lahaina Center, 900 Front St., Lahaina* ☎*808/667–7400.*

★ **Lahaina Store Grille & Oyster Bar.** The Oyster Bar, as locals fondly call it, saved West Maui's discerning night owls from overpriced admission, long waits, and trance music. Enjoy a wonderful dinner on the open rooftop, then stay for some cool tunes afterwards. The place features free admission, drink specials, hip-hop and house DJs from Thursday to Saturday, and live bands on Sunday. ⊠*744 Front St., Lahaina* ☎*808/661–9090* ⊡*Free* ⊙*10 PM–2 AM.*

Longhi's. This upscale, open-air restaurant is the spot on Friday nights, when there's usually live island rock or reggae music and a bumping dance floor. Here you'll mingle with what locals call Maui's beautiful people, so be sure to dress your casual best ($5 occasional cover, 10 PM). ⊠*Lahaina Center, 888 Front St., next to Hard Rock Cafe, Lahaina* ☎*808/667–2288.*

The Sly Mongoose. Off the beaten tourist path, the Sly Mongoose is the seediest dive bar in town, and one of the friendliest. The bartender will know your name and half your life history inside of 10 minutes, and she makes the strongest mai tai on the island. ⊠*1036 Limahana Pl., Lahaina* ☎*808/661–8097.*

CLUBS
Moose McGillycuddy's. The Moose offers no-cover live or DJ music on most nights, drawing a young, mostly single crowd who come for the burgers, beer, and dance-floor beats. Live music on Sunday. ⊠*844 Front St., Lahaina* ☎*808/667–7758.*

THE SOUTH SHORE

BARS & RESTAURANTS
Lulu's. Lulu's could be your favorite bar in any beach town. It's a second-story, open-air tiki and sports bar, with a pool table, small stage, and dance floor to boot. The most popular night is Salsa Thursday, with dancing and lessons until 11. Wednesday is karaoke night, Friday is reggae night, and Saturday features guest DJs. ⊠*1945 S. Kīhei Rd., Kīhei* ☎*808/879–9944*

★ **Mulligan's on the Blue.** Frothy pints of Guinness and late-night fish-and-chips—who could ask for more? Sunday nights feature foot-stomping Irish jams that will have you dancing a jig, and singing something about "a whiskey for me-Johnny." On Thursday and Friday, Mulligan's also brings you the more mellow *Wailea Nights,* an inspired and very popular dinner show performed by members of the band Hapa. ⊠*Blue Golf Course, 100 Kaukahi St., Wailea* ☎*808/874–1131*

South Shore Tiki Lounge. Good eats are paired with the island's most progressive DJs in this breezy, tropical tavern. Local DJs are featured every day of the week; if you're craving some heady electronica, Thursday is your night. ✉*1913-J S. Kihei Rd., Kihei* ☎*808/874-6444*

UPCOUNTRY & THE NORTH SHORE

BARS & RESTAURANTS

Casanova Italian Restaurant and Deli. Casanova can bring in some big acts, which in the past have included Kool and the Gang, Los Lobos, and Taj Majal. Most Friday and Saturday nights, though, it attracts a hip, local scene with live bands and eclectic DJs spinning house, funk, and world music. Don't miss the costume theme nights. Wednesday is for Wild Wahines (code for ladies drink half price), which can be on the smarmy side. $5 to $15 cover. ✉*1188 Makawao Ave., Makawao* ☎*808/572-0220*

Charley's. The closest thing to country Maui has to offer, Charley's is a down-home, dive bar in the heart of Pā'ia. It recently expanded its offerings to include disco, house, industry, and lounge nights. If you're lucky, you might even see Willy Nelson hanging here. ✉*142 Hāna Hwy., Pā'ia* ☎*808/579-9453.*

Stopwatch Sportsbar & Grill. This friendly dive bar books favorite local bands on Friday and charges only $3. ✉*1127 Makawao Ave., Makawao* ☎*808/572-1380*

CLUBS

Jacques. Who could resist a place once voted by locals as the "best place to see suspiciously beautiful people from around the world"? On Friday nights, the crowd spills onto the cozy streets of Pā'ia, as funky DJs spin Latino, world lounge, salsa, and live jazz. ✉*120 Hāna Hwy., Pā'ia* ☎*808/579-8844.*

Where to Eat

WORD OF MOUTH

"We still love the informal atmosphere of the Hula Grill bar. You and your husband would have fun and have what we value most—dinner on the beach with the sand under your feet and the sound of the waves."

—chicgeek

By Carla
Tracy

IN THE MID-1990S, Maui and the rest of Hawai'i emerged as a gastronomic force, as menus were infused with bold colors and bold flavors with the freshest island ingredients. Hawai'i Regional Cuisine (modern Hawaiian fare) was born, and whether you're dining at an upscale restaurant or at a casual café, you're likely to be the beneficiary.

Forget old clichés of foods frozen in a time when top island chefs dished up bland Dover sole and iceberg lettuce. Instead, picture Asian guacamole enticing with ginger and sake; nori fettuccine with fresh *'opihi* (limpets) and garlic-chile-lime butter; and Ho'okipa Bay *limu* (seaweed) poke salad made with chunks of broiled yellowfin tuna and blood-orange dressing. Imagine desserts that bend all culinary conventions, such as macadamia-nut tacos packed with tropical fruits and *liliko'i* (passion fruit) custard.

This sustainable style of cooking is no flash in the pan. The premise is to raise awareness of the state's indigenous cuisine, and to encourage farmers to grow more produce and fisherfolk to know they have a source for their days of work on the water. Now Maui has everything from award-winning Surfing Goat Dairy cheeses to a host of lavender food products from Ali'i Kula Lavender.

Some of Hawai'i Regional Cuisine's original 12 chefs still live on the island and remain successful restaurateurs. They include Beverly Gannon of Hāli'imaile General Store and Joe's, Peter Merriman of Hula Grill, and Mark Ellman of Mala Ocean Tavern, Maui Tacos, and Penne Pasta fame. Countless chefs in small mom-and-pop shops also buy locally and support the vast agricultural resources in this tropical island state.

If you want to get off the beaten path and hunt down ethnic and local-style restaurants, you can eat well at thrifty prices. Check out historic downtown Wailuku on First Friday of every month with its market-style atmosphere. Restaurants take their foods out onto the sidewalks, and entertainment is on every corner. Head Upcountry to Makawao for a taste of *paniolo* (cowboy) country or to the beach in little Pā'ia, packed with fun restaurants and bars on the booming North Shore. You will find bistros, creperies, cafés, and sushi bars. Maui really is *nō ka 'oi* (the best).

RESERVATIONS

Maui is one of the top tourist islands in the world, and in peak months, it's best to make reservations in advance, at your earliest convenience. If you're dying to go to Mama's Fish House or the Old Lahaina Lūʻau, make reservations before leaving home. Everywhere else you may be able to squeeze into, at least at the bar, at the last minute.

WHAT TO WEAR

Maui's last jacket-required dining room closed years ago. Wear evening resort attire, meaning covered shoes and collared shirts for men (you can get away with dress shorts) and a nice outfit for women at the better restaurants. Refrain from tank tops at family establishments as it's still considered too casual. Bring a sweater or cover-up in winter months—many restaurants are breezy and open-air.

HOURS & PRICES

Many restaurants on Maui are packed from 5 PM to 7 PM— the early-bird special hours and the best time for viewing sunsets. By 8:30 many dining rooms have quieted down, and by 9:30 most are closed. If the place has a rowdy bar (or is a karaoke hangout), you may be able to get food until 10 or even midnight.

Unless a resort is noted for its culinary department, you may find hotel restaurants somewhat overpriced and underwhelming. We've listed the best of the bunch. To dine well on the cheap, go for coupons advertised in the *Maui News*. Even upscale restaurants go half-price during the slow months (September through November). As for tips, 18% to 20% is standard for quality service.

WHAT IT COSTS				
¢	$	$$	$$$	$$$$
AT DINNER				
Under $10	$10–$17	$18–$26	$27–$35	Over $35

Restaurant prices are for a main course at dinner.

WEST MAUI

AMERICAN

$$$$ ✕ **Lahaina Grill.** Open since 1990, Lahaina Grill lost the "David Paul's" part of its name late in 2007, but under the latest owner Jurg Munch, executive chef at the Mandarin Oriental in Hong Kong for years, the celebrated updated American food and the service remain consistent. Beautifully designed with tin-stamped ceilings, splashy artwork, and overhead fans, it is part of an elegant older building and has an extensive wine cellar and an in-house bakery. Try the signature tequila shrimp and firecracker rice; veal chop with Pommery mustard, wild mushrooms, and truffle risotto; and the sesame-seed-crusted seared 'ahi paired with vanilla jasmine rice. Save room for the scrumptious triple-berry pie. Smaller portions are available at the bar. ⊠ *127 Lahainaluna Rd., Lahaina* ☎*808/667–5117* ⊟ *AE, DC, MC, V* ⊘*No lunch.*

DINER

¢ ✕ **The Gazebo Restaurant.** Even locals will stand in line up to half an hour to have diner fare at a table overlooking the beach at this slightly hard-to-find restaurant, an open-air gazebo (albeit an old and funky one) overlooking magnificent Nāpili Bay. Sunsets are phenomenal, and turtle and spinner dolphin sightings are common. The food is standard diner fare, but it's thoughtfully prepared. Breakfast choices include macadamia-nut pancakes and Portuguese-sausage omelets, and there are satisfying burgers and salads at lunch. The friendly hotel staff puts out coffee for those waiting in line. ⊠*Nāpili Shores Resort, 5315 Lower Honoapi'ilani Hwy., Nāpili* ☎*808/669–5621* ⊟*No credit cards* ⊘*No dinner.*

FRENCH

$$$ ✕ **Chez Paul.** Open since 1975, this intimate restaurant in tiny Olowalu on the ride between Mā'alaea and Lahaina remains the best place for French cuisine on Maui. Owner-chef Patrick Callarec hails from Provence, and he honed his skills at many Ritz-Carltons. Let the Edith Piaf music and sensual artwork transport you to France as you dine on magret of duck with raspberry vinegar sauce; fresh island fish poached in champagne with caper berries; and rack of lamb paniolo-style with fruit marinade. For dessert, try the vanilla crème brûlée in a pineapple shell. Chef Patrick is lively, so do chat him up. The restaurant's offbeat exterior belies the fine art, linen-draped tables, and wine cel-

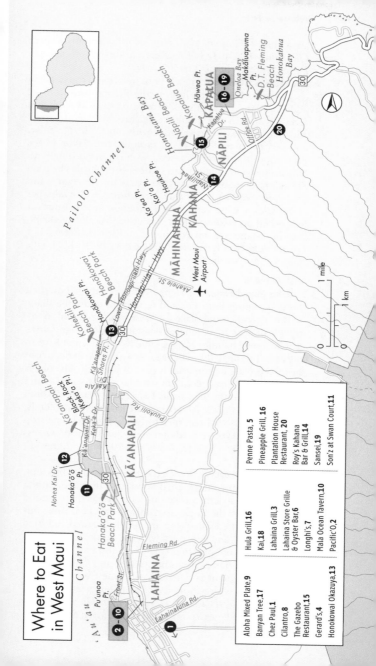

Where to Eat in West Maui

Aloha Mixed Plate,**9**	Hula Grill,**16**
Banyan Tree,**17**	Kai,**18**
Chez Paul,**1**	Lahaina Grill,**3**
Cilantro,**8**	Lahaina Store Grille
The Gazebo	& Oyster Bar,**6**
Restaurant,**15**	Longhi's,**7**
Gerard's,**4**	Mala Ocean Tavern,**10**
Honokowai Okazuya,**13**	Pacific'O,**2**

Penne Pasta, **5**	
Pineapple Grill, **16**	
Plantation House	
Restaurant, **20**	
Roy's Kahana	
Bar & Grill,**14**	
Sansei,**19**	
Son'z at Swan Court,**11**	

lar within. ⊠*Honoapi'ilani Hwy., 4 mi south of Lahaina, Olowalu*🕾*808/661–3843* ⩘*Reservations essential*🍴*AE, D, MC, V*⊘*No lunch.*

★ **Fodor's**Choice ✕**Gerard's.** French-born owner and top Lahaina
$$$$ chef Gerard Reversade honors the French tradition yet adds an island twist in such exquisite dishes as fresh 'ahi tartare with taro chips; shiitake mushrooms in puff pastry; and roasted Hawaiian snapper with olive oil, star anise, and savory fennel fondue. All explode with flavor. In the Plantation Inn, Gerard's resembles a country estate with balustrades and gingerbread lattice work. Birds chirp on the palms, mangos hang on the trees in the courtyard, and fans spin overhead. Antique furnishings and wallpaper along with a wide veranda for dining make this perfect for special occasions. A first-class wine list and celebrity-spotting round out the experience. ⊠*Plantation Inn, 174 Lahainaluna Rd., Lahaina* 🕾*808/661–8939* 🍴*AE, D, DC, MC, V* ⊘*No lunch.*

HAWAIIAN

$ ✕**Aloha Mixed Plate.** Set right on the ocean in Lahaina, this walk-up open-air bar and restaurant under the shade trees is a great casual place for *'ono grinds*—"good food" in Hawaiian slang. Chinese roast duck, Hawaiian *laulau* (leaf-wrapped bundles of meats and fish) plate, and Korean *kalbi* ribs (marinated and cooked on a grill) are indicative of the mixed-plate culture that is part of Hawai'i. The plates come piled with two scoops of rice and macaroni salad and go well with drinks such as the Lava Flow, Peachy Passion, and Hawaiian Punch. All are favorite island comfort foods, and this place is well-regarded by locals. It's a good pit stop for lunch when you're tired of more expensive sit-down restaurants. ⊠*1286 Front St., Lahaina*🕾*808/661–3322*🍴*AE, D, DC, MC, V.*

¢ ✕**Honokowai Okazuya.** Don't expect to sit down at this miniature restaurant sandwiched between a dive shop and a salon—this is strictly a take-out joint. It has quite a good reputation with the locals, so it's always packed. Sink your teeth into chicken *katsu* (Japanese-style breaded and fried chicken), pork, and peas piled with the requisite two scoops rice and macaroni-potato salad. You'll also find lighter fare such as vegetarian plates, sandwiches, and Chinese food. The spicy eggplant is delicious, and the fresh *chow fun* noodles (flat, wide Chinese rice noodles) are purchased quickly. ⊠*3600-D Lower Honoapi'ilani Hwy., Lahaina* 🕾*808/665–0512* 🍴*No credit cards* ⊘*Closed Sun.*

A hula performance is always part of a lūau; one of the favorites on Maui is the Old Lahaina Lū'au.

ITALIAN

$$$$ ✕**Longhi's.** A Lahaina landmark, Longhi's has been drawing in throngs of visitors since 1976, serving great Italian pasta as well as sandwiches and seafood, beef, and chicken dishes from the menu created by Bob Longhi, "the man who loves to eat." The pasta is homemade and the in-house bakery turns out breakfast pastries, desserts, and pizza bread, the latter complimentary with your meal. Definitely for two, the signature lobster Longhi includes two lobsters over linguine and pomodoro sauce with mussels, clams, and prawns. Even on a warm day, you won't need air-conditioning with two spacious, breezy, open-air levels to choose from. The black-and-white marble tile floors and the feng shui–inspired rounded archways are a classic touch. There's a second restaurant on the South Shore, at the Shops at Wailea. ✉ *888 Front St., Lahaina* ☎ *808/667–2288* ✉ *The Shops at Wailea, 3750 Wailea Alanui Dr., Wailea* ☎ *808/891–8883* ▭ *AE, D, DC, MC, V.*

$ ✕**Penne Pasta.** A couple of blocks off the beaten path in Lahaina, little Penne Pasta packs a powerhouse of a menu, as might be expected from a place owned by chef Mark Ellman of the Mala Ocean Tavern. Heaping plates of reasonably priced, flavorful pasta and low-key, unobtrusive service make this restaurant the perfect alternative to an expensive night out down the street. The osso buco (Wednesday's special) is sumptuous, and the traditional salade niçoise overflows with olives, peppers, garlic 'ahi, and potatoes.

Couples should split a salad and entrée, as portions are large. House favorites are baked penne and linguine in clam sauce. Nothing is priced over $13.95, and aloha is practiced here. ⊠*180 Dickenson St., Lahaina* ☎*808/661–6633* ⊟*AE, D, DC, MC, V* ⊘*No lunch weekends.*

JAPANESE

$$$✕ **Kai.** The popular sushi bar in the Ritz-Carlton, Kapalua takes design inspiration from the arrival of the ancient Hawaiians over the sea. Hand-carved ceiling beams resemble outrigger canoes, and the back wall of the bar glows like lava. This is a great place to meet your friends and lift your chopsticks to rainbow roll and fresh 'ahi sashimi before you head to the Lobby Lounge. The menu also includes hot Japanese entrées such as baked crab dynamite; your best bet is to let chef Yoshino design the meal. He might have yellowtail cheeks, fresh sea urchin, and raw lobster, and he makes lobster-head soup, a Japanese comfort food. The kitchen is open until 10 PM. ⊠*Ritz-Carlton, Kapalua, 1 Ritz-Carlton Dr., Kapalua* ☎*808/669–6200* ⊟*AE, D, DC, MC, V.*

SUSHI FOR ALL. On Maui, there's a sushi restaurant for everyone—even those who don't like sushi! Sansei has the most diverse menu: everything from lobster ravioli to sea urchin. People love designer rolls such as the "69"—unagi eel slathered in sweet sauce paired with crab, or the "caterpillar"—avocado and tuna wrapped around rice, complete with radish-sprout antennae.

MEDITERRANEAN

$$$✕ **Plantation House Restaurant.** It's hard to decide which is better here, the food or the view. Nestled above Kapalua's coastline, this restaurant at the Plantation Course has the misty Maui Mountains behind, with their grassy volcanic ridges. Facing the ocean are the famous fairways as well as views of Moloka'i and the Pailolo Channel. The menu is on par with these surroundings and features Mediterranean flavors blended with local ingredients. Revel in chef Alex Stanislaw's 'ahi in the style of Italy with cannelloni beans and olives, and the pistachio-crusted fresh catch called Taste of Maui. The breeze through the open-air windows can be cool, so bring a sweater or sit by the fireplace. Breakfast here is luxurious. ⊠*Plantation Course Clubhouse, 2000 Plantation Club Dr., past Kapalua* ☎*808/669–6299*⊟*AE, MC, V.*

$$$$ ✕ **Son'z at Swan Court.** Robin Leach once named this the most romantic restaurant in the world in *Lifestyles of the Rich and Famous*, and it's perfect for couples celebrating special occasions. Descend the grand staircase into an amber-lit dining room with soaring ceilings and a massive artifical lagoon with swans, waterfalls, and tropical gardens. Choose your evening's libation from one of 3,000 bottles of wine, the largest cellar in the state. Must-haves on chef George Gomes Jr.'s contemporary, Mediterranean-influenced menu are goat-cheese ravioli of fresh Kula corn, edamame, and Hamakua mushrooms; and the fresh opakapaka (blue snapper) served with artichokes, sweet-potato hash browns, and tomato puree. ⊠*Hyatt Regency Maui, Kā'anapali Beach Resort, 200 Nohea Kai Dr., Kā'anapali* ☎*808/661–1234* ⊟*AE, D, DC, MC, V* ⊗*No lunch.*

MEXICAN

$ ✕**Cilantro.** The flavors of Old Mexico are given new life here, where the tortillas are hand-pressed and no fewer than nine chilies are used to create the salsas. The style explores 80- to 90-year-old Baja, Sonoran, and Yucatán roots, with modern sauces put into the mix. Owner Paris Nabavi spent three years doing research, visiting authentic eateries in 40 Mexican cities. Rotisserie chicken tacos with jicama slaw are both mouthwatering and healthy, and the Mother Clucker flautas with *crema fresca* (crème fraiche) and jalapeño jelly are not to be missed. Look for Nabavi's collection of tortilla presses worn from duty, now hand-painted and displayed up on the wall. ⊠*Old Lahaina Center, 170 Papalaua Ave., Lahaina* ☎*808/667–5444* ⊟*AE, MC, V.*

MODERN HAWAIIAN

$$$$ ✕**The Banyan Tree.** The signature restaurant of the Ritz-Carlton, Kapalua is better than ever after the resort's late 2007 makeover. Drink in views of the Pailolo Channel and Moloka'i from the outdoor bar and lounge with covered terrace. Indoors are light fixtures and artwork inspired by sea urchins and vibrant corals. The *dukka* (Middle Eastern spices) delivered with your bread is a tip that this elegant dining hall has something different to offer discerning palates. Chef Jojo Vasquez excels with pine-nut crusted 'ahi with cucumber noodles and Thai basil pesto; organic chicken fricassee; and chocolate cake trio with vanilla sorbet and peanut brittle. The open-beam restaurant's subdued atmosphere is charged with the sounds of live world music by Ranga Pae. ⊠*Ritz-Carlton, Kapalua, 1 Ritz-Carlton Dr., Kapalua* ☎*808/669–6200* ⊟*AE, D, DC, MC, V.*

$$$ ✕**Hula Grill.** Genial chef-restaurateur Peter Merriman, the pied piper and founder of Hawai'i Regional Cuisine, has teamed with TS Restaurant Group in this bustling, family-oriented restaurant. They have re-created a 1930s Hawaiian beach house, and every table has an ocean view. You can also dine on the beach, toes in the sand, at the Barefoot Bar, where Hawaiian entertainment is presented every evening. South Pacific snapper is baked with tomato, chili, and cumin aioli, and served with a black bean, Maui onion, and avocado relish. Spareribs are steamed in banana leaves, then grilled with mango barbecue sauce. Children of all ages scream for the ice-cream sandwich made with baked brownies and drizzled with raspberry sauce. ⊠*Whalers Village, 2435 Kā'anapali Pkwy., Kā'anapali*☎808/667–6636⊟*AE, DC, MC, V.*

$$ ✕**Mala Ocean Tavern.** On the water's edge, above the tide-tossed rocks, stands this cheery yellow-walled, open-air restaurant owned by noted Hawai'i Regional Cuisine chef Mark Ellman and his wife, Judy. The menu, composed of mostly organic and locally sourced ingredients, includes flavorful flatbreads and a Kobe burger with Maytag blue cheese. Don't miss the calamari, battered and fried with lemon slices and served with a spicy mojo verde (jalapeño cilantro pesto). This is a good place to try *moi,* the fish of Hawaiian royalty, wok-fried with ginger and spicy black-bean sauce. Fans of the Caramel Miranda dessert at Avalon (Ellman's former restaurant) can find it here. In the evening, the bar is a coveted hangout, and weekend brunch is lively. ⊠*1307 Front St., Lahaina*☎808/667–9394⊟*AE, MC, V.*

$$$ ✕**Pineapple Grill.** With a menu built almost entirely around local ingredients, Pineapple Grill attracts those foodies who appreciate exceptional Pacific Island cuisine such as Asian braised short ribs, pistachio–wasabi pea seared rare 'ahi, and desserts such as Maui Gold pineapple upside-down cake. A Maui Seafood Watch participant, the restaurant agrees to serve only seafood that has been harvested sustainably. So go on—order the Kona lobster. The restaurant also features *Wine Spectator*'s annual top 100 wines by the glass. At night, you can witness spectacular sunsets overlooking the golf greens and the Pacific. If the weather isn't too cold, the outdoor tables facing the West Maui Mountains can be even nicer than those with an ocean view. ⊠*200 Kapalua Dr., Kapalua*☎808/669–9600⊟*AE, D, DC, MC, V.*

$$$ ✕**Roy's Kahana Bar & Grill.** Founder Roy Yamaguchi's own sake brand ("Y") and Hawaiian-fusion specialties, such as shrimp with sweet-and-spicy chili sauce and *miso yaki* (a sake and miso marinade) butterfish, keep regulars returning for more. You can watch signature items such as macadamia-nut mahimahi, honey-mustard short ribs, and hibachi grilled salmon come out of the open kitchen. Locals know to order the incomparable chocolate soufflé immediately after being seated. Both branches, in Kahana and Kīhei, are in supermarket parking lots—it's not the view that excites; it's the fantastic food. ✉*Kahana Gateway Shopping Center, 4405 Honoapi'ilani Hwy., Kahana* ☎808/669–6999 ✉*Safeway Shopping Center, 303 Pi'ikea Ave., Kīhei* ☎808/891–1120 ▬*AE, D, DC, MC, V.*

PACIFIC RIM

$$ ✕**Sansei.** One of the best-loved restaurants on the island, Sansei is Japanese with a Hawaiian twist. Inspired dishes include *panko* (Japanese breadcrumb)-crusted 'ahi sashimi roll, rock shrimp in creamy garlic aioli, spicy fried calamari, and the signature mango-and-crab-salad roll. Those who love goose liver will appreciate a decadent foie gras nigiri sushi. Desserts such as deep-fried tempura ice cream are worth the calories. The Kapalua location uses colors such as pumpkin, butterscotch and sage that all add a tasty touch. Both this and the Kīhei locations are popular karaoke hangouts, serving late-night sushi at half price. ✉*600 Office Rd., Kapalua* ☎808/666–6286 ✉*Kīhei Town Center, 1881 S. Kīhei Rd., Kīhei* ☎808/879–0004 ▬*AE, D, MC, V* ☉*No lunch.*

SEAFOOD

$$$ ✕**The Lahaina Store Grille & Oyster Bar.** Overlooking the seawall near Lahaina Harbor, the rooftop tables at this seafood restaurant are wonderfully romantic. Inside, antique fans, Roaring '20s decor, and the giant etched mirror give a nod to this whaling town's past. You get views of Lāna'i and Moloka'i here, along with the surfers and the sunsets; and in season, humpback whales jump offshore. Join your friends in the Martini Raw Bar Lounge for oysters, crabs, sashimi, and other appetizers from around the globe. Be sure to try the yellowfin 'ahi seared with *togarashi* (Asian seven spice) and served with wasabi aioli and sweet soy reduction. Lahaina Store is also known as the one-stop hot spot for late-night excitement, entertainment, music, and dancing. ✉*744 Front St., Lahaina* ☎808/661–9090 ▬*AE, D, MC, V.*

$$$ ✕ **Pacific'O.** You can sit outdoors at umbrella-shaded tables near the water's edge, or find a spot in the breezy, marble-floor interior of this seafood haven. The exciting menu features fresh 'ahi-and-ono tempura, in which the two kinds of fish are wrapped around *tobiko* (flying-fish roe), then wrapped in nori, and wok-fried. There's a great lamb dish, too—a whole rack of sweet New Zealand lamb, sesame-crusted and served with roasted macadamia sauce and Hawaiian chutney. Live jazz is played Friday and Saturday from 9 to midnight. ⊠ *505 Front St., Lahaina* ☎ *808/667–4341* ▭ *AE, D, DC, MC, V.*

THE SOUTH SHORE

Besides restaurants listed below, you'll find branches of Roy's, Sansei, and Longhi's in this area. For reviews of these establishments, *see* the West Maui section. A branch of Fiesta Time is here, too; *see* the North Shore section for a review.

AMERICAN

★ Fodor'sChoice ✕ **Cafe O'Lei.** Chef-owners Michael and Dana
$$ Pastula work their kitchen magic on ample, tasty midprice dishes at lunch and dinner, including Manoa lettuce wraps filled with chicken, mushrooms and water chestnuts; crab cakes; and hefty salads. This is where locals go on their day off. For dinner, order sushi from the bar in back, or roast duck and baked clams from the brick oven. Other popular items are fresh fish, lamb shank, prime rib, and Asian short ribs. Gauze curtains separate tables nicely set with white linens and bright tableware, and the spacious octagonal bar is great for sharing pūpū and sipping cocktails. The Pastulas also have Café O'Lei restaurants in Kahului and Wailuku. ⊠ *2439 S. Kīhei Rd., Kīhei* ☎ *808/891–1368* ▭ *AE, MC, V.*

$$$$ ✕ **Joe's Bar & Grill.** Owners Joe and Beverly Gannon, who run the immensely popular Hāli'imaile General Store in Upcountry Maui, have brought their flair for food to this comfortable treetop-level restaurant at the Wailea Tennis Club. You can dine while watching night play from a balcony seat. This place is named after Joe, who's been in show biz for decades, instead of his celebrity chef wife, and gold records and other memorabilia hang on the walls. With friendly service and such dishes as Joe's favorite meat loaf, grilled thick-cut pork chop, seafood potpie, and Joe's pastry chef daughter Cheech's chocolate bread pudding,

there are lots of reasons to stop in at this hidden spot. ⊠*131 Wailea Ike Pl., Wailea* ☎*808/875–7767* ▭*AE, MC, V* ⊙*No lunch.*

$$ ✕**Māʻalaea Grill.** Large French doors are kept open so that you can view Māʻalaea Harbor and feel the ocean breezes in this casual seaside restaurant. The teak and bamboo furniture, open kitchen, and walk-in wine cellar lend sophistication to this otherwise happily relaxed establishment. Enjoy a light but satisfying seared ʻahi salad, kiawe-wood grilled beef tenderloin, or shrimp prepared a variety of ways: coconut fried, sautéed Provençal, or garlic grilled with pesto. Live jazz music is performed Wednesday through Sunday. This may be one of the few restaurants on Maui in which you can enjoy ocean views until 10 PM, as the harbor and Kīhei beyond are backlighted. ⊠*In the Harbor Shops, 300 Māʻalaea Rd., Māʻalaea* ☎*808/243–2206* ▭*AE, MC, V.*

$$$ ✕**Seawatch.** The Plantation House's South Shore sister restaurant has equally outstanding views and an equally delicious menu. Breakfast is especially nice here—the outdoor seating is cool in the morning and overlooks the parade of boats heading out to Molokini. The crab-cake Benedicts are a well-loved standard. For dinner, try longtime chef Todd Carlos' fresh opakapaka topped with mango chutney and macadamia nuts; or grilled with Grand Marnier and orange glaze. Meat lovers have options including rack of lamb and duck breast pan-seared with cranberry-guava port wine glaze. Regarding the "brownie all the way" dessert, one regular says it "serves a deep need." Avoid seats above their private catering section, which can be noisy. ⊠*100 Golf Club Dr., Wailea* ☎*808/875–8080* ▭*AE, D, DC, MC, V.*

⟲ ✕**Stella Blues.** Parked in humble Azeka Mauka marketplace,
$$ this affordable spot wins die-hard fans for unpretentious service and cuisine in an open-beam, warmly lit dining room that's unexpectedly classy. The menu is a major hit, especially with families, and the bar is great for surfer-dude watching. Comfort food of every sort is served at breakfast, lunch, and dinner—everything from Toby's Tofu Tia (a tofu and veggie-packed tortilla) to "Mama Tried" Meatloaf and the classic spinach salad. The ample dessert tray, including chocolate bread pudding big enough to feed four, is bound to tempt someone in your party; if it doesn't, the cocktails from the swank bar will. ⊠*1279 S. Kīhei Rd., Kīhei* ☎*808/874–3779* ▭*AE, D, DC, MC, V.*

6

The heart of any lū'au is the imu, the earth oven in which a whole pig is roasted.

CAFÉ

¢ ✕**Kihei Caffe.** People-watching is fun over a cup of coffee at this casual breakfast and lunch joint right on the main drag in Kīhei. Hearty, affordable portions will prepare you for surfing across the street at Kalama Park. The bowl-shaped egg scramble is tasty and almost enough for two, or try signature dishes such as the Hawaiian favorite *loco moco* (a hamburger patty and over-easy egg on top of scoops of rice in a bowl, slathered in brown gravy), pork fried rice, and chorizo and eggs. Opakapaka (blue snapper) with *liliko'i* (passion fruit) beurre blanc is popular lunch fare, and fish preparations change daily. The resident rooster, one of many that live under the building, may come a-beggin' for some of your muffin. This place closes at 3. ⊠*1945 S. Kīhei Rd., Kīhei* ☎*808/879–2230* ⊟*MC, V* ⊗*No dinner.*

IRISH

$$ ✕**Mulligan's on the Blue.** When you have a hankering for Irish fare such as bangers and mash, shepherd's pie, and corned beef and cabbage, head to this popular pub and restaurant on the Wailea Blue golf course. A nearly all-Irish staff greets you, and before you know it, you'll be sipping a heady pint of Guinness. Some bartenders even score a four-leaf clover in the head. The Wailea Nights dinner show with different kinds of live music is outstanding—and a terrific deal to boot. Breakfast is a good value for the area, and the view of

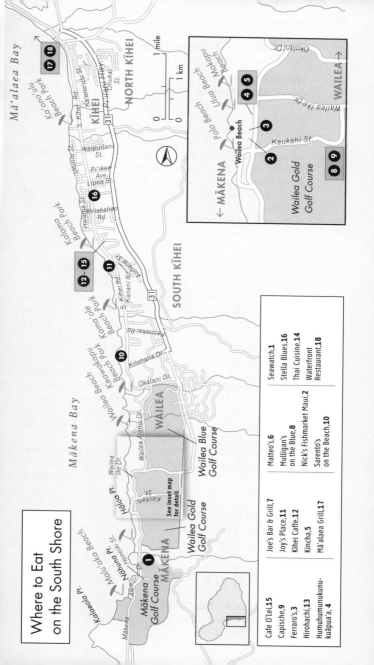

Where to Eat on the South Shore

Cafe O'Lei, **15**	Joe's Bar & Grill, **7**
Capische, **9**	Joy's Place, **11**
Ferraro's, **3**	Kihei Caffe, **12**
Hirohachi, **13**	Kincha, **5**
Humuhumunukunuku- āpua'a, **4**	Ma'alaea Grill, **17**

Matteo's, **6**	Seawatch, **1**
Mulligan's on the Blue, **8**	Stella Blues, **16**
Nick's Fishmarket Maui, **2**	Thai Cuisine, **14**
Sarento's on the Beach, **10**	Waterfront Restaurant, **18**

the golf course and ocean is one of the best. ✉ *100 Kaukahi St., Wailea* ☎ *808/874–1131* ▭ *AE, D, DC, MC, V.*

ITALIAN

★ **Fodor'sChoice** ✕ **Capische.** Hidden up at the quiet Diamond
$$$$ Hawaii Resort & Spa, this Italian restaurant is one local
patrons would like kept secret. A circular stone atrium
with soaring ceilings gives way to a small piano lounge,
where you can find some of the best sunset views on the
island. It's as romantic as it gets, and you'll want to be
dressed up for your date. Capische favorites include ciop-
pino, braised lamb shank with lemon risotto, and herb-
crust opakapaka with whipped potatoes and sun-dried
tomato relish. Intimate and well conceived, this restaurant, with its seductive flavors and ambience, ensures a
lovely night out. ✉ *Diamond Hawaii Resort & Spa, 555
Kaukahi St., Wailea* ☎ *808/879–2224* ▭ *AE, D, DC, MC,
V* ⊘ *No lunch.*

$$$$ ✕ **Ferraro's.** Overlooking Wailea Beach, this outdoor Italian
restaurant at the Four Seasons Resort Maui is beautiful
both day and night, with unparalleled service. For lunch,
indulge in a lobster sandwich, salade niçoise, or a bento
(Japanese divided box filled with savory items). At dinner
you might begin your feast with the arugula and endive
salad and move on to the lobster risotto and veal Milanese
while enjoying live classical music. Try the wine list's excellent Italian choices, and if chef Paul Luna is offering one of
his periodic tasting menus—such as white Alba truffles in
fall—go for it. Occasionally you can catch celebrities gos-
siping at the bar. ✉ *Four Seasons Resort Maui at Wailea,
3900 Wailea Alanui Dr., Wailea* ☎ *808/874–8000* ▭ *AE,
D, DC, MC, V.*

☾ ✕ **Matteo's.** Chef Matteo Mitsura—a bona-fide Italian—may
$$ be heard singing as he pounds dough in the kitchen of this
miraculous pizzeria. (Trust us, discovering handsomely
sized Margherita and Portofino pizzas for $17 in Wailea is
truly a miracle.) Handmade pastas are loaded with luxuri-
ous braised lamb, wild mushrooms, and fresh-shaved Par-
mesan. Located on the Wailea Blue golf course, this casual,
open-air restaurant benefits from gentle trade winds in the
afternoon and a sky full of stars at night. A salad bar, a
voluptuous wine list, and desserts such as tiramisu top it
off. ✉ *100 Wailea Ike Dr., Wailea* ☎ *808/874–1234* ▭ *AE,
D, MC, V.*

$$$$ ✕ **Sarento's on the Beach.** The setting right on spectacular
Keawakapu Beach, with views of the islands of Molokini

and Kahoʻolawe, at this upscale Italian restaurant is irresistible. Chef George Gomes Jr. heads the kitchen, which turns out both traditional dishes—like penne Calabrese and seafood *fra diavolo* (in a tomato sauce spiced with chilies)—as well as inventions such as swordfish saltimbocca, a strangely successful entrée with a prosciutto, Bel Paese cheese, radicchio, and porcini sauce. Meat lovers should try the fall-off-the-bone tender osso buco. The wine list includes some great finds. ⊠*2980 S. Kīhei Rd., Kīhei* ☎*808/875–7555* ⊟*AE, D, DC, MC, V* ☺*No lunch.*

JAPANESE

$$ ✕**Hirohachi.** A stone's throw from the flashier Sansei, Hirohachi has been serving authentic Japanese fare for years. This is where all the Maui restaurant owners and workers hang out, because the fish is fresh and it's more down home than the other sushi bars. Owner Hiro has discerning taste: he buys only the best from local fishermen and imports many ingredients from Japan. Order with confidence even if you can't read the Japanese specials posted on the wall; everything on the menu is high quality. ⊠*1881 S. Kīhei Rd., Kīhei* ☎*808/875–7474* ⊟*AE, MC, V* ☺*Closed Mon.*

★ **Fodor'sChoice** ✕**Kincha.** At the Grand Wailea Resort, take your
$$$$ taste buds into the heart of Tokyo with superb if expensive Japanese fare as you dine amid tranquil gardens, waterfalls, and 800 tons of rock imported from the base of Mt. Fuji. Sit Japanese-style at low tables with pits underneath to save your feet from falling asleep, or dine in a private tatami room. The seafood buffet ($52) showcases lobster tails and more, and the sushi bar is one of the best on the island. Even visitors from Japan are impressed with the decor and the quality of the cuisine. ⊠ *3850 Wailea Alanui Dr., Wailea* ☎*808/875–1234* ⊟*AE, MC, V* ☺*No lunch*

MODERN HAWAIIAN

$$$$ ✕**Humuhumunukunukuāpuaʻa.** You don't have to wrestle with the restaurant's formidable name (it's Hawaiʻi's state fish); simply tell the valet or concierge that you're headed to Humuhumu. Romantic, exotic, and good for a special occasion, this oceanfront thatched-roof restaurant at the Grand Wailea has delectable sunsets. You may select your own lobster from the surrounding saltwater lagoon and also watch the fish swim by in the tank at the bar. As for the food, the chef who creates it rocks: try his Malaysian-style rack of lamb finished with mustard, mild sambal (an Asian condiment), and brioche crust; and blue-crab-stuffed hamachi (yellowtail) with garlic-sautéed baby spinach. The

cocktails are over the top. ⊠*Grand Wailea Resort Hotel & Spa, 3850 Wailea Alanui Dr., Wailea* ☎*808/875–1234* ⊜*AE, D, DC, MC, V.*

SEAFOOD

$$$$ ✕**Nick's Fishmarket Maui.** This romantic spot serves fresh seafood using the simplest preparations: original Tiger Eye sushi, mahimahi with Kula-corn relish, 'ahi pepper fillet, and *opakapaka* (Hawaiian pink snapper) with rock shrimp in a lemon-butter-caper sauce, to name a few. Everyone seems to love the Greek Maui Wowie salad made with local onions, tomatoes, avocado, feta cheese, and bay shrimp. The team service is formal—even theatrical—but it befits the beautiful food presentations and extensive wine list. If you are a repeat diner, the staff will even remember what drink is your favorite. ⊠*Fairmont Kea Lani, 4100 Wailea Alanui Dr., Wailea* ☎*808/879–7224* ⊜*AE, D, DC, MC, V* ⊘*No lunch.*

★ Fodor'sChoice ✕**Waterfront Restaurant.** The Smith family lures
$$$$ you in hook, line, and fresh catch at this well-regarded harborside establishment with an outstanding wine list. Sit in cushy leather booths or on the lānai and choose from six types of fresh fish prepared in nine different ways, including baked in buttered parchment paper; captured in ribbons of angel-hair potato; and topped with tomato salsa, smoked chili pepper, and avocado. The varied menu also lists an outstanding rack of lamb and veal scaloppine. Visitors like to come early to dine at sunset on the outdoor patio. Enter Mā'alaea at the Maui Ocean Center and then follow the blue WATERFRONT RESTAURANT signs to the third condominium. ⊠*50 Hau'oli St., Mā'alaea* ☎*808/244–9028* ⊜*AE, D, DC, MC, V* ⊘*No lunch.*

THAI

$ ✕**Thai Cuisine.** Fragrant tea and coconut-ginger chicken soup begin a satisfying meal at this excellent Thai restaurant, set unassumingly in the back of a casual shopping mall. The care that goes into the decor—reflected in the glittering Buddhist shrines, fancy napkin folds, and matching blue china—also applies to the cuisine. The lean, moist meat of the red-curry duck rivals similar dishes at resort restaurants, and the fried bananas with ice cream are wonderful. ⊠*In Kukui Mall, 1819 S. Kīhei Rd., Kīhei* ☎*808/875–0839* ⊜*AE, D, DC, MC, V.*

The Plate Lunch Tradition

To experience island history first-hand, take a seat at one of Hawai'i's ubiquitous "plate lunch" eateries, and order a segmented Styrofoam plate piled with rice, macaroni salad, and maybe some fiery pickled vegetable condiment. On the sugar plantations, native Hawaiians and immigrant workers from many different countries ate together in the fields, sharing food from their kaukau kits, the utilitarian version of the Japanese *bento* lunchbox. From this melting pot came the vibrant language of pidgin and its equivalent in food: the plate lunch.

At beaches and events, you can probably see a few tiny kitchens-on-wheels, another excellent venue for sampling plate lunch. These portable restaurants are descendants of lunch wagons that began selling food to plantation workers in the 1930s. Try the deep-fried chicken *katsu* (rolled in Japanese panko flour and spices). The marinated beef teriyaki is another good choice, as is miso butterfish. The noodle soup, *saimin,* with its Japanese fish stock and Chinese red-tinted barbecue pork, is a distinctly local medley. Koreans have contributed spicy barbecue *kalbi* ribs, often served with chili-laden kimchi (pickled cabbage). Portuguese bean soup and tangy Filipino adobo stew are also favorites. The most popular Hawaiian contribution to the plate lunch is the *laulau,* a mix of meat and fish and young taro leaves, wrapped in more taro leaves and steamed.

6

VEGETARIAN

$ ✕ **Joy's Place.** You may see Joy in the back of this small spot, whipping up one of the fantastic, vitamin-packed soups that reflect her healthful culinary wizardry. Try a sandwich or collard-green wrap filled with veggies and a creamy spread, or a nut burger and nondairy cheese. Joy's is also known for free-range turkey sandwiches, and they poach tuna for fresh tuna salad. Organic cookies and vegan brownies top it off. If you have a hint of a cold, a spicy potion called Cold Buster is available to ward it off. ✉ *In Island Surf Bldg., 1993 S. Kīhei Rd., Suite 17, Kīhei* ☎ *808/879–9258* ▭ *MC, V.*

CENTRAL MAUI

AMERICAN

¢ ×**Maui Bake Shop.** Wonderful breads baked in old brick ovens (dating to 1935), hearty lunch fare, and irresistible desserts make this a popular lunch spot in Central Maui. Baker José Krall was trained in his homeland of France, and his wife, Claire, is a Maui native whose friendly face you often see when you walk in. Standouts include the focaccia, Caesar salads, and homemade soups. José also creates impressive wedding and other specialty cakes. ⊠*2092 Vineyard St., Wailuku* ☎*808/242–0064* ⊟*AE, D, MC, V* ⊗*Closed Sun. No dinner.*

CHINESE

$$ ×**Dragon Dragon.** Whether you're a party of 10 or two, this is the place to share seafood-tofu soup, spareribs with garlic sauce, or fresh Dungeness crab with four sauces. Tasteful, simple decor that focuses on feng shui and sharp angles complements the solid Chinese menu. The restaurant shares parking with the Maui Megaplex and makes a great pre- or postmovie stop. ⊠*In Maui Mall, 70 E. Ka'ahumanu Ave., Kahului* ☎*808/893–1628* ⊟*AE, D, MC, V.*

HAWAIIAN

$ ×**A.K.'s Café.** Nearly hidden between auto-body shops and karaoke bars is this wonderful, bright café serving good Hawaiian fare. Affordable, tasty entrées such as grilled tenderloin with wild mushrooms or garlic-crusted ono with ginger relish come with a choice of two sides. The flavorful dishes are healthy, too—chef Elaine Rothermal previously instructed island nutritionists on how to prepare health-conscious versions of local favorites. (She's trying to get away from that somewhat, as most people like the bad stuff at least sometimes.) Try the Hawaiian french-fried sweet potatoes or the poi, the Hawaiian classic made from taro root. Single musicians entertain you on weekends. ⊠*1237 Lower Main, Wailuku* ☎*808/244–8774* ⊟*D, MC, V* ⊗*Closed Sun.*

ITALIAN

$$ ×**Marco's Grill & Deli.** Outside Kahului Airport, this convenient eatery (look for the green awning) serves perhaps the best Italian food in Central Maui. Owner Marco Defanis was a butcher in his former life, and his meatballs and sausages are housemade. Homemade pastas appear on the extensive menu, along with an unforgettably good Reuben sandwich and the best tiramisu on the island. Even the

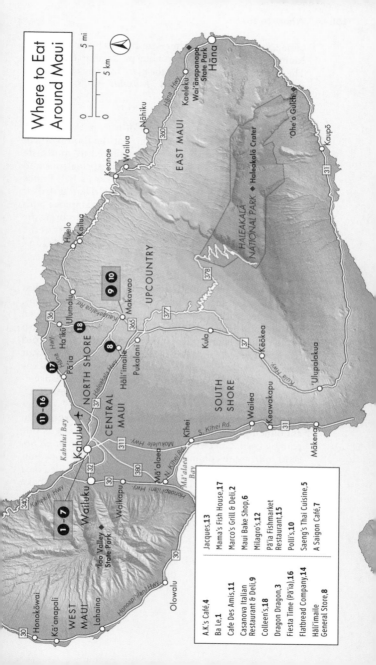

Where to Eat Around Maui

5 mi
5 km

WEST MAUI

Honokōwai
Kāʻanapali
Lahaina

Kahului Bay
Kahului

Wailuku

ʻIao Valley State Park

CENTRAL MAUI

Māʻalaea
Māʻalaea Bay

SOUTH SHORE

Kihei
Wailea
Keawakapu
Makena

NORTH SHORE

Pāʻia
Haʻikū
Ulumalu

UPCOUNTRY

Makawao
Pukalani
Kula
Keōkea
ʻUlupalakua

EAST MAUI

Nāhiku
Wailua
Keʻanae
Hāna
Koʻeleku
Waiʻānapanapa State Park
ʻOheʻo Gulch
Kaupō

HALEAKALĀ NATIONAL PARK
Haleakalā Crater

A.K.'s Café, **4**
Ba le, **1**
Cafe Des Amis, **11**
Casanova Italian Restaurant & Deli, **9**
Colleen's, **18**
Dragon Dragon, **3**
Fiesta Time (Pā'ia), **16**
Flatbread Company, **14**
Hāli'imaile General Store, **8**
Jacques, **13**
Mama's Fish House, **17**
Marco's Grill & Deli, **2**
Maui Bake Shop, **6**
Milagro's, **12**
Pā'ia Fishmarket Restaurant, **15**
Polli's, **10**
Saeng's Thai Cuisine, **5**
A Saigon Café, **7**

coffee, served in Mad Hatter–size cups, is made by nearby Maui Coffee Roasters; you can buy packages to take home. The local business crowd fills the place for breakfast, lunch, and dinner. ⊠*444 Hāna Hwy., Kahului* ☏*808/877–4446* ⊟*AE, D, DC, MC, V.*

THAI

$$ ✕**Saeng's Thai Cuisine.** Choosing a dish from the six-page menu here requires determination, but the food is worth the effort, and most dishes can be tailored to your taste buds: hot, medium, or mild. Begin with spring rolls and a dipping sauce, move on to such entrées as Evil Prince Chicken (cooked in coconut sauce with Thai herbs) or red-curry shrimp, and finish up with tea and tapioca pudding. Asian artifacts, flowers, and a waterfall decorate the dining room, and tables on a veranda satisfy lovers of the outdoors. ⊠*2119 Vineyard St., Wailuku* ☏*808/244–1567* ⊟*AE, MC, V.*

VIETNAMESE

¢ ✕**Ba Le.** Tucked into a mall's food court is the best, cheapest Vietnamese fast food on the island. *Pho*, the famous soups, come laden with seafood or rare beef, fresh basil, bean sprouts, and lime. Tasty sandwiches are served on crisp French rolls—lemongrass chicken is a favorite. The word is out, so the place gets busy at lunchtime, though the wait is never long. Make sure to try one of the flavored tapiocas for dessert. ⊠*Kau Kau Corner food court, Maui Marketplace, 270 Dairy Rd., Kahului* ☏*808/877–2400* ⊟*AE, D, DC, MC, V.*

★ **Fodor's**Choice ✕**A Saigon Café.** The only storefront sign
$$ announcing this delightful Vietnamese hideaway is one reading OPEN. Once you find it, treat yourself to *banh hoi chao tom,* more commonly known as "shrimp pops burritos" (ground marinated shrimp, steamed and grilled on a stick of sugarcane). Wok-fried or steamed whole opakapaka is always available, and vegetarian fare is well represented— try the green-papaya salad. The simple white interior serves as a backdrop for Vietnamese carvings, and booths make for some privacy. Owner Jennifer Nguyen really makes the place, so ask to talk story with her if she's in. ⊠*1792 Main St., Wailuku* ☏*808/243–9560* ⊟*D, MC, V.*

UPCOUNTRY

ITALIAN

$$$ ✕**Casanova Italian Restaurant & Deli.** An Italian dinner house and nightclub, this place is smack in the middle of paniolo (cowboy) country, yet it remains an Upcountry institution. The pizzas, baked in a brick wood-burning oven imported from Italy, are the best on the island, especially the *tartufo,* or truffle oil pizza. All entrées come with either creamy risotto, steamy polenta, or garlicky mashed potatoes. The daytime deli serves outstanding sandwiches and espresso. After dining hours, local and visiting entertainers heat up the dance floor. ✉ *1188 Makawao Ave., Makawao* ☎808/572–0220 ▤D, DC, MC, V.

MEXICAN

$$ ✕**Polli's.** Not only does this Mexican restaurant offer standards such as enchiladas, chimichangas, and fajitas, but it will also prepare any item on the menu with seasoned tofu or vegetarian taco mix—and the meatless dishes are just as good as the real thing. A special treat are the *buñuelos*—light pastries topped with cinnamon, maple syrup, and ice cream. The intimate interior is plastered with colorful sombreros and other cantina knickknacks. The bar is always packed with the same regulars, just as it has been for decades. ✉ *1202 Makawao Ave., Makawao* ☎808/572–7808 ▤AE, D, DC, MC, V.

MODERN HAWAIIAN

$$$$ ✕**Hāli'imaile General Store.** What do you do with a lofty wooden building surrounded by sugarcane and pineapple fields that was a tiny town's camp store in the 1920s? If you're Beverly and Joe Gannon, you invent a now legendary restaurant known for Hawaii Regional Cuisine. The Szechuan barbecued salmon and Hunan-style rack of lamb are classics, as is the sashimi napoleon appetizer: a tower of crispy wontons layered with 'ahi and salmon. The back room houses a rotating art exhibit, courtesy of some of the island's top artists. The restaurant even has its own cookbook, but Beverly will never reveal the recipe for her famous crab dip. ✉ *900 Hāli'imaile Rd., take left exit halfway up Haleakalā Hwy., Hāli'imaile* ☎808/572–2666 ▤MC, V.

6

Lū'au food is typically served buffet-style and always includes lomi lomi salmon.

THE NORTH SHORE

AMERICAN

$ ✕**Colleen's.** On the main road in jungly Ha'ikū, this is the neighborhood hangout for windsurfers, yoga teachers, and just plain beautiful people. Many regulars prefer takeout on their way home from commutes in the touristy areas. At breakfast, pastries tend to be jam-packed with berries and nuts, rather than being flaky and full of butter. Sandwiches are especially good, served on giant slices of homemade bread. For dinner you can't go wrong with the pan-seared 'ahi with ginger-scented rice, bok-choy stir-fry, and miso butter sauce; and red-ale and mango-glazed ribs with sour cream and herb mashed potatoes. ⊠*In Ha'ikū Cannery, 810 Kokomo Rd., Ha'ikū* ☎808/575–9211 ▭*AE, DC, MC, V.*

ECLECTIC

$ ✕**Jacques.** An amiable French chef, Jacques won the hearts of the windsurfing crowd when he opened this hip, ramshackle bar and restaurant. It's a youthful hangout with fairly sophisticated fare for the price, and makes a great dating spot for twentysomethings on a budget. French-Caribbean dishes like Jacques' Crispy Little Poulet (chicken) reveal the owner's expertise. The outdoor seating can be a little chilly at times; coveted spots at the sushi bar inside are snatched up quickly. On Friday nights, a DJ moves in and the dining room becomes a packed dance floor. ✉*120 Hāna Hwy., Pāʻia* ☎*808/579–8844* ▭*AE, D, MC, V.*

FRENCH

$ ✕**Cafe Des Amis.** Papier-mâché wrestlers pop out from the walls at this small creperie. French crepes with Gruyère, and Indian wraps with lentil curry are among the choices, all served with wild greens and sour cream or chutney on the side. The giant curry bowls are mild but tasty, served with delicious chutney. For dessert there are crepes filled with chocolate, Nutella, cane sugar, or banana. Bring your newspaper and relax; it may take some time for your order to arrive. The people-watching in eccentric Pāʻia makes it worth the wait—so do the smoothies. ✉*42 Baldwin Ave., Pāʻia* ☎*808/579–6323* ▭*AE, D, MC, V.*

LATIN-AMERICAN

$$ ✕**Milagro's.** Delicious fish tacos are found at this corner restaurant, along with a fine tequilas and Latin-fusion recipes that ignite the taste buds. For instance, try the lava-rock grilled ʻahi burrito with house-made beans and rice; and the seafood enchiladas with ʻahi, ono, and mild green Anaheim chile sauce. The location at the junction of Baldwin Avenue and Hāna Highway makes watching the scene from under the awning shade fun, but the constant stream of traffic makes it a bit noisy. Mostly tourists dine here as it's such a convenient location. Lunch and happy hour (3 to 5) are the best values; prices jump at dinnertime. ✉*3 Baldwin Ave., Pāʻia* ☎*808/579–8755* ▭*AE, D, DC, MC, V.*

MEXICAN

¢ ✕**Fiesta Time.** Little tastes better, after a hard day of snorkeling, watching whales, and catching waves, than fish tacos with rice and beans slathered in melted cheese and fresh salsa. At three locations, Fiesta Time can fill your belly with burritos, enchiladas, and chiles rellenos. The pickled vegetables available in take-home tubs are especially tasty. Decorated with fanciful Mexican murals, the Wailuku and Pāʻia locations have limited seating and are mainly takeout. The Māʻalaea restaurant serves alcohol. This is the Mexicans' Mexican restaurant; it's as authentic as it gets on Maui. ✉ *149 Hāna Hwy., Pāʻia* ☎*808/579–8269* ✉*1132 Lower Main St., Wailuku* ☎*808/249–8463* ✉ *In the Harbor Shops, 300 Māʻalaea Rd., Māʻalaea* ☎*808/244–5862* ▭*AE, MC, V.*

PIZZA

C ✕**Flatbread Company.** Sit inside this popular pizzeria and
$$ watch the chef stir the giant cauldron of organic fresh toma-
toes over kiawe wood and sweeten it with maple syrup.
Next to him, another chef caramelizes organic onions.
Every item on the menu screams that it's fresh, sustainable,
and oh-so-good for you. Wood-fired pizzas are baked in
a clay oven, and meats include nitrate-free pepperoni and
free-range pork. Partake in the "Punctuated Equilibrium"
with Kalamata olives and Surfing Goat cheese; or "Mopsy's
Pork Pie" with *kālua* (baked underground) pork and bar-
becue sauce. The terrific mesclun salad arrives dressed with
arame seaweed and ginger-tamari vinaigrette. Portions are
large and service is prompt and friendly, despite the near-
constant crowds. ✉*375 Hāna Hwy., Pā'ia* ☎*808/579–8989*
🖃*MC, V.*

SEAFOOD

★ Fodor'sChoice ✕**Mama's Fish House.** For 35 years Mama's has
$$$$ been *the* Maui destination for special occasions. A stone-
and shell-engraved path leads you up to what would be,
in an ideal world, a good friend's house. The Hawaiian
nautical theme is hospitable and fun—the menu even names
which boat reeled in your fish. Despite its high prices—even
for Maui—the restaurant is always full; dinner reservations
start at 4:30 PM. The daily catch steamed in traditional lū'au
leaves is outstanding—and worth the cash. Follow up with
the Polynesian Pearl—a gorgeous affair of chocolate mousse
and passion-fruit cream. A tiny fishing boat is perched
above the entrance to Mama's, about 1½ mi east of Pā'ia
on Hāna Highway. ✉*799 Poho Pl., Kū'au* ☎*808/579–8488*
⌖*Reservations essential* 🖃*AE, D, DC, MC, V.*

$ ✕**Pā'ia Fishmarket Restaurant.** The line leading up to the
counter of this tiny corner fishmarket should attest to the
popularity of the tasty fish sandwiches. But it's really the
great location, on the corner of Hāna Highway and Bald-
win Avenue, right in the middle of Pā'ia. Bench seating is
somewhat grimy (you aren't the only one to have enjoyed
fries here), but you will find a good fish sandwich. Don't
bother with the other items—go for your choice of fillet on
a soft bun with a dollop of slaw and some grated cheese.
As we say in Hawai'i, *'ono* (delicious)! ✉*2A Baldwin Ave.,
Pā'ia* ☎*808/579–8030* 🖃*AE, DC, MC, V.*

Where to Stay

WORD OF MOUTH

"We spent time on the entire island and were glad we chose Wailea . . . The beaches were perfect. The drive to Lahaina is a bit long, but we weren't crazy about Lahaina—too busy for us."

—jess_honeymoon

Updated
by Bonnie
Friedman

MAUI'S ACCOMMODATIONS RUN THE GAMUT from a rural B&B listed on the State and National Historic Registers to one particularly over-the-top, super-opulent megaresort. But hey, each to his or her own taste, right? In between the extremes, there's something for every vacation style and budget.

If the latest and greatest is your style, be prepared to spend a small fortune. Newly renovated properties like the Ritz-Carlton, Kapalua and the Four Seasons Resort Maui at Wailea and the newest condo complexes such as the Wailea Beach Villas may well set you back at least $600 a night. Consider the alternatives.

Although there aren't many of them, small bed-and-breakfasts are charming. They tend to be in residential or rural neighborhoods around the island, sometimes beyond the resort areas of West Maui and the South Shore. The B&Bs offer both a personalized experience and a window onto authentic local life. The prices tend to be the lowest available on Maui, often less than $200 per night.

Apartment and condo rentals are perfect for modest budgets, for two or more couples traveling together, and for families. Not only are the nightly rates lower than hotel rooms, but "eating in" (all have kitchens of some description) is substantially less expensive than dining out. There are literally hundreds of these units, ranging in size from studios to luxurious four-bedrooms with multiple baths, all over the island. The vast majority are along the sunny coasts—from Mākena to Kīhei on the South Shore and Lahaina up to Kapalua on West Maui. Prices are dependent on the size of the unit and its proximity to the beach, as well as on the amenities and services offered. For about $250 a night, you can get a perfectly lovely one-bedroom apartment without many frills or flourishes, close to but probably not on the beach. Many rentals have minimum stays (usually three to five nights), and don't forget to ask if a discount is offered on stays of a week or more.

Most of Maui's resorts—several are megaresorts—have opulent gardens, fantasy swimming pools, championship golf courses, and the latest "must," full-service fitness centers and spas. Expect to spend at least $350 a night at the resort hotels; they are all located in the Wailea and Mākena resort area on the South Shore and Kā'anapali and Kapalua on West Maui. If you're staying more than a week, consider staying in two different areas. It may rule out longer-stay discounts but can make exploring Maui easier.

RESERVATIONS

The further ahead you book, the more likely you are to get exactly the room you want. This is especially true at the big resort hotels for December 20 through April, and again during July and August, Maui's busiest times. At these times, booking a year in advance is not uncommon. Even at other times, booking less than four to six months ahead may mean settling for a second, third, or fourth choice.

PRICES

Assume that hotels have private bath, phone, and TV and that prices do not include meals unless we state otherwise. We always list facilities but not whether you'll be charged an extra fee to use them; ask when you book. Most resorts charge parking and facility fees—a "resort fee." Ask about packages and discounts. In Hawai'i room prices can rise dramatically if a room has an ocean view. To save money, ask for a garden or mountain view.

WHAT IT COSTS IN HOTELS				
¢	$	$$	$$$	$$$$
FOR 2 PEOPLE				
Under $100	$100–$180	$181–$260	$261–$340	Over $340

Hotel prices are for two people in a double room in high season. Condo price categories reflect studio and one-bedroom rates. Prices exclude 11.41% tax.

WEST MAUI

Along the coast, West Maui is a long string of small communities, beginning with Lahaina at the south end and meandering north into Kā'anapali, Honokowai, Kahana, Nāpili, and Kapalua. Here's the breakdown on what's where: Lahaina, a former whaling town, is the business district with all the action: shops, shows, restaurants, historic buildings, churches, and rowdy side streets. Kā'anapali, the island's original resort area, is all glitz: fancy resorts set on Kā'anapali Beach. Honokōwai, Kahana, and Nāpili are quiet little nooks characterized by comfortable condos built in the late 1960s. All face the same direction and get

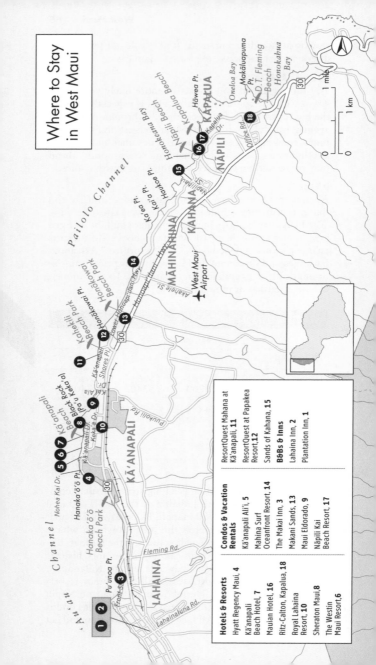

Where to Stay in West Maui

Hotels & Resorts
Hyatt Regency Maui, **4**
Kā'anapali
Beach Hotel, **7**
Mauian Hotel, **16**
Ritz-Calton, Kapalua, **18**
Royal Lahaina
Resort, **10**
Sheraton Maui, **8**
The Westin
Maui Resort, **6**

Condos & Vacation
Rentals
Kā'anapali Ali'i, **5**
Mahina Surf
Oceanfront Resort, **14**
The Makai Inn, **3**
Makani Sands, **13**
Maui Eldorado, **9**
Nāpili Kai
Beach Resort, **17**

ResortQuest Mahana at
Kā'anapali, **11**
ResortQuest at Papakea
Resort, **12**
Sands of Kahana, **15**

B&Bs & Inns
Lahaina Inn, **2**
Plantation Inn, **1**

the same consistently hot, humid weather. Kapalua, at the northern tip, faces windward, and has a cooler climate and slightly more rain. It has become synonymous with the utmost in luxury in accommodations from hotels to condos to residences.

HOTELS & RESORTS

$$$$ ⌖**Hyatt Regency Maui Resort & Spa.** Fantasy landscaping with splashing waterfalls, swim-through grottoes, a lagoonlike swimming pool, and a 130-foot waterslide wow guests of all ages at this active Kāʻanapali resort. Stroll through the lobby past museum-quality art, brilliant parrots, and South African penguins (as we said, this is not reality). The Hyatt is not necessarily Hawaiian, but it is photogenic. The grounds are the big deal, but rooms are elegantly decorated with plantation-style wood furniture and Hawaiian quilts on the walls; each has a private sitting area and lānai. At the southern end of Kāʻanapali Beach, this resort is in the midst of the action. Also on the premises is Spa Moana, an oceanfront, full-service facility. **Pros:** nightly lūʻau show on-site, recent upgrades of linens, refurbished restaurant. **Cons:** it can be difficult to find a space in self-parking, the hotel staff's service can be uneven. ⌂*200 Nohea Kai Dr., Kāʻanapali* ☎*808/661–1234 or 800/233–1234* ⊕*www. maui.hyatt.com* ⬎*815 rooms* ⌂*In-room: safe, refrigerator, Ethernet. In-hotel: 4 restaurants, bars, golf courses, tennis courts, pool, gym, spa, beachfront, children's programs (ages 3–12)* ▤*AE, D, DC, MC, V.*

$$$–$$$$ ⌖**Kāʻanapali Beach Hotel.** Older but still attractive, this small hotel is full of aloha. Locals say that it's one of the few resorts on the island where visitors can get a true Hawaiian experience. The entire staff takes part in the hotel's ongoing Poʻokela program to learn about the history, traditions, and values of Hawaiian culture, and shares its knowledge and stories with guests. Also, you can take complimentary classes in authentic hula dancing, lei-making, lauhala weaving, and ʻukulele playing. The spacious rooms are decorated with Hawaiian motifs, wicker, and rattan; each has a lānai and faces the beach beyond the courtyard. The departure ceremony makes you want to come back. **Pros:** exceptional Hawaiian culture program, friendly staff. **Cons:** a bit run-down, no fine-dining option on-site, fewer amenities than other places along this beach. ⌂*2525 Kāʻanapali Pkwy., Kāʻanapali* ☎*808/661–0011 or 800/262–8450* ⊕*www.kbhmaui.com* ⬎*432 rooms* ⌂*In-*

7

room: safe, refrigerator, Ethernet. In-hotel: 3 restaurants, bar, pool, beachfront☰*AE, D, DC, MC, V.*

$–$$ ☷ **Mauian Hotel.** If you're looking for a quiet place to stay, this nostalgic hotel way out in Nāpili may be for you. The rooms have neither TVs nor phones—such noisy devices are relegated to the 'Ohana Room, where a Continental breakfast is served daily. The simple two-story buildings date from 1959 but have been renovated with bright islander furnishings. Rooms include well-equipped kitchens. Best of all, the 2-acre property opens out onto lovely Nāpili Bay. **Pros:** reasonable rates, friendly staff. **Cons:** older building, few amenities. ✉*5441 Lower Honoapi'ilani Hwy., Nāpili* ☎*808/669–6205 or 800/367–50349*⊕*www.mauian. com*⊅*44 rooms*⚐*In-room: no a/c, no phone, kitchen, no TV. In-hotel: pool, beachfront, laundry facilities, public Wi-Fi*☰*AE, D, MC, V.*

★ **Fodor's**Choice ☷ **Ritz-Carlton, Kapalua.** After a multimillion-
$$$$ dollar going-over, this elegant hillside property reopened in early 2008 with upgraded accommodations, spa, restaurants, and pool, along with a new education center and an enhanced Hawaiian sense of place. The result is one of Maui's most notable resorts. Refurbished guest rooms and 107 newly created one- and two-bedroom condominium residential suites (some of which are available for rent) are decorated in themes incorporating the rich colors of the ocean, mountains, and rain forests that surround the resort. The expanded spa facility includes a fitness center, yoga studio, 15 treatment rooms, private outdoor shower gardens, and Hawaiian design elements. Set amid the lush grounds of the resort, the renovated multilevel pool and hot tubs are open 24 hours. There is a new Environmental Education Center, as well as a full-time cultural advisor who instructs employees and guests in Hawaiian traditions. Although not set directly on the sand, the Ritz does front D. T. Fleming beach, recognized as one of America's best. **Pros:** luxury and service you'd expect from a Ritz, newly renovated, many cultural and recreational programs. **Cons:** can be windy on the grounds and at the pool, the hotel is not on the beach and is far from major attractions such as Lahaina and Hāleakala. ✉*1 Ritz-Carlton Dr., Kapalua* ☎*808/669–6200 or 800/262–8440*⊕*www.ritzcarlton. com/resorts/kapalua*⊅*450 rooms*⚐*In-room: safe, Wi-Fi. In-hotel: 6 restaurants, bar, tennis courts, pool, gym, spa, beachfront, children's programs (ages 5–12), laundry service*☰*AE, D, DC, MC, V.*

Ritz-Carlton, Kapalua

$$$–$$$$  **Royal Lahaina Resort.** Major upgrades have taken place here since 2006, including renovation of the rooms in the 12-story Lahaina Kai Tower. The 333-room tower has Hawaiian canoe–theme rooms with dark teak furnishings set against light-color walls, plush beds with 300-count Egyptian cotton linens, sound systems with an iPod and MP3 docking station, and 32-inch, high-definition flat-screen TVs. The resort's low-rise cottages are being replaced with 126 individually owned luxury villas. Visitors should be aware that renovations will continue through 2009 on the new villas and grounds. The dozen-tennis-court stadium is going, but four upgraded tennis courts remain. Overall, the $300 million renovation project upgrades this property from midprice to deluxe or luxury status. The aim is to return the Royal Lahaina to its glory days, when, as the first property in the resort, it hosted millionaires and Hollywood stars. **Pros:** now an upscale resort with new amenities, on-site lū'au nightly. **Cons:** you may feel it has lost its "old-Hawaiian resort" charm; construction in some areas. ⊠*2780 Keka'a Dr., Kā'anapali* ☎*808/661–3611 or 800/447–6925* ⬜*808/661–3538* ⊕*www.hawaiianhotels. com* ⇥*333 rooms* △*In-room: safe, refrigerator, Ethernet, Wi-Fi. In-hotel: 2 restaurants, tennis courts, pools, beach-front* ⊟*AE, D, DC, MC, V.*

$$$$  **Sheraton Maui Resort.** Set among dense gardens on Kā'anapali's best stretch of beach, the Sheraton offers a quieter, more low-key atmosphere than its neighboring

VACATION RENTAL COMPANIES

There are many real-estate companies that specialize in short-term vacation rentals. They may represent an entire resort property, most of the units at one property, or even individually owned units. The companies listed here have a long history of excellent service to Maui visitors.

AA Oceanfront Condominium Rentals. As the name suggests, the specialty is "oceanfront." With rental units in more than 25 condominium complexes on the South Shore from the northernmost reaches of Kīhei all the way to Wailea, there's something for everyone at prices that range from $130 to $435 a night. ✉ 1279 S. Kīhei Rd., Kīhei ☎ 808/879-7288 or 800/488-6004 ⊕ www. aaoceanfront.com

Bello Maui Vacations. The Bellos are Maui real-estate experts and have a full range of vacation rentals in 20 South Shore condominium complexes. They also have gorgeous houses for rent. Condos start at right around $100 per night (most are $200 or less); a seven-bedroom oceanfront estate rents for $1,500 per night. ✉ 115 E. Lipoa #101, Kīhei ☎ 808/879-3328 or 800/541-3060 ⊕ www. bellomauivacations.com

Chase 'n Rainbows. Family-owned and -operated, this is the largest property management company on West Maui, with the largest selection of rentals from studios to three-bedrooms. Rentals are everywhere from Lahaina town up to Kahana. Prices range from about $100 to $525 per night. The company has been in business since 1980, and it's good. ✉ 118 Kupuohi St., Lahaina ☎ 808/667-7088 or 800/367-6092 ⊕ www. chasenrainbows.com

Destination Resorts. If it's the South Shore luxury of Wailea and Mākena you seek, look no further. This company has a full complement of many dozens of condominiums and villas ranging in size from studios to four bedrooms, and in price from $240 a night for a studio at Wailea 'Ekahi, an older property, to more than $3,500 for the new Wailea Villas. The company offers excellent personalized service and is known for particularly fine housekeeping services. ✉ 3750 Wailea Alanui Dr., Wailea ☎ 808/879-1595 or 866/384-1365 ⊕ www.drhmaui.com

resorts. The open-air lobby has a crisp, cool look with understated furnishings and decor, and sweeping views of the pool area and beach. The majority of the spacious rooms come with ocean views; only one of the six buildings has rooms with mountain or garden views. All rooms have plenty of amenities, including a 32-inch flat-screen TV with video games and on-command movies; all suites also have Bose stereo systems. The huge swimming pool looks like a natural lagoon, with rock waterways and wooden bridges. Best of all, the hotel sits next to and on top of the 80-foot-high Pu'u Keka'a (Black Rock), from which divers leap in a nightly torch-lighting and cliff-diving ritual. **Pros:** luxury resort with terrific beach location, great snorkeling right off the beach. **Cons:** extensive property can mean a long walk from your room to the lobby, restaurants, and beach; staff not overly helpful. ✉2605 Kā'anapali Pkwy., Kā'anapali ☎808/661–0031 or 888/488–35358 ⊕www.sheraton-maui. com ⌖476 rooms, 34 suites △In-room: safe, refrigerator, Ethernet. In-hotel: 2 restaurants, bar, tennis courts, pool, gym, spa, beachfront, children's programs (ages 5–12), laundry facilities, public Wi-Fi⊟AE, D, DC, MC, V.

$$$$ 🚇**The Westin Maui Resort & Spa.** The cascading waterfall in the 🐊 lobby of this hotel gives way to an "aquatic playground" with five heated swimming pools, abundant waterfalls (15 at last count), lagoons complete with pink flamingos, and a premier beach. The water features combined with a spa and fitness center and privileges at two 18-hole golf courses make this an active resort—great for families. Relaxation is by no means forgotten, though. The 15,000-square-foot Heavenly Spa has 16 treatment rooms and a yoga studio. Elegant dark-wood furnishings in the rooms accentuate the crisp linens of the chain's "Heavenly Beds." Rooms in the Beach Tower are newer and slightly larger than those in the Ocean Tower. Farther up the beach, the newly built Westin Ka'anapali Ocean Resort Villas offer studio and one-bedroom units with full kitchens. The Villas have their own restaurants, tennis courts, and three pools, including one for kids with a pirate ship. **Pros:** complimentary shuttle between both Westin properties and to Lahaina, where parking can be difficult; activity programs for all ages; one pool just for adults. **Cons:** you could end up with fantasy overload, luxury chain hotel can seem a bit stuffy at times. ✉2365 Kā'anapali Pkwy., Kā'anapali ☎808/667–2525 or 888/488–3535 ⊕www.starwood.com/hawaii ⌖758 rooms, 500 studios, 521 1-bedroom units △In-room: Ethernet. In-hotel: 6 restaurants, bar, pools, gym, spa, beachfront, children's programs (all ages), public Wi-Fi ⊟AE, D, DC, MC, V.

CONDOS & VACATION RENTALS

$$$$ ⬛ **Kā'anapali Ali'i.** Four 11-story buildings are laid out so well that the feeling of seclusion you enjoy may make you forget you're in a condo complex. Instead of tiny units, you'll be installed in an ample (1,500–1,900 square feet) one- or two-bedroom apartment. All units have great amenities: a chaise in an alcove, a sunken living room, a whirlpool, and a separate dining room, though some of the furnishings are dated. It's the best of both worlds: homelike condo living with hotel amenities—daily maid service, an activities desk, small store with video rentals, and 24-hour front-desk service. **Pros:** large, comfortable units on the beach, good location in heart of the action in Kā'anapali Resort. **Cons:** elevators are notoriously slow, crowded parking, no on-site restaurant. ✉*50 Nohea Kai Dr., Kā'anapali* ☎*808/667–1400 or 800/642–6284*⊕*www.kaanapalialii.com* ⌂*264 units* ⌂*In-room: safe, kitchen, DVD. In-hotel: golf course, tennis courts, pools, beachfront, laundry facilities*=*AE, D, DC, MC, V.*

$–$$ ⬛ **Mahina Surf Oceanfront Resort.** Mahina Surf stands out from the many condo complexes lining the oceanside stretch of Honoapi'ilani Highway by being both well-managed and affordable. You won't be charged fees for parking, check-out, or local phone use, and discount car rentals are available. The individually owned units are typically overdecorated (lots of rattan furniture, silk flowers, and decorative items), but each one has a well-equipped kitchen and an excellent ocean view. The quiet complex is a short amble away from Honokōwai's grocery shopping, beaches, and restaurants. **Pros:** oceanfront barbecues, no "hidden" fees. **Cons:** set among a row of relatively nondescript condo complexes, oceanfront but with rocky shoreline rather than a beach. ✉*4057 Lower Honoapi'ilani Hwy., Mahinahina* ☎*808/669–6068 or 800/367–60864*⊕*www.mahinasurf.com*⌂*50 units* ⌂*In-room: safe, kitchen, Ethernet. In-hotel: pool, laundry facilities, concierge*= *MC, V.*

$ ⬛ **The Makai Inn.** Right on the ocean, this pleasant inn consists of 18 units, all at least 400 square feet, with four special "Hideaway" rooms with private lānai 9 feet from the water. All are one-bedroom except for the two-bedroom "Pineapple Sweet." The furnishings aren't terribly attractive and you might find a smudge of red Lahaina dirt here and there (there is no daily maid service, and towels are replaced only on request), but the lānai are perfect for daydreaming. Suzie, the landlord, lives on the property, and keeps a flock of cheerful Java sparrows well fed; there's a lovely garden courtyard. **Pros:** oceanfront location, full kitchens, reasonable rates. **Cons:** older building, a few blocks walk to center of Lahaina, small units. ⊠ *1415 Front St., Lahaina* ☎ *808/662–3200 or 808/870–9004* ⊕ *www. makaiinn.net* ↷ *18 units* ⬄ *In-room: no a/c (some), kitchen, no TV. In-hotel: no elevator, laundry facilities, public Wi-Fi* ⊟ *AE, MC, V.*

$–$$ 🆃**Makani Sands.** Centrally located in Honokāwai on the lower road between two roads that access West Maui's main highway, this slightly older complex offers an economical way to see West Maui. Rooms have wide lānai, which hang over a small sandy beach below. The corner rooms (ending in 01) are best, with wraparound views. A small freshwater pool is available for cooling off. The back bedrooms may be noisy at night, as they're close to the road. **Pros:** beachfront, reasonable rates. **Cons:** older buildings, few amenities, road noise. ⊠ *3765 Lower Honoapi'ilani Hwy., Honokōwai* ☎ *808/669–8223 or 800/227–8223* ⊕ *www. makanisands.com* ↷ *21 units* ⬄ *In-room: kitchen, DVD, dial-up, Wi-Fi (some). In-hotel: pool, beachfront, laundry facilities* ⊟ *AE, MC, V.*

$$$–$$$$ 🆃**Maui Eldorado.** This fine condo complex, which wraps around the Kā'anapali golf course's sixth fairway, offers several perks, most notably air-conditioning in the units and access to a fully outfitted beach cabana on a semiprivate beach. The complex itself isn't exactly on the beach—it's a quick golf-cart trip away. While resort guests get scolded for dragging lounge chairs onto neighboring resort beaches, here you can relax in luxury. Not only will you have beach chairs at your disposal, but a full kitchen and lounge area at the cabana, too. The privately managed units are tastefully decorated with modern appliances and have spacious bathrooms. Those overseen by the Outrigger aren't as up-to-date, but are still a good value for pricey Kā'anapali. **Pros:** privileges at five resort golf courses, daily maid service. **Cons:** not right on beach, some distance from attractions of the Kā'anapali Resort, some units are privately rented and some are managed by Outrigger Resorts, so the condition of the units may vary. ⊠ *2661 Keka'a Dr., Kā'anapali* ☎ *808/661–0021* ⊕ *www.lahainagrill.com/eldorado.htm* ↷ *204 units* ⬄ *In-room: kitchen, Ethernet (some). In-hotel: golf course, pools, laundry facilities, concierge* ⊟ *AE, D, DC, MC, V.*

$$$–$$$$ 🆃**Nāpili Kai Beach Resort.** On 10 beautiful beachfront acres—the beach here is one of the best on West Maui for swimming and snorkeling—the Nāpili Kai draws a loyal

7

following. Hawaiian-style rooms have plantation-theme furnishings with shoji doors opening onto a private lānai. The rooms closest to the beach have no air-conditioning, but ceiling fans usually suffice. "Hotel" rooms have only mini-refrigerators and coffeemakers, whereas studios and suites have fully equipped kitchenettes. This is a family-friendly place, with children's programs and free classes in hula and lei-making. A 5th Night Free package is offered seasonally. **Pros:** free kids' hula performance every week, fantastic swimming and sunning beach, old Hawaiian feel. **Cons:** older property, some might call it "un-hip." ⊠*5900 Lower Honoapi'ilani Hwy., Nāpili* ☎*808/669–6271 or 800/367–5030* 🖷*808/669–5740* ⊕*www.napilikai.com* ➳*163 units* ◊*In-room: no a/c (some), kitchen (some), Ethernet. In-hotel: pools, beachfront, children's programs (ages 6–10), laundry service, concierge* ⊟*AE, D, MC, V.*

WORD OF MOUTH. "Nāpili is great. Close to Kā'anapali, great views, nice condos in several price ranges. The beaches are rocky, but the sea life is incredible. It is quiet and peaceful, good for active people, but still close to shopping and restaurants."—Julia_E

$$$–$$$$ ⛱ **ResortQuest Mahana at Kā'anapali.** Though the address claims Kā'anapali, this 12-story condominium complex is really in quiet, neighboring Honokowai. All of the studio, one- and two-bedroom units in this building are ocean-front, with views of the ocean and nearby islands, and the spacious rooms and living areas can accommodate families easily. Built in 1974, the property has been regularly updated since, but the decor in individually owned units may vary. An elegant pool faces a sandy beach, which isn't, unfortunately, recommended for swimming because of the shallow reef. **Pros:** the private lānai and floor-to-ceiling windows are great for watching Maui's spectacular sunsets, daily maid service. **Cons:** high-rise with an elevator, not on a swimming beach.⊠*110 Kā'anapali Shores Pl., Honokowai* ☎*808/661–8751*🖷*808/661–5510*⊕*www.themahana.com*➳*145 units*◊*In-room: safe, kitchen, Ethernet, Wi-Fi (some), laundry facilities. In-hotel: tennis courts, pool, beachfront, concierge, public Wi-Fi*⊟*AE, MC, V.*

$$$–$$$$ ⛱ **ResortQuest at Papakea Resort.** Although this oceanfront condominium with studios to two-bedrooms units has no beach, there are several close by. And with classes on swimming, snorkeling, pineapple cutting, and more, you'll have plenty to keep you busy. Papakea has built-in privacy because its units are spread out among 11 low-

rise buildings on about 13 acres of land; bamboo-lined walkways between buildings and fish-stocked ponds add to the serenity. Fully equipped kitchens and laundry facilities make longer stays easy here. There are air-conditioning units in the living rooms of each condo. **Pros:** units have large rooms, lovely garden landscaping. **Cons:** no beach in front of property, pool can get crowded, no on-site shops or restaurants. ✉ *3543 Lower Honoapi'ilani Hwy., Honokōwai* ☎ *808/669–4848 or 800/922–78665* ⊕ *www.resortquesthawaii.com* ⊃ *364 units* ⚲ *In-room: kitchen, Wi-Fi, laundry facilities. In-hotel: tennis courts, pools, children's programs (ages 5–12)* ⊟ *AE, MC, V.*

$$–$$$ 🏨**Sands of Kahana.** Meandering gardens, spacious rooms, and an on-site restaurant distinguish this large condominium complex. Primarily a time-share property, a few units are available as vacation rentals; those are managed by Sullivan Properties. The upper floors benefit from their height—matchless ocean views stretch away from private lānai. The oceanfront penthouse, which accommodates up to eight, is a bargain at $495 during peak season. One-, two-, and three bedroom units are also available in the rental pool. Kids can enjoy their own swimming pool area near a putting green and ponds filled with giant koi. **Pros:** spacious units at reasonable prices, restaurant on the premises. **Cons:** you may be approached about buying a unit, street-facing units may get a bit noisy. ✉ *4299 Lower Honoapi'ilani Hwy., Kahana* ☎ *808/669–0400* 🖷 *808/669–8409* ⊕ *www.sands-of-kahana.com* ⊃ *162 units* ⚲ *In-room: no a/c (some), kitchen, Ethernet. In-hotel: restaurant, tennis courts, pools, beachfront, concierge* ⊟ *AE, D, MC, V.*

B&BS & INNS

$–$$ 🏨**Lahaina Inn.** An antique jewel in the heart of town, this two-story wooden building is classic Lahaina and will transport romantics back to the turn of the 20th century. The small rooms shine with authentic period furnishings, including antique lamps and bed headboards. You can while away the hours in a wooden rocking chair on your balcony, sipping coffee and watching Old Lahaina town come to life. Beverages are served in the Community Room, which has a microwave and toaster for guests. The renowned restaurant Lahaina Grill is downstairs. **Pros:** just a half block off Front Street, the location is within easy walking distance of shops, restaurants, and historical attractions; lovely antiques. **Cons:** rooms are really small, bathrooms

CONDO COMFORTS

When you stay in a condo, you'll want to find the best places for food shopping, takeout, and other comforts. Here's a rundown of the best sports around Maui.

WEST MAUI

Foodland. This large grocery store should have everything you need, including video rentals and a Starbucks. ⊠*Old Lahaina Center, 845 Waine'e St., Lahaina* ☎*808/661-0975.*

Gaby's Pizzeria and Deli. The friendly folks here will toss a pie for takeout. ⊠*505 Front St., Lahaina* ☎*808/ 661-8112.*

The Maui Fish Market. It's worth stopping by this little fish market for an oyster or a cup of fresh-fish chowder. You can also get live lobsters and fillets marinated for your barbecue. ⊠*4405 Lower Honoapi'ilani Hwy., Honokowai* ☎*808/665-9895.*

SOUTH SHORE

Eskimo Candy. Stop here for fresh fish or fish-and-chips. ⊠*2665 Wai Wai Pl., Kīhei* ☎*808/879-5686.*

Premiere Video. This is the best video store around. ⊠*North Kīhei, 357 Huku Li'i Pl.* ☎*808/875-0500*

Safeway. Find every variety of grocery at this giant super-store. ⊠*277 Pi'ikea Ave., Kīhei* ☎*808/891-9120.*

Who Cut the Cheese. This shop has great party foods. ⊠*Azeka Marketplace, 1279 S. Kīhei Rd., Suite 309, Kīhei* ☎*808/874-3930.*

CENTRAL MAUI

Safeway. Newly renovated to look more like a gourmet grocery than a supermarket, this store has a deli, prepared foods section, and bakery that are all fantastic. There's a great wine selection, tons of pro-duce, and a flower shop where you can treat yourself to a fresh lei. ⊠*170 E. Ka'ahumanu Ave., Kahului* ☎*808/877-3377.*

UPCOUNTRY

Pukalani Terrace Center. Stop by for pizza, a bank, post office, hardware store, and Starbucks. Also here are a **Foodland** (☎*808/572-0674*), which has fresh sushi and a good seafood section in addi-tion to the usual grocery store fare, and **Paradise Video** (☎*808/572-6200*). ⊠*55 Pu-kalani St., Pukalani.*

NORTH SHORE

Ha'ikū Cannery. This mar-ketplace is home to **Ha'ikū Grocery** (☎*808/575-9291*), a somewhat limited grocery store where you can find the basics: veggies, meats, wine, snacks, and ice cream. Also part of the cannery are a few restaurants, a laundromat, pharmacy, and yoga studio. ⊠*810 Ha'ikū Rd., Ha'ikū.*

particularly so; some street noise. ⊠*127 Lahainaluna Rd., Lahaina* ☎*808/661–0577 or 800/669–3444* ⊕*www. lahainainn.com* ⤐*10 rooms, 2 suites* ⚌*In-room: no TV. In-hotel: no elevator, public Internet, no-smoking rooms* ⊟*AE, MC, V.*

$$–$$$ ☒**Plantation Inn.** Charm and some added amenities set this inn, tucked into a corner of a busy street in the heart of Lahaina, apart. Filled with Victorian and Asian furnishings, it's reminiscent of a southern plantation home. Secluded lānai draped with hanging plants face a central courtyard, pool, and a garden pavilion perfect for morning coffee. Each guest room or suite is decorated differently, with hardwood floors, French doors, slightly dowdy antiques, and four-poster beds. (We think No. 10 is nicest.) Suites have kitchenettes and whirlpool baths. A generous breakfast is included in the room rate, and one of Hawai'i's best French restaurants, Gerard's, is on-site. Breakfast, coupled with free parking in downtown Lahaina, makes this a truly great value, even if it's 10 minutes from the beach. **Pros:** guests have full privileges at the sister Kā'anapali Beach Hotel, 3 mi north; walk to shops, sights, and restaurants. **Cons:** Lahaina Town can be noisy, Wi-Fi connection is hit-or-miss (try the lānai). ⊠*174 Lahainaluna Rd., Lahaina* ☎*808/667–9225 or 800/433–6815* ⊕*www. theplantationinn.com* ⤐*15 rooms, 4 suites* ⚌*In-room: safe, kitchen (some), refrigerator, Wi-Fi. In-hotel: restaurant, pool, no elevator* ⊟*AE, D, DC, MC, V.*

THE SOUTH SHORE

The South Shore is composed of two main communities: resort-filled Wailea and down-to-earth Kīhei. In general, the farther south you go, the fancier the accommodations get. ■TIP➔**North Kīhei tends to have great prices, but it has windy beaches scattered with seaweed. (This isn't a problem if you don't mind driving 5 to 10 minutes to save a few bucks.)** As you travel down South Kīhei Road, you can find condos both fronting and across the street from inviting beach parks, and close to shops and restaurants. Once you hit Wailea, the opulence quotient takes a giant leap—this is the land of perfectly groomed resorts. Wailea and West Maui's Kā'anapali continuously compete over which is more exclusive and which has better weather—in our opinion it's a draw.

WORD OF MOUTH. "We stayed in the Kahana area of West Maui this time and have stayed before in both North and South

Kīhei. Next time we have decided that we will stay in Wailea. It is just way less crowded and also seems to be less windy than Kīhei."—lunabug

HOTELS & RESORTS

$$$$ ⊠ **Fairmont Kea Lani Hotel Suites & Villas.** Gleaming white ☾ spires and tiled archways are the hallmark of a stunning resort that's particularly good for families. Spacious suites have microwaves, stereos, and marble bathrooms. The villas are the real lure, though. Each is two-story and has a private plunge pool, two (or three) large bedrooms, a laundry room, and a fully equipped kitchen—barbecue and margarita blender included. Best of all, maid service does the dishes. A fantastic haven for families, the villas are side by side, creating a sort of miniature neighborhood. Request one on the end, with an upstairs sundeck. The resort offers good dining choices, a gourmet deli, and a small, almost private beach. **Pros:** for families, this is the best of the South Shore luxury resorts; on-site Caffe Ciao serves up good, casual Italian fare; adjacent deli good for picnic fare. **Cons:** some feel the architecture and design scream anything but Hawai'i, great villas but prices put them out of range for many. ⊠*4100 Wailea Alanui Dr., Wailea* ☎*808/875–4100 or 800/659–4100*📠*808/875–1200*⊕*www.kealani.com*⊸*413 suites, 37 villas*⚬*In-room: kitchen (some), refrigerator, DVD, Ethernet. In-hotel: 3 restaurants, bar, pools, gym, spa, beachfront, children's programs (ages 5–13)*▭*AE, D, DC, MC, V.*

★ **Fodor's**Choice ⊠ **Four Seasons Resort Maui at Wailea.** Impeccably
$$$$ stylish, subdued, and relaxing describe most Four Seasons properties; this one fronting award-winning Wailea beach is no exception. Thoughtful luxuries—like Evian spritzers poolside and twice-daily housekeeping—earned this Maui favorite its reputation. The property has an understated elegance, with beautiful floral arrangements, courtyards, and private cabanas. Most rooms have an ocean view (avoid those over the parking lot in the North Tower), and terry robes and a mini-refrigerator on request are among the amenities. Choose among three restaurants, including Wolfgang Puck's Spago and DUO. The spa is small but expertly staffed and impeccably appointed, or you can opt for poolside spa mini-treatments. Honeymooners: request Suite 301, with its round tub and private lawn. **Pros:** the most low-key elegance on Maui, known for exceptional service. **Cons:** extremely expensive; for some, a bit too pretentious. ⊠*3900 Wailea Alanui Dr., Wailea* ☎*808/874–8000*

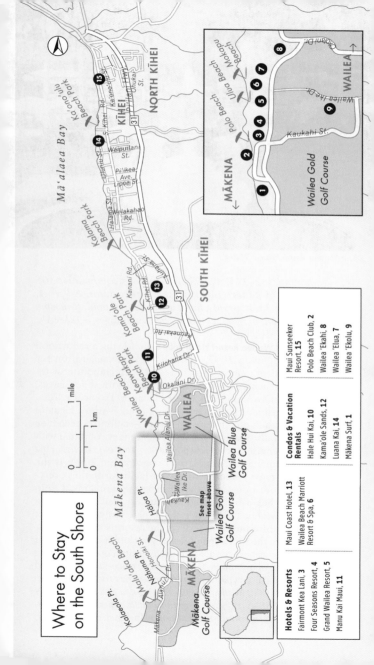

Where to Stay on the South Shore

Hotels & Resorts
Fairmont Kea Lani, **3**
Four Seasons Resort, **4**
Grand Wailea Resort, **5**
Manu Kai Maui, **11**

Maui Coast Hotel, **13**
Wailea Beach Marriott Resort & Spa, **6**

Condos & Vacation Rentals
Hale Hui Kai, **10**
Kama'ole Sands, **12**
Luana Kai, **14**
Mākena Surf, **1**

Maui Sunseeker Resort, **15**
Polo Beach Club, **2**
Wailea 'Ekahi, **8**
Wailea 'Elua, **7**
Wailea 'Ekolu, **9**

Four Seasons Resort Maui at Wailea

or 800/ 332–3442 ⊕*www.fourseasons.com/maui* ⤳*305 rooms, 75 suites* ⌂*In-room: safe, refrigerator, Ethernet. In-hotel: 3 restaurants, bars, tennis courts, pool, gym, spa, beachfront, bicycles, children's programs (ages 5–12)* ▭*AE, D, DC, MC, V.*

$$$$ 🏨**Grand Wailea Resort Hotel & Spa.** Following a renovation of all rooms in 2007, "Grand" is no exaggeration for this opulent, sunny 40-acre resort with elaborate water features such as a "canyon riverpool" with slides, caves, a Tarzan swing, and a water elevator. Tropical garden paths meander past artwork by Léger, Warhol, Picasso, Botero, and noted Hawaiian artists—sculptures even hide in waterfalls. Spacious ocean-view rooms are outfitted with stuffed chaises, comfortable desks, and oversize marble bathrooms. Spa Grande, also upgraded in 2007, is the island's most comprehensive spa facility, offering everything from mineral baths to massage. For kids, Camp Grande has a full-size soda fountain, game room, and movie theater. Definitely not the place to go for a quiet retreat or for attentive service, the resort is astounding or way over the top, depending on your point of view. **Pros:** you can meet every vacation need without ever leaving the property; many shops. **Cons:** at these prices, service should be extraordinary, and it isn't; sometimes too much is too much. ⊠*3850 Wailea Alanui Dr., Wailea* ☎*808/875–1234 or 800/888–6100* ⊕*www.grandwailea.com* ⤳*728 rooms, 52 suites* ⌂*In-room: safe, Ethernet. In-hotel: 5 restaurants,* *bars, pools, gym, spa, beachfront, children's programs (ages 5–12)* ☐AE, D, MC, V.

$$–$$$ ☺**Mana Kai Maui.** An unsung hero of South Shore hotels, this place may be older than its competitors, but you cannot get any closer to gorgeous Keawakapu Beach than this. Hotel rooms with air-conditioning are remarkably affordable for the location. One- and two-bedroom condos—very well-priced—with private lānai benefit from the hotel amenities, such as daily maid service and discounts at the oceanfront restaurant downstairs. Also, prices are discounted for stays of seven nights and longer. The ocean views are marvelous; you may see the visiting humpback whales. **Pros:** arguably the best beach on the South Shore, great value, Maui Yoga Path is on property and offers classes (additional cost). **Cons:** older property, the decor of some of the individually decorated condos is a little rough around the edges. ☒*2960 S. Kīhei Rd., Kīhei* ☎*808/879–2778 or 800/367–5242* ⊕*www.crhmaui.com* ⬅*50 hotel rooms, 57 1-bedroom condos, 57 2-bedroom condos* ⏃*In-room: safe, refrigerator, dial-up (some), Wi-Fi (some). In-hotel: restaurant, pool, beachfront, laundry facilities* ☐ *MC, V.*

$$$ ☺**Maui Coast Hotel.** You might never notice this lovely hotel because it's set back off the street, but it's worth a look. The standard rooms are fine—very clean and modern—but the best deal is to pay a little more for one of the suites. In these you'll get an enjoyable amount of space and jet nozzles in the bathtub. All rooms and suites have lānai. You can sample nightly entertainment by the large, heated pool or work out in the fitness center until 10 PM. The 6-mi-long stretch of Kama'ole Beach I, II, and III is across the street. **Pros:** closest thing to a boutique hotel on the South Shore; Spices Restaurant on property is open for breakfast, lunch, and dinner. **Cons:** right in the center of Kīhei, so traffic and some street noise are issues. ☒*2259 S. Kīhei Rd., Kīhei* ☎*808/874–6284 or 800/895–6284* ☏*808/875–4731* ⊕*www.mauicoasthotel.com* ⬅*151 rooms, 114 suites* ⏃*In-room: safe, refrigerator. In-hotel: 2 restaurants, tennis courts, pool, laundry service* ☐*AE, D, DC, MC, V.*

$$$$ ☺**Wailea Beach Marriott Resort & Spa.** The Marriott was built before current construction laws, so rooms sit much closer to the crashing surf than at most resorts. If you like to be lulled to sleep by the sound of the ocean, this is the place. Wailea Beach is a few steps away, as are the Shops at Wailea. In 2007, the hotel completed a $60 million renovation with redesigned guest rooms, the new 10,000-square-foot

Mandara Spa, a gorgeous, adults-only "Serenity" pool, and Maui celebrity chef Mark Ellman's Mala Ocean Tavern. All rooms have private lānai and have been restyled with a contemporary residential feel; the new mattresses, quilts, and bed linens make for a great night's sleeep. You have golf privileges at three nearby courses, as well as tennis privileges at the Wailea Tennis Club. **Pros:** spa is one of the best in Hawai'i, Mala restaurant is outstanding, near good shopping. **Cons:** it's not quite "beachfront" but has a rocky shore, so you must walk left or right to sit on the sand; building exteriors are showing their age. ⊠ *3700 Wailea Alanui Dr., Wailea* ☎ *808/879–1922 or 800/922–7866* ⊕ *www.waileamarriott.com* ⬯ *499 rooms, 47 suites* ⬧ *In-room: safe, Ethernet. In-hotel: 2 restaurants, pools, gym, spa, beachfront, children's programs (ages 5–12), laundry service* ▭ *AE, D, DC, MC, V.*

CONDOS & VACATION RENTALS

$$–$$$$ ▣ **Hale Hui Kai.** Bargain hunters who stumble across this small three-story condo complex of two-bedroom units will think they've died and gone to heaven. The beachfront units are older, but many of them have been renovated. Some have marble countertops in the kitchens and all have outstanding views. But never mind the interior; you'll want to spend all of your time outdoors—in the shady lava-rock lobby that overlooks a small pool perfect for kids, or on gorgeous Keawakapu Beach just steps away. Light sleepers should avoid the rooms just above the neighboring restaurant, Sarento's, but do stop in there for dinner. **Pros:** far enough from the noise and tumult of "central" Kīhei, close enough to all the conveniences. **Cons:** "older" can sometimes mean a bit shabby, nondescript '70s architecture. ⊠ *2994 S. Kīhei Rd., Kīhei* ☎ *808/879–1219 or 800/809–6284* ⎙ *808/879–0600* ⊕ *www.halehuikaimaui.com* ⬯ *40 units* ⬧ *In-room: no a/c (some), safe, kitchen, DVD. In-hotel: pool, beachfront, laundry facilities* ▭ *D, DC, MC, V.*

$$–$$$ ▣ **Kama'ole Sands.** At this south Kīhei property, a good ☾ choice for the active traveler, there are tennis and volleyball courts to keep you in shape, and the ideal family beach (Kama'ole III) is just across the street. Ten four-story buildings wrap around 15 acres of grassy slopes with swimming pools, a small waterfall, and barbecues. Condos with one to three bedrooms are equipped with modern conveniences, but there's a relaxed, almost retro feel to the place. All units have kitchens, laundry facilities, and private lānai. The

property has a 24-hour front desk and an activities desk. ■TIP→**Attention home-owners: privately owned house-trade options are available at** ⊕ **www.kamaole-sands.com.** Pros: in the seemingly endless strip of Kīhei condos, this stands out for its pleasant grounds and well-cared-for units. **Cons:** for some, the complex of buildings is bit too"city"; all buildings look alike, so remember a landmark so you can find your unit. ⊠2695 S. Kīhei Rd., Kīhei ☎808/270–1200 🖷808/879–3273 ⊕www.castleresorts.com ⇥309 units ⚭In-room: kitchen, DVD, Ethernet (some), Wi-Fi (some). In-hotel: tennis courts, pool ☰AE, D, DC, MC, V.

$ 🖵**Luana Kai.** If you don't need everything to be totally modern, consider setting up house at this North Kīhei condominium-by-the-sea. Units are older and some have slightly dated furnishings, but each one comes with everything you need to make yourself at home: a fully equipped kitchen with dishwasher, laundry facilities, TV, DVD, and stereo equipment. There are three different room plans, suited for couples, families, or friends traveling together. The pool area and its new deck area are a social place, with five gas grills, a full outdoor kitchen, hot tub, men's and women's sauna rooms, and a shuffleboard court. The property adjoins a grassy county park with tennis courts, and the beach is a short way down the road. **Pros:** great value, meticulously landscaped grounds, excellent management team. **Cons:** it's not right on the beach, and it's not sleek and modern. ⊠940 S. Kīhei Rd., Kīhei ☎808/879–1268 or 800/669–1127 ⊕www.luanakai.com ⇥113 units ⚭In-room: no a/c (some), kitchen, DVD, Wi-Fi. In-hotel: tennis courts, pool, no elevator☰ MC, V.

$$$–$$$$ 🖵**Mākena Surf.** For travelers who've done all there is to do on Maui and just want simple but luxurious relaxation, this is the spot. The security-gate entrance gives way to manicured landscaping dotted with palm trees. The secluded complex is designed so that it's hard to tell from the road that they're actually three-story buildings. "B" building is oceanfront; "A," "C," and "G" are the best value, just a bit farther from the shore. Water aerobics and tennis clinics are regularly offered. Privacy envelops the grounds—which makes the place a favorite with visiting celebrities. **Pros:** get away from it all, still close enough to "civilization." **Cons:** too secluded and "locked-up" for some, Hawaiian legend has it that spirits may have been disturbed here. ⊠3750 Wailea Alanui Dr., Wailea ☎808/879–1595 or 800/367–5246 ⊕www.drhmaui.com ⇥107 units ⚭In-room:

safe, kitchen, DVD, Wi-F, laundry facilities. In-hotel: tennis courts, pools, beachfront ⊟*AE, MC, V.*

$–$$ ⊡**Maui Sunseeker Resort.** The care put into this small North Kīhei property, which is particularly popular with a gay and lesbian clientele, is already noticeable from the sign on the road. A great value for the area, it's private and relaxed. You can opt for the simple but attractively furnished studio and one-bedroom units, or the incredible, more expensive penthouse decked out in French Provincial antiques (really); all have kitchenettes and full baths. There's a lovely gazebo with two gas grills in the courtyard. The 4-mi stretch of beach across the street isn't the best for swimming, but it's great for strolling and watching windsurfers, whales (in winter), and sunsets. **Pros:** impeccably maintained; there's a hair salon and a wedding officiate on property. **Cons:** no pool, no frills. ⊠*551 S. Kīhei Rd., Kīhei* ☏*808/879–1261 or 800/532–6284* 🖷*808/874–3877* ⊕*www.mauisunseeker. com* ⬠*17 units* ⬧*In-room: kitchen, DVD. In-hotel: no elevator, laundry facilities, public Wi-Fi* ⊟*AE, D, DC, MC, V.*

$$$$ ⊡**Polo Beach Club.** Lording over a hidden section of Polo Beach, this wonderful old eight-story property somehow manages to stay under the radar. From your giant corner window, you can look down at the Fairmont Kea Lani villas and know you've scored the same great locale at a fraction of the price (and also including daily housekeeping service). Individually owned one- and two-bedroom apartments are well cared for and feature top-of-the-line amenities, such as stainless-steel kitchens, marble floors, and valuable artwork. An underground parking garage keeps vehicles out of the blazing Kīhei sun. **Pros:** you can pick fresh herbs for dinner out of the garden, beach fronting the building is a beautiful, very private crescent of sand. **Cons:** some may feel isolated. ⊠*3750 Wailea Alanui Dr., Wailea* ☏*808/879–1595 or 800/367–5246* 🖷*808/874–3554* ⊕*www.drhmaui. com* ⬠*71 units* ⬧*In-room: kitchen, DVD, Wi-Fi. In-hotel: pool, beachfront, laundry facilities* ⊟*AE, MC, V.*

$$$$ ⊡**Wailea Beach Villas.** The most luxurious vacation rentals on Maui include units that are bigger than many houses—about 3,000 square feet. The furnishings and accessories are gorgeous; some kitchens are fit for the likes of Wolfgang Puck, some units have plunge pools, some have outdoor showers. Combined with stunning grounds and all the services of the finest resort hotel—the concierge will arrange anything from in-room spa treatments to a personal trainer or a chef—you've got the vacation accommodation of a lifetime. **Pros:** steps away from the luxurious Shops at Wailea, near several excellent restaurants. **Cons:** lots of walking and up and down steps required, certainly not in everyone's budget. ✉*3750 Wailea Alanui, Wailea* ☎*808/879–1595 or 800/367–5246* ⊕*www.drhmaui.com* ☞*98 units* ⌂*In-room: safe, DVD, kitchen, Wi-Fi. In-hotel: pools, beachfront, gym, laundry facilities, parking, concierge* ⊟*AE, MC, V.*

$$–$$$$ 🏠**Wailea 'Ekahi, 'Elua, and 'Ekolu.** The Wailea Resort started out with three upscale condominium complexes named, appropriately, 'Ekahi, 'Elua, and 'Ekolu (One, Two, and Three). The individually owned units, managed by Destination Resorts Hawai'i, represent some of the best values in this high-class neighborhood; there's a wide range of prices. All benefit from daily housekeeping, air-conditioning, high-speed Internet, free long distance, lush landscaping, and preferential play at the neighboring world-class golf courses and tennis courts. You're likely to find custom appliances and sleek furnishings befitting the million-dollar locale. ■TIP➜**The concierges here will stock your fridge with groceries—even hard-to-find dietary items—for a nominal fee.** 'Ekolu, farthest from the water, is the most affordable, and benefits from a hillside view; 'Ekahi is a large V-shaped property focusing on Keawakapu Beach; 'Elua has 24-hour security and overlooks Ulua Beach. **Pros:** probably the best value in this high-rent district, close to good shopping and dining. **Cons:** the oldest complexes in the neighborhood, it can be tricky to find your way around the buildings. ✉*3750 Wailea Alanui Dr., Wailea* ☎*808/879–1595 or 800/367–5246* 🖷*808/874–3554* ⊕*www.drhmaui.com* ☞*594 units* ⌂*In-room: kitchen, DVD, Wi-Fi. In-hotel: pools, beachfront, laundry facilities* ⊟*AE, MC, V.*

CENTRAL MAUI

Kahului and Wailuku, the commercial, residential, and government centers that make up Central Maui, are not known for their lavish accommodations, but there are options that meet some travelers' needs perfectly.

B&BS & INNS

★ Fodor'sChoice 🏠**The Old Wailuku Inn at Ulupono.** Built in 1924 $ and listed on the State and National Registers of Historic Places, this home may be the ultimate Hawaiian B&B. Each room is decorated with the theme of a Hawaiian flower, and the flower motif appears in the heirloom Hawaiian quilt on each bed. Other features include 10-foot ceilings and floors of native hardwoods; some rooms have delightful whirlpool tubs. The first-floor rooms have private gardens. A newer addition has three gorgeous rooms, each with a standing spa shower and bed coverings designed by Hawai'i's premier fabric designer, Sig Zane. A hearty and delicious breakfast is included. **Pros:** the charm of old Hawai'i, knowledgeable innkeepers, walking distance to Maui's best ethnic restaurants. **Cons:** closest beach is a 20-minute drive away, you may hear some traffic at certain times. ⊠*2199 Kaho'okele St., Wailuku* ☎*808/244–5897 or 800/305–4899* ⊕*www.mauiinn.com* ⌖*10 rooms* ⌂*In-room: VCR, Ethernet. In-hotel: no elevator* ⊟*AE, D, DC, MC, V.*

HOSTELS

c ▣**Banana Bungalow Maui Hostel.** A typical lively and cosmopolitan hostel, the yellow Banana Bungalow offers the cheapest accommodations on the island. Private rooms have one queen or two single beds; bathrooms are down the hall. Dorm rooms are available for $29 per night. Free daily tours to waterfalls, beaches, and Haleakalā Crater make this a stellar deal. The property's amenities include free high-speed Internet access in the common room, kitchen privileges, a Jacuzzi, and banana and mango trees ripe for the picking. Though it's tucked in a slightly rough-around-the-edges corner of Wailuku, the old building does have mountain views. **Pros:** on an expensive island, this is as inexpensive as it gets; you can walk to Takamiya Market for some of the island's best bento boxes (lunches). **Cons:** you get what you pay for, no luxury or serenity here. ⊠*310 N. Market St., Wailuku* ☎*808/244–5090 or 800/846–7835* ⊕*www.mauihostel.com* ⌖*26 rooms* ⌂*In-room: no a/c. In-hotel: no elevator, laundry facilities, public Internet* ⊟*MC, V.*

UPCOUNTRY

Upcountry accommodations (those in Kula, Makawao, and Hāli'imaile) are generally on country properties—with the exception of Kula Lodge—and are privately owned vacation rentals. At high elevation, these lodgings offer splendid views of the island, temperate weather, and a "getting away from it all" feeling—which is actually the case, as most shops and restaurants are a fair drive away, and beaches even farther. You'll definitely need a car here.

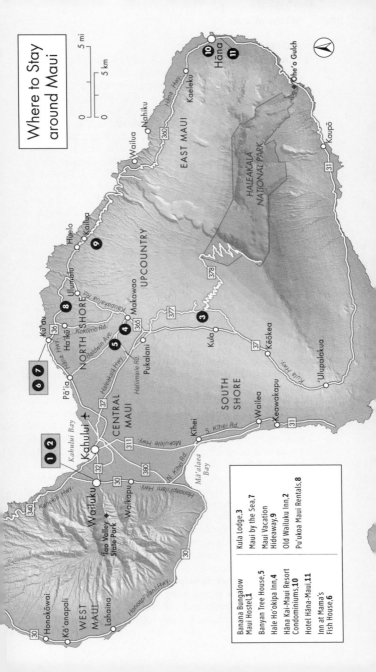

Where to Stay around Maui

Banana Bungalow
Maui Hostel, **1**

Banyan Tree House, **5**

Hale Ho'okipa Inn, **4**

Hāna Kai-Maui Resort
Condominums, **10**

Hotel Hāna-Maui, **11**

Inn at Mama's
Fish House, **6**

Kula Lodge, **3**

Maui by the Sea, **7**

Maui Vacation
Hideaway, **9**

Old Wailuku Inn, **2**

Pu'ukoa Maui Rentals, **8**

HOTELS & RESORTS

$ ⊠**Kula Lodge.** Don't expect a local look despite being out in the country: the lodge inexplicably resembles a chalet in the Swiss Alps, and two units even have gas fireplaces. Charming and cozy in spite of the nontropical ambience, it's a good spot for a short romantic stay. Units are in two wooden cabins; four have lofts in addition to the ample bed space downstairs. On 3 acres, the lodge has striking, expansive views of Haleakalā and two coasts, enhanced by the surrounding tropical gardens. The property has an art gallery and a protea store that will pack flowers for you to take home; next door you'll find a gourmet and gift shop. **Pros:** a quiet and peaceful place in the country, excellent shopping right next door. **Cons:** it's a long, long way to the beach; in the winter, it can get downright cold. ⊠*15200 Haleakalā Hwy., Rte. 377, Kula* ☎*808/878–1535 or 800/233–1535* ⊕*www.kulalodge.com* ⤴*5 units* ⌂*In-room: no a/c, no phone, no TV. In-hotel: restaurant, no elevator* ⊟*AE, MC, V.*

B&BS & INNS

$ ⊠**The Banyan Tree House.** If a taste of rural Hawai'i life in
☾ plantation days is what you crave, you'll find it here. The setting is pastoral—the 2-acre property is lush with tropical foliage, has an expansive lawn, and is fringed with huge monkeypod and banyan trees. The cottages (bedrooms, really, with updated baths and kitchenettes) are simple and functional. The gem, though, is the 1927 plantation house with its sprawling living and dining rooms, a kitchen any cook will adore, and a lānai that will take you back in time. The configuration of the property allows for lots of combinations; you can rent one, two, or all three bedrooms in the house or even add the adjoining one-bedroom cottage. And you can rent the entire property for a family reunion or a retreat and have access to a large activities room complete with audio and video capabilities. **Pros:** one cottage and the pool are outfitted for travelers with disabilities, you can walk to Makawao town for dining and shopping. **Cons:** the furniture in the cottages is pretty basic, few amenities. ⊠*3265 Baldwin Ave., Makawao* ☎*808/572–9021* ⊕*www. banyantreehouse.com* ⤴*7 rooms* ⌂*In-room: kitchen, Wi-Fi. In-hotel: pool, laundry facilities* ⊟*AE, D, MC, V.*

★ **Fodor's**Choice ⊠**Hale Ho'okipa Inn.** A handsome 1924 Crafts-
$ man-style house in the heart of Makawao town, this inn on both the Hawai'i and the National Historic Registers provides a great base for excursions to Haleakalā or to

Hāna. Owner Cherie Attix has furnished it with antiques and fine art, and she allows guests to peruse her voluminous library of Hawai'i-related books. She's also a fount of local knowledge. The house is divided into three single rooms, each prettier than the next, and the South Wing, which sleeps four and includes the kitchen. Two rooms have wonderful claw-foot tubs. The lush, serene grounds have a koi pond and the biggest Norfolk Pine tree you've ever seen. **Pros:** genteel rural setting, price includes full island-style breakfast including organic fruit from the garden. **Cons:** a 20-minute drive to the nearest beach; this is not the sun, sand, and surf surroundings of travel posters. ✉*32 Pakani Pl., Makawao* ☎*808/572–6698* 📠*808/572–2580* ⊕*www.maui-bed-and-breakfast.com* ⤶*3 rooms, 1 suite* ♿*In-room: Wi-Fi* ▭ *MC, V.*

THE NORTH SHORE

You won't find any large resorts or condominium complexes along the North Shore, yet there are a variety of accommodations along the coastline from the surf town of Pā'ia, through tiny Kū'au, and along the rain-forested Hāna Highway through Ha'ikū. Some are oceanfront but not necessarily beachfront (with sand); instead, look for tropical gardens overflowing with ginger, bananas, papayas, and nightly bug symphonies. Some have heart-stopping views or the type of solitude that seeps in, easing your tension before you know it. You may encounter brief, powerful downpours, but that's what makes this part of Maui green and lush. You'll need a car to enjoy staying on the North Shore.

B&BS. Additional B&Bs on Maui can be found by contacting **Bed & Breakfast Hawai'i** (☎*808/ 822–7771 or 800/733–1632* ⊕*www. bandb-hawaii.com*). **Bed and Breakfast Honolulu** (☎*808/595– 7533 or 800/288–4666* ⊕*www.hawaiibnb.com*) is another good source. It's always a good idea to ask specifically if a property is licensed by Maui County.

CONDOS & VACATION RENTALS

$$ ☒**The Inn at Mama's Fish House.** Nestled in gardens adjacent to one of Maui's most popular dining spots, Mama's Fish House ($$$$), these well-maintained one- and two-bedroom cottages have a retro-Hawaiian style with rattan furnishings and local artwork. Each has a kitchen and a private garden patio. There is a small beach in front of the property known as Kūʻau Cove. It's best to make reservations for the restaurant when you book your accommodations or you may not get a table. **Pros:** daily maid service, free parking, next to Hoʻokipa Beach. **Cons:** Mama's Fish House is very popular, so there can be a lot of people around in the evenings (it's more mellow during the day). ⊠799 *Pono Pl., Kūʻau* ☏808/579–9764 *or* 800/860–4852 ⊕*www. mamasfishhouse.com* ⬎9 *units* ⌂*In-room: safe, kitchen, DVD, Wi-Fi. In-hotel: restaurant, laundry facilities*═AE, D ,DC, MC, V.

$$ ☗**Maui by the Sea.** Just past Pāʻia, on the other side of a stucco wall from Hāna Highway, this cute, small but clean one-bedroom apartment decorated with tropical prints and Hawaiian quilts is bright and airy. You can park your car in the garage below and climb the stairs to this second-floor unit, which has a broad lānai with a gas grill and a dining table. The lānai captures gentle cooling breezes, and it has a fantastic ocean view. You're just steps away from the ocean here, although there is no sand beach, just a rocky access; Tavares Bay is a mere 200 yards away for launching windsurfing or swimming. **Pros:** free interisland, mainland, and Canada phone calls; host is lifelong Maui resident and will share island stories with you. **Cons:** road noise from Hāna Highway, room for only one or two people, another house is right next door, no resort amenities. ⊠*523 Hāna Hwy., Pāʻia* ☏808/579–9865 ⊕*www.mauibythesea.com*⬎1 *unit* ⌂*In-room: kitchen, DVD, Ethernet. In-hotel: laundry facilities* ═AE, MC, V

$ ☗**Maui Vacation Hideaway.** The warm ocean breeze rolls through these pretty rentals and shoos the mosquitoes away, making this a perfect spot if you want quiet, gorgeous scenery. The decor is both whimsical and calming—expect colorfully painted walls and sheer curtains. The saltwater pool is fed by a waterfall. Fully equipped kitchens and Wi-Fi make these studios an ideal home away from home. Allergy-prone travelers can relax here—no chemicals or pesticides are used on the property. Although it seems far from civilization, you are only 5 minutes from Haʻikū and 10 minutes from Pāʻia. **Pros:** good for people sensitive to harsh chemicals, one of few licensed rentals in area. **Cons:** 15 minutes from closest beach, rather remote location. ⊠*240 N. Holokai Rd., Haʻikū 96708* ☏808/572–2775 ⊕*www. mauivacationhideaway.com*⬎3 *units* ⌂*In-room: no a/c, kitchen, Wi-Fi. In-hotel: pool, no elevator, laundry facilities*═MC, V.

¢ ⌚Pu'ukoa Maui Rentals. Off a peaceful cul-de-sac in a residential area, these two well-maintained and immaculately clean homes offer studio and one-bedroom accommodations. Studios have an efficiency-style kitchen with a small refrigerator, hot plate, microwave, toaster oven, and coffeemaker. One-bedroom apartments have fully equipped kitchens, a separate bedroom, and a large living area. All units have private bathrooms and a lānai or patio, some with ocean views. The large yard with tropical flowers and fruit trees is great for a sunset barbecue or just relaxing. **Pros:** very clean, reasonable rates, good spot for a group attending a wedding or family reunion. **Cons:** it's a 10-minute drive to the beach, set in quiet residential area. ⌂*Pu'ukoa Pl., Ha'ikū* ☎*808/573–2884* ⌖*www.puukoa. com* ⌸*7 rooms* ♿ *In-room: no a/c, kitchen, DVD, Wi-Fi. In-hotel: no elevator* ▭ AE, MC, V.

HĀNA

Why stay in Hāna when it's so far from everything? In a world where everything moves at high speed, Hāna still travels on horseback, ambling along slowly enough to smell the flowers. But old-fashioned and remote do not mean tame—this is a wild coast, known for heart-stopping scenery and downpours. Leave city expectations behind: the single grocery may run out of milk, and the only videos to rent may be several years old. The dining options are slim. ■TIP➔**If you're staying for several days, or at a vacation rental, stock up on groceries before you head out to Hāna.** Even with these inconveniences, Hāna is a place you won't want to miss.

SHOPPING IN HĀNA. **Hasegawa General Store.** Hāna's one-stop shopping option is charming, filled-to-the-rafters Hasegawa's. Buy fishing tackle, hot dogs, ice cream, and eggs here. You can rent videos and buy the newspaper, which isn't always delivered on time. Check out the bulletin board for local events. ⌂*5165 Hāna Hwy.* ☎*808/248–8231.*

HOTELS & RESORTS

★ **Fodor'sChoice** ⌚**Hotel Hāna-Maui.** Small, secluded, and quietly luxurious, with unobstructed views of the Pacific, this tranquil property is a departure from the usual resort destinations on Maui. Here, horses nibble wild grass on the sea cliff nearby. Spacious rooms (680 to 830 square feet) have bleached-wood floors, authentic kapa-print fab-

$$$$

ric furnishings, and sumptuously stocked minibars at no extra cost. Spa suites and a heated *watsu* (massage performed in warm water) pool complement a state-of-the-art spa-and-fitness center. The Sea Ranch Cottages with individual hot tubs are the best value. A shuttle takes you to beautiful Hāmoa Beach. **Pros:** if you want to get away from it all, there's no better or more beautiful place; spa is incredibly relaxing. **Cons:** everything moves slowly; if you can't live without your Blackberry, this is not the place for you; it's oceanfront but does not have a sandy beach (red-and black-sand beaches are nearby). ✉*5031 Hāna Hwy.* ✉*Box 9, Hāna 96713* ☎*808/248–8211 or 800/321–4262* ⊕*www.hotelhanamaui.com* ⇨*69 rooms, 7 cottages, 1 house* ⌖*In-room: refrigerator, no TV, dial-up. In-hotel: 2 restaurants, bar, tennis courts, pools, gym, spa, no elevator, public Internet* ⊟*AE, D, DC, MC, V.*

CONDOS & VACATION RENTALS

$$–$$$ 🖵 **Hāna Kai-Maui Resort Condominiums.** Perfectly situated close to Hāna Bay, this resort complex has a long history (it opened in 1970) and excellent reputation for visitor hospitality. All you have to do is take your morning coffee out onto the lānai of any of these lovely units to know why Hāna is often referred to as "heavenly." The units are tastefully and comfortably furnished with tropical-pattern fabrics and light-color wood, and have well-equipped kitchens with all the appliances, table settings, and tools you need to prepare meals. They even have 100% Egyptian cotton sheets on the beds. **Pros:** it's a stone's throw to Hāna Bay, where you can take a swim or have a Roselani mac-nut ice-cream cone at Tutu's. **Cons:** early to bed and early to rise—no nightlife or excitement here. ✉*1533 Uakea Rd., Hāna* ☎*808/248–8426 or 800/346–2772* ⊕*www. hanakaimaui.com* ⇨*6 studios, 11 1-bedroom units* ⌖*In-room: kitchen, no TV, Wi-Fi* ⊟ *MC, V*

Maui Essentials

PLANNING TOOLS, EXPERT INSIGHT, GREAT CONTACTS

There are planners and there are those who, excuse the pun, fly by the seat of their pants. We happily place ourselves among the planners. Our writers and editors try to anticipate all the issues you may face before and during any journey, and then they do their research. This section is the product of their efforts. Use it to get excited about your trip to Maui, to inform your travel planning, or to guide you on the road should the seat of your pants start to feel threadbare.

www.fodors.com/forums

GETTING STARTED

We're proud of our Web site: Fodors.com is a great place to begin any journey. Scan Travel News for suggested itineraries, travel deals, restaurant and hotel openings, and other up-to-the-minute info. Check out Book It to research prices and book plane tickets, hotel rooms, rental cars, and vacation packages. Head to Talk for on-the-ground pointers from travelers who frequent our message boards. You can also link to loads of other travel-related resources.

▌ RESOURCES

ONLINE TRAVEL TOOLS

ALL ABOUT MAUI

Resources **Hawai'i Beach Safety** (⊕www.hawaiibeachsafety.org) has the latest updates on Maui's beaches, including surf forecasts and safety tips.

Hawai'i Department of Land and Natural Resources (⊕www.state. hi.us/dlnr) has information on hiking, fishing, and camping permits and licenses; online brochures on hiking safety and mountain and ocean preservation; and details on volunteer programs.

Kā'anapali Beach Resort Association (⊕www.kaanapaliresort. com) provides detailed information about the resorts, condominiums, attractions, activities, and special events at this 1,200-acre resort in West Maui. **Lāna'i Visitors Bureau** (⊕www.visitlanai.net) has good introductory information about

the island. **Maui Visitors Bureau** (⊕www.visitmaui.com) has special-interest sections on wellness and honeymoons, among other topics. **Moloka'i Visitors Association** (⊕www.molokai-hawaii.com) includes information on golf, transportation, and special events. **Nā Ala Hele** (⊕www.hawaiitrails.org), the state's trail and access program, has online maps and directions for hikes on Maui, Moloka'i, and Lāna'i.

VISITOR INFORMATION

Before you go, contact the Hawai'i Visitors & Convention Bureau (HVCB) for general information on Maui, Lāna'i, or Moloka'i, and to request a free official vacation planner with information on accommodations, transportation, sports and activities, dining, arts and entertainment, and culture.

The Hawai'i Tourism Authority's Travel Smart Hawaii site offers tips on everything from packing to flying. Also visit the Hawai'i State Vacation Planner for all information on the destination, including camping.

Contacts **Hawai'i State Vacation Planner** (⊕www.bestplaceshawaii.

com). **Hawai'i Tourism Authority** (⊕www.travelsmarthawaii.com). **Hawai'i Visitors & Convention Bureau** (✉2270 Kalakaua Ave., Suite 801, Honolulu 96815 ☎808/923–1811, 800/464–2924 for brochures ⊕www.gohawaii.com).

∎ THINGS TO CONSIDER

GEAR

Probably the most important thing to tuck into your suitcase is sunscreen. There are many tanning oils on the market in Hawai'i, including coconut and *kukui* (the nut from a local tree) oils, but they can cause severe burns. Hats and sunglasses offer important sun protection, too. All major hotels in Hawai'i provide beach towels.

Hawai'i is casual: sandals, bathing suits, and comfortable, informal cotton clothing are the norm. In summer, synthetic slacks and shirts, although easy to care for, can be uncomfortably warm. The aloha shirt is accepted dress in Hawai'i for business and most social occasions.

Shorts are acceptable daytime attire, along with a T-shirt or polo shirt. There's no need to buy expensive sandals on the mainland—here you can get flip-flops for a couple of dollars and off-brand sandals for $20. Many golf courses have dress codes requiring a collared shirt; call courses for details. If you're visiting in winter or planning to visit a high-altitude area, bring a sweater, a light- to medium-weight jacket, or a polar-fleece pullover.

If your vacation plans include an exploration of Maui's northeast-ern coast, including Hāna and Upcountry Maui, you'll want to pack a light raincoat. And if you'll be exploring Haleakalā National Park, make sure you pack appropriately as weather at the summit can be very cold and windy. Bring good boots for hiking.

TRIP INSURANCE

We believe that comprehensive trip insurance is especially valuable if you're booking a very expensive or complicated trip (particularly to an isolated region) or if you're booking far in advance.

Comprehensive travel policies typically cover trip-cancellation and interruption, letting you cancel or cut your trip short because of a personal emergency, illness, or, in some cases, acts of terrorism in your destination. Such policies also cover evacuation and medical care. Some also cover you for trip delays because of bad weather or mechanical problems as well as for lost or delayed baggage. Another type of coverage to look for is financial default—that is, when your trip is disrupted because a tour operator, airline, or cruise line goes out of business. Generally you must buy this when you book your trip or shortly thereafter, and it's only available to you if your operator isn't on a list of excluded companies.

Expect comprehensive travel-insurance policies to cost about 4% to 7% of the total price of your trip (it's more like 12% if you're over age 70).

Trip Insurance Resources

INSURANCE COMPARISON SITES		
Insure My Trip.com	800/487-4722	www.insuremytrip.com
Square Mouth.com	800/240-0369 or 727/490-5803	www.quotetravelinsurance.com
COMPREHENSIVE TRAVEL INSURERS		
Access America	866/807-3982	www.accessamerica.com
CSA Travel Protection	800/873-9855	www.csatravelprotection.com
HTH Worldwide	610/254-8700 or 888/243-2358	www.hthworldwide.com
Travelex Insurance	800/228-9792	www.travelex-insurance.com
Travel Guard International	715/345-0505 or 800/826-4919	www.travelguard.com
Travel Insured International	800/243-3174	www.travelinsured.com
MEDICAL-ONLY INSURERS		
International Medical Group	800/628-4664 or 317/655-4500	www.imglobal.com
International SOS	215/942-8000 or 713/521-7611	www.internationalsos.com
Wallach & Company	800/237-6615 or 540/687-3166	www.wallach.com

BOOKING YOUR TRIP

■ ONLINE

You really have to shop around. A travel wholesaler such as Hotels. com or HotelClub.net can be a source of good rates, as can discounters such as Hotwire or Priceline, particularly if you can bid for your hotel room or airfare. Indeed, such sites sometimes have deals that are unavailable elsewhere. They do, however, tend to work only with hotel chains (which makes them just plain useless for getting hotel reservations outside of major cities) or big airlines (so that often leaves out upstarts like jetBlue and some foreign carriers like Air India).

Also, with discounters and wholesalers you must generally prepay, and everything is nonrefundable. And before you fork over the dough, be sure to check the terms and conditions, so you know what a given company will do for you if there's a problem and what you'll have to deal with on your own.

■ WITH A TRAVEL AGENT

If this is your first visit to Maui, a travel agent or vacation packager specializing in Hawai'i can be extremely helpful in planning a memorable vacation. Not only do they have the knowledge of the destination, but they can save you money by packaging the costs of airfare, hotel, activities, and car rental. In addition, many Hawai'i-specialist travel agents may offer added values or special deals (i.e., resort food and beverage credit, a free night's stay) when you book a package with them. The Hawai'i Visitors & Convention Bureau provides a list of member travel agencies and tour operators.

Agent Resources American Society of Travel Agents (☎703/739–2782 ⊕www.travelsense.org).

Maui Travel Agents AA Vacations (☎800/321–2121 ⊕www.aavacations.com). **AAA Travel** (☎800/436–4222 ⊕www.aaa.com). **All About Hawai'i** (☎800/274–8687 ⊕www.allabouthawaii.com). **Aloha Destinations Vacations** (☎800/256–4280 ⊕www.mccoyvacations.com). **Blue Hawai'i Vacation** (☎800/315–1812 ⊕www.blue-hawaii.com). **Continental Airlines Vacations** (☎800/301–3800 ⊕www.covacations.com). **Delta Vacations** (☎800/654–6559 ⊕www.deltavacations.com). **Dream-Catcher Vacations** (☎916/927–0445 ⊕www.dreamcatchervacations.com).**Funjet Vacations** (☎888/558–6654 ⊕www.funjet.com). **Hello Hawai'i** (☎800/809–9844 ⊕www.hellohawaii.com). **Incredible Journey Travel** (☎888/729–6899 ⊕www.incrediblejourney.net). **Maui Travel Services** (☎877/628–4386 ⊕www.mauitravelservices.com). **Travel-Hawaii.com** (☎800/373–2422 ⊕www.travel-hawaii.com). **Travel Wizard.com** (☎800/330–8820 ⊕www.travelwizard.com). **United Vacations** (☎800/699–6122 ⊕www.unitedvacations.com).

Online Booking Resources

AGGREGATORS

Cheapflights	www.cheapflights.com	compares airfares.
Kayak	www.kayak.com	looks at cruises, airfares, and vacation packages.
Mobissimo	www.mobissimo.com	examines airfare, hotels, cars, and activities.
Qixo	www.qixo.com	compares cruises, airfares, vacation packages, and even travel insurance.
Sidestep	www.sidestep.com	compares vacation packages and lists travel deals.
Travelgrove	www.travelgrove.com	compares cruises and vacation packages and lets you search by themes.

BOOKING ENGINES

Cheap Tickets	www.cheaptickets.com	a discounter.
Expedia	www.expedia.com	a large online agency that charges a booking fee for airline tickets.
Hotwire	www.hotwire.com	a discounter.
lastminute.com	www.uslastminute.com	specializes in last-minute travel.
Luxury Link	www.luxurylink.com	has auctions (surprisingly good deals) as well as offers on the high-end side of travel.
Onetravel.com	www.onetravel.com	a discounter for hotels, car rentals, airfares, and packages.
Orbitz	www.orbitz.com	charges a booking fee for airline tickets, but gives a clear breakdown of fees and taxes.
Priceline.com	www.priceline.com	a discounter that also allows bidding.
Travel.com	www.travel.com	allows you to compare its rates with those of other booking engines.
Travelocity	www.travelocity.com	charges a booking fee for airline tickets, but promises good problem resolution.

ONLINE ACCOMMODATIONS

Hotelbook.com	www.hotelbook.com	focuses on independent hotels worldwide.
Hotel Club	www.hotelclub.net	good for major cities and some resort areas.

Online Booking Resources

Hotels.com	www.hotels.com	a big Expedia-owned wholesaler that offers rooms in hotels all over the world.
Quikbook	www.quikbook.com	offers "pay when you stay" reservations that let you settle your bill at checkout.
OTHER RESOURCES		
Bidding For Travel	www.biddingfor-travel.com	a good place to figure out what you can get and for how much before you start bidding on, say, Priceline.

❚ RENTAL CARS

It is best to rent a car in Maui. Even if all you want to do is relax at your resort, you may want to hop in the car to check out one of the island's popular restaurants.

Rates begin at about $25 to $35 a day for an economy car with air-conditioning, automatic transmission, and unlimited mileage, depending on your pickup location. This does not include the airport concession fee, general excise tax, rental-vehicle surcharge, or vehicle license fee. When you reserve a car, ask about cancellation penalties and drop-off charges should you plan to pick up the car in one location and return it to another. Many rental companies in Hawai'i offer coupons for discounts at attractions that could save you money later in your trip.

How about seeing the island in your own VW camper? Aloha Campers rents older VW Westfalia Campers for $115 per day that accommodate up to four adults. And if exploring the island on two wheels is more your speed, Maui Harley-Davidson and Island Rental Cars both rent motorcycles; Island

Rental Cars also rents exotic cars. Want to drive an earth-friendly automobile that gets 30–45 mi to the gallon? Bio-Beetle Eco Rental Cars run on clean-burning diesel fuel that comes from renewable sources like recycled vegetable oil.

In Hawai'i you must be 21 years of age to rent a car and you must have a valid driver's license and a major credit card. Those under 25 will pay a daily surcharge of $15 to $25. Request car seats and extras such as a GPS when you make your reservation. Hawai'i's Child Restraint Law requires that all children three years and younger be in an approved child-safety seat in the backseat of a vehicle. Children ages four to seven must be seated in a rear booster seat or child restraint such as a lap and shoulder belt. Car seats and boosters range from $5 to $8 per day. Your unexpired mainland driver's license is valid for rental for up to 90 days.

Since many of Maui's roads are mostly two lanes, be sure to allow plenty of time to return your vehicle so that you can make your flight. Traffic can be bad during morning and afternoon rush hour.

Car Rental Resources

LOCAL AGENCIES		
AA Aloha Cars-R-Us	800/655-7989	www.hawaiicarrental.com
Adventure Lāna'i Eco-Centre (Lāna'i)	808/565-7373	www.adventurelanai.com
Aloha Campers (Maui)	808/268-9810	www.alohacampers.com
Aloha Rent A Car (Maui)	877/452-5642	www.aloharentalcar.com
Bio-Beetle Eco Rental Cars	877/873-6121	www.bio-beetle.com
Discount Hawaii Car Rentals	888/292-3307	www.discounthawaiicarrental.com
Hawaiian Discount Car Rentals	800/882-9007	www.hawaiidrive-o.com
Island Kine Auto Rental (Moloka'i)	866/527-7368	www.molokai-car-rental.com
Island Rental Cars (Maui)		www.hawaiianriders.com
Maui Harley Davidson	808/877-7433	www.hawaiiharleyrental.com
MAJOR AGENCIES		
Alamo	800/462-5266	www.alamo.com
Avis	800/331-1212	www.avis.com
Budget	800/527-0700	www.budget.com
Dollar	800/800-4000	www.dollar.com
Enterprise	800/261-7331	www.enterprise.com
Hertz	800/654-3131	www.hertz.com
National Car Rental	800/227-7368	www.nationalcar.com
Thrifty	800/847-4389	www.dollar.com

Give yourself about 3½ hours before departure time to return your vehicle.

CAR-RENTAL INSURANCE

If you own a car and carry comprehensive car insurance for both collision and liability, your personal auto insurance will probably cover a rental, but read your policy's fine print to be sure. Some credit cards offer CDW coverage, but it's usually supplemental to your own insurance and rarely covers SUVs, minivans, luxury models, and the like. If your coverage is secondary, you may still be liable for loss-of-use costs from the car-rental company (again, read the fine print). But no credit-card insurance is valid unless you use that card for *all* transactions, from reserving to paying the final bill.

■TIP→**Diners Club offers primary CDW coverage on all rentals reserved and paid for with the card. This means that Diners Club's company—not your own car insurance—pays in case of an accident. It doesn't mean that your car-insurance company won't raise your rates once it discovers you had an accident.**

You may also be offered supplemental liability coverage; the car-rental company is required to carry a minimal level of liability coverage insuring all renters, but it's rarely enough to cover claims in a really serious accident if you're at fault. Your own auto-insurance policy will protect you if you own a car; if you don't, you have to decide whether you are willing to take the risk.

U.S. rental companies sell CDWs and LDWs for about $15 to $25 a day; supplemental liability is usually more than $10 a day. The car-rental company may offer you all sorts of other policies, but they're rarely worth the cost. Personal accident insurance, which is basic hospitalization coverage, is an especially egregious rip-off if you already have health insurance.

■TIP→**You can decline the insurance from the rental company and purchase it through a third-party provider such as Travel Guard (www. travelguard.com)—$9 per day for** $35,000 of coverage. That's sometimes just under half the price of the CDW offered by some car-rental companies.

■ VACATION PACKAGES

About half of the visitors to Maui travel on package tours. All of the wholesalers specializing in Hawai'i offer a range of packages from the low to the high end. Because of the volume of business they do, wholesalers typically have great deals. Combine that with their knowledge of the destination and wholesale packages make a lot of sense. However, shop around and compare before you book to make sure you are getting a good deal.

Yours truly, can check on a tour operator's reputation among travelers by posting an inquiry on one of the Fodors.com forums.

Hawai'i Tour Operators **American Express Vacations** (☎800/528–4800 ⊕www.americanexpress-vacations.com). **Apple Vacations** (☎ 800/517–2000 ⊕www.apple-vacations.com). **Classic Vacations** (☎800/635–1333 ⊕www.classic-vacations.com). **Creative Leisure** (☎800/413–1000 ⊕www.creative-leisure.com). **Pleasant Holidays** (☎800/742–9244 ⊕www.pleasant-holidays.com).

■TIP→**Local tourism boards can provide information about lesser-known and small-niche operators that sell packages to only a few destinations.**

TRANSPORTATION

Getting around Maui is relatively easy as there are really only a few major roads leading to and from the major towns and must-see sights. Honoapiʻilani Highway will get you from the central Maui towns of Wailuku and Kahului to the leeward coast and the towns and resorts of Lahaina, Kāʻanapali, Kahana, and Kapalua. Depending on traffic, it should take about 30 to 45 minutes to travel this route. Those gorgeous mountains that hug Honoapiʻilani Highway are the West Maui Mountains.

North and South Kīhei Road will take you to the town of Kīhei and the resort area of Wailea on the South Shore. The drive from Kahului to Wailea should take about 30 minutes, and the drive from Kāʻanapali to Wailea will take about 45 to 60 minutes.

Your vacation to Maui must include a visit to Haleakalā National Park and you should plan on 2 to 2½ hours driving time from Kāʻanapali or Wailea. Hoʻokipa and Baldwin beaches are on the Island's North Shore, just a stone's throw from Kahului, and could easily be combined with a day in Upcountry Maui. The drive from Kāʻanapali or Wailea to the charming towns of Makawao and Kula will take about 45 to 60 minutes. And you must not miss the Road to Hāna, a 55-mi stretch with one-lane bridges, hairpin turns, and some of the most breathtaking views you will ever see.

▌ BY AIR

Flying time is about 10 hours from New York, eight hours from Chicago, and five hours from Los Angeles.

Hawaiʻi is a major destination link for flights traveling to and from the U.S. mainland, Asia, Australia, New Zealand, and the South Pacific. Some of the major airline carriers serving Hawaiʻi fly direct to Maui, allowing you to bypass connecting flights out of Honolulu, on Oʻahu. For the more spontaneous traveler, island-hopping is easy, with flights departing every 20 to 30 minutes daily until mid-evening. International travelers also have options: Oʻahu and the Big Island are gateways to the United States.

Although Maui's airports are smaller and more casual than Honolulu International, during peak times they can also be quite busy. Allow extra travel time to either airport during morning and afternoon rush-hour traffic periods, and allow time if you are returning a rental car. Plan to arrive at the airport 60 to 90 minutes before departure for interisland flights.

Plants and plant products are subject to regulation by the Department of Agriculture, both on entering and leaving Hawaiʻi. Upon leaving the Islands, you're required to have your bags X-rayed and tagged at one of the airport's agricultural-inspection stations before you proceed to check-in. Pineapples and coconuts with the packer's agricultural-inspection stamp pass freely; papayas must be treated, inspected, and stamped. All other fruits are banned for export to the U.S. mainland. Flowers pass except for gardenia, rose leaves, jade vine, and mauna loa. Also banned are insects, snails, soil, cotton, cacti, sugarcane, and all berry plants.

You'll have to leave dogs and other pets at home. A 120-day quarantine is imposed to keep out rabies, which is nonexistent in Hawai'i. If specific pre- and postarrival requirements are met, animals may qualify for 30-day or 5-day-or-less quarantine.

■ TIP→ If you travel frequently, look into the TSA's Registered Traveler program (⊕ www.tsa.gov). The program, which is still being tested in several U.S. airports, is designed to cut down on gridlock at security checkpoints by allowing pre-screened travelers to pass quickly through kiosks that scan an iris and/ or a fingerprint.

Air-Travel Resources in Maui
State of Hawaii Airports Division Offices (☎808/836–6417 ⊕www. hawaii.gov/dot/airports).

AIRPORTS

All of Hawai'i's major islands have their own airports, but Honolulu's International Airport on O'ahu is the main stopover for most U.S.–mainland and international flights. From Honolulu, there are departing flights to Maui leaving almost every hour from early morning until evening. In addition, some carriers now offer nonstop service directly from the U.S. mainland to Maui on a limited basis. Flights from Honolulu into Lāna'i and Moloka'i are offered several times a day.

MAUI AIRPORTS

Maui has two major airports. Kahului Airport handles major airlines and interisland flights; it's the only airport on Maui that has direct service from the mainland. Kapalua–West Maui Airport is served by Aloha Airlines, go!Express, and Hawaiian Air. If you're staying in West Maui and you're flying in from another island, you can avoid the hour drive from the Kahului Airport by flying into Kapalua–West Maui Airport. Hāna Airport is very small.

Information Kahului Airport (OGG) (☎808/872–3893). **Kapalua–West Maui Airport (JHM)** (☎808/669–0623). **Hāna Airport (HNM)** (☎808/248–8208).

GROUND TRANSPORTATION

If you're not renting a car, you'll need to take a taxi. Maui Airport Taxi serves the Kahului Airport and charges $3.50, plus $3 for every mile, with a 30¢ surcharge per bag. Cab fares to locations around the island are estimated as follows: Kā'anapali $87, Kahului town $13 to $18, Kapalua $105, Kīhei town $33 to $53, Lahaina $74 to $79, Mākena $65, Wailea $57, and Wailuku $20 to $27.

SpeediShuttle offers transportation between the Kahului Airport and hotels, resorts, and condominium complexes throughout the island. There is an online reservation and fare-quote system for information and bookings.

Information Maui Airport Taxi (☎808/877–0907). **SpeediShuttle Hawai'i** (☎877/242–5777 ⊕www. speedishuttle.com).

FLIGHTS

ATA flies into Maui from Los Angeles, Oakland, and Phoenix; and also serves O'ahu and the Big Island. America West flies into Maui and Honolulu from Las Vegas and Phoenix. Delta and Northwest serve Maui and O'ahu. American has daily nonstop flights into Maui from Los Angeles, Chicago, and Dallas-Fort Worth; and also serves O'ahu, Kaua'i, and the Big Island. United flies from Chicago, Los Angeles, and San Francisco to Maui; and also serves O'ahu and the Big Island. Continental flies into Honolulu.

In addition to offering very competitive rates and online specials, all have frequent-flyer programs that will entitle you to rewards and upgrades the more you fly. Be sure to compare prices offered by all of the interisland carriers. If you are somewhat flexible with your dates and times for island-hopping, you should have no problem getting a very affordable round-trip ticket.

Airline Contacts America West/ US Airways (☎800/428–4322 ⊕www.usairways.com). **American Airlines** (☎800/433–7300 ⊕www. aa.com). **Continental Airlines** (☎800/523–3273 for U.S. and Mexico reservations, 800/231–0856 for international reservations ⊕www.continental.com). **Delta Airlines** (☎800/221–1212 for U.S. reservations, 800/241–4141 for international reservations ⊕www. delta.com).**Northwest Airlines** (☎800/225–2525 ⊕www.nwa.com). **Southwest Airlines** (☎800/435–9792 ⊕www.southwest.com). **United Airlines** (☎800/864–8331 for U.S. reservations, 800/538–2929 for international reservations ⊕www.united.com).

INTERISLAND FLIGHTS

Hawaiian and Island Air offer regular interisland service to Maui's Kahului and Kapalua airports, as well as the Moloka'i and Lāna'i airports. go! Airlines/go! Express provides interisland service between Maui (Kahului and Kapalua), Lāna'i, Moloka'i, O'ahu, Kaua'i, and the Big Island. Mokulele Airlines flies between Maui's Kahului and Hāna Airports and Kona on the Big Island. PWExpress serves Maui's Kahului and Hāna airports, Moloka'i's Ho'olehua and Kalaupapa airports and Lāna'i City, and also flies into O'ahu and the Big Island. Pacific Wings has regular and charter service between Honolulu and Maui (all three airports), Moloka'i, Lāna'i, and the Big Island.

Interisland Flights Hawaiian Airlines (☎800/367–5320 ⊕www.hawaiianair.com). **Island Air** (☎800/323–3345 ⊕www. islandair.com). **Mokulele Airlines** (☎866/260–7070 ⊕www. mokuleleairlines.com). **PWExpress** (☎888/866–5022 ⊕www.flypwx. com). **Pacific Wings** (☎888/575–4546 ⊕www.pacificwings.com).

∎ BY BOAT

There is daily ferry service between Lahaina or Maʻalaea Harbor, Maui, and Mānele Bay, Lānaʻi, with Expeditions Lānaʻi Ferry. The 9-mi crossing costs $50 cash (or $52 if you pay with a credit card) round-trip, per person, and takes about 45 minutes or so, depending on ocean conditions (which can make this trip a rough one).

Molokaʻi Ferry offers twice-daily ferry service between Lahaina, Maui, and Kaunakakai, Molokaʻi. Travel time is about 90 minutes each way and the one-way fare is $42.40 per person (including taxes and fees); a book of six one-way tickets costs $196.10 (including taxes and fees). Reservations are recommended.

Hawaiʻi Superferry, a high-speed interisland ferry service, runs between Oʻahu and Maui. Features include a passenger deck with floor-to-ceiling windows, big-screen entertainment, video games for kids, and dining areas. The ferry departs Honolulu daily at 6:30 AM and arrives into Kahului at 10:15 AM. The Kahului to Honolulu ferry departs at 11:15 AM and arrives at 2:15 PM. One-way, 14-day advance purchase Web fares are $44, Tuesday through Thursday, and $54, Friday through Monday. One-way base passenger fares are $52, Tuesday through Thursday, and $62, Friday through Monday. Discounts are offered for children, seniors, and retired military personnel.

Hawaiʻi Superferry suspended service between Oʻahu and Kauaʻi due to environmental concerns, but hopes to resume this route in the future. In 2009, the company expects to have a second daily Oʻahu to Maui ferry, as well as service between Oʻahu and the Big Island. Check the Hawaiʻi Superferry Web site for the latest route information.

Information Expeditions Lānaʻi Ferry (☎800/695-2624 ⊕www.go-lanai.com). **Hawaiʻi Superferry** (☎877/443-3779 ⊕www.hawaiisuperferry.com). **Molokaʻi Ferry** (☎866/307-6524 ⊕www.molokaiferry.com).

∎ BY BUS

Maui Bus, operated by Roberts Hawaiʻi, offers 11 routes in and between various Central, South, and West Maui communities, seven days a week, including all holidays. Passengers can travel in and around Wailuku, Kahului, Lahaina, Kāʻanapali, Kapalua, Kīhei, Wailea, Māʻalaea, and Upcountry (including Pukalani, Hāliʻimaile, Haʻikū, and Pāʻia). The Upcountry and Haʻikū Islander routes include a stop at Kahului Airport. The Kahului and Wailuku loops are free; others are $1.

For travelers who prefer not to rent a car, Maui Bus is a great way to go. It runs from early morning to late evening daily, including holidays, and can get you to most of the major towns and sightseeing destinations. And you can't beat the price.

Bus Information Roberts Hawaiʻi (☎808/871-4838 ⊕www.co.maui.hi.us/bus).

█ BY CAR

Asking for directions will almost always produce a helpful explanation from the locals, but you should be prepared for an island term or two. Hawai'i residents refer to places as being either *mauka* (toward the mountains) or *makai* (toward the ocean) from one another.

Hawai'i has a strict seat-belt law. Those riding in the front seat must wear a seat belt and children under the age of 17 in the backseat must be belted. The fine for not wearing a seat belt is $92. Jaywalking is also very common so please pay careful attention to the roads.

Traffic on Maui can be very bad branching out from Kahului to and from Pā'ia, Kīhei, and Lahaina. Parking along many streets is curtailed during rush hours, and towing is strictly practiced. Read curbside parking signs before leaving your vehicle.

GASOLINE

You can pretty much count on having to pay more for gasoline on Maui than on the U.S. mainland. At the time of this writing, the average price of a gallon of gas is about $3.89.

PARKING

With a population of more than 119,000 and nearly 30,000 visitors on any given day, Maui has parking challenges. Lots sprinkled throughout West Maui charge by the hour. There are about 700 parking spaces in the Lahaina Center; shoppers can get validated parking. *This Week Maui* often has coupons

for free parking at this lot, as well as at Whalers Village.

ROAD CONDITIONS

It's difficult to get lost throughout most of Maui as there are really only four major roads. The Hawai'i Visitors and Convention Bureau's red-caped King Kamehameha signs mark major attractions and scenic spots. Ask for a map at the car-rental counter. Free publications containing good-quality road maps can be found at airports, hotels, and shops.

Maui has its share of impenetrable areas, although four-wheel-drive vehicles rarely run into problems. Moloka'i and Lāna'i have fewer roadways, but car rental is worthwhile. On these smaller islands, opt for a four-wheel-drive vehicle if dirt-road exploration holds any appeal.

In rural areas, it's not unusual for gas stations to close early. In Hawai'i, turning right on a red light is legal, except where noted. Use caution during heavy downpours, especially if you see signs warning of falling rocks. If you're enjoying views from the road or need to study a map, pull over to the side. Remember the aloha spirit; allow other cars to merge, don't honk (it's considered rude); use your headlights and turn signals.

ON THE GROUND

▮ COMMUNICATIONS

INTERNET

If you've brought your laptop with you to Maui, you should have no problem checking e-mail or connecting to the Internet. Most of the major hotels and resorts offer high-speed access in rooms and/or lobbies. If you're staying at a small inn or B&B without Internet access, ask the proprietor for the nearest café or coffee shop with wireless access.

Contacts Cybercafes (⊕www. cybercafes.com) lists more than 4,000 Internet cafés worldwide. **JiWire** (⊕www.jiwire.com) features a directory of Wi-Fi hotspots around the world.

▮ HEALTH

Hawai'i is known as the Health State. The life expectancy here is 79 years, one of the longest in the nation. Balmy weather makes it easy to remain active year-round, and the low-stress aloha attitude certainly contributes to general well-being. When visiting the Islands, however, there are a few health issues to keep in mind.

The Hawai'i State Department of Health recommends that you drink 16 ounces of water per hour to avoid dehydration when hiking or spending time in the sun. Use sunblock, wear UV-reflective sunglasses, and protect your head with a visor or hat for shade. If you're not acclimated to warm, humid weather, allow plenty of time for rest stops and refreshments.

When visiting freshwater streams, be aware of the tropical disease leptospirosis, which is spread by animal urine and carried into streams and mud. Symptoms include fever, headache, nausea, and red eyes. If left untreated it can cause liver and kidney damage, respiratory failure, internal bleeding, and even death. To avoid this, don't swim or wade in freshwater streams or ponds if you have open sores and don't drink from any freshwater streams or ponds.

On the Islands, fog is a rare occurrence, but there can often be "vog," an airborne haze of gases released from volcanic vents on the Big Island. During certain weather conditions such as "Kona Winds," the vog can settle over the Islands and wreak havoc with respiratory and other health conditions, especially asthma or emphysema. If susceptible, stay indoors and get emergency assistance if needed.

The Islands have their share of bugs and insects. Most are harmless but annoying. When planning to spend time outdoors in hiking areas, wear long-sleeved clothing and pants and use mosquito repellent containing deet. In very damp places you may encounter the dreaded local centipede. On the Islands they usually come in two colors, brown and blue, and they range from the size of a worm to an 8-inch cigar.

Their sting is very painful, and the reaction is similar to bee- and wasp-sting reactions. When camping, shake out your sleeping bag before climbing in, and check your shoes in the morning, as the centipedes like cozy places. If planning on hiking or traveling in remote areas, always carry a first-aid kit and appropriate medications for sting reactions.

For information on travel insurance and medical-assistance companies see Trip Insurance under Things to Consider in Getting Started, above.

▌ HOURS OF OPERATION

Even people in paradise have to work. Generally local business hours are weekdays 8 to 5. Banks are usually open Monday through Thursday 8:30 to 3 and until 6 on Friday. Some banks have Saturday-morning hours.

Many self-serve gas stations stay open around-the-clock, with full-service stations usually open from around 7 AM until 9 PM. U.S. post offices are generally open weekdays 8:30 AM to 4:30 PM and Saturday 8:30 to noon.

Most museums generally open their doors between 9 AM and 10 AM and stay open until 5 PM, Tuesday through Saturday. Many museums operate with afternoon hours only on Sunday and close on Monday. Visitor-attraction hours vary throughout the state, but most sights are open daily with the exception of major holidays such as Christmas. Check local newspapers or visitor publications upon arrival for attraction hours and schedules if visiting over holiday periods. The local dailies carry a listing of "What's Open/What's Not" for those time periods.

Stores in resort areas sometimes open as early as 8, with shopping-center opening hours varying from 9:30 to 10 on weekdays and Saturday, a bit later on Sunday. Bigger malls stay open until 9 weekdays and Saturday and close at 5 on Sunday. Boutiques in resort areas may stay open as late as 11.

▌ MONEY

Prices throughout this guide are given for adults. Substantially reduced fees are almost always available for children, students, and senior citizens.

CREDIT CARDS

Throughout this guide, the following abbreviations are used: **AE**, American Express; **D**, Discover; **DC**, Diners Club; **MC**, MasterCard; and **V**, Visa.

Reporting Lost Cards American Express (☎800/528–4800 in the U.S. or 336/393–1111 collect from abroad ⊕www.americanexpress.com). **Diners Club** (☎800/234–6377 in the U.S. or 303/799–1504 collect from abroad ⊕www.dinersclub.com). **Discover** (☎800/347–2683 in the U.S. or 801/902–3100 collect from abroad ⊕www.discovercard.com). **MasterCard** (☎800/627–8372 in the U.S. or 636/722–7111 collect from abroad ⊕www.mastercard.com). **Visa** (☎800/847–2911 in the U.S. or 410/581–9994 collect from abroad ⊕www.visa.com).

▌SAFETY

Hawai'i is generally a safe tourist destination, but it's still wise to follow common sense safety precautions. Rental cars are magnets for break-ins, so don't leave any valuables in the car, not even in a locked trunk. Avoid poorly lighted areas, beach parks, and isolated areas after dark as a precaution. When hiking, stay on marked trails, no matter how alluring the temptation might be to stray. Weather conditions can cause landscapes to become muddy, slippery, and tenuous, so staying on marked trails will lessen the possibility of a fall or getting lost. *For advice on beach and sun safety, see chapter 3, Beaches.*

Women traveling alone are generally safe on the Islands, but always follow the safety precautions you would use in any major destination. When booking hotels, request rooms closest to the elevator and always keep your hotel-room door and balcony doors locked. Stay away from isolated areas after dark; camping and hiking solo are not advised. If you stay out late visiting nightclubs and bars, use caution when exiting night spots and returning to your lodging.

▌TAXES

There's a 4.16% state sales tax on all purchases, including food. A hotel room tax of 7.25%, combined with the sales tax of 4.16%, equals an 11.41% rate added onto your hotel bill. A $3-per-day road tax is also assessed on each rental vehicle.

▌TIME

Hawai'i is on Hawaiian standard time, 5 hours behind New York, 2 hours behind Los Angeles, and 10 hours behind London.

When the U.S. mainland is on daylight saving time, Hawai'i is not, so add an extra hour of time difference between the Islands and U.S. mainland destinations. You may find that things generally move more slowly here. That has nothing to do with your watch—it's just the laid-back way called Hawaiian time.

▌TIPPING

As this is a major vacation destination and many of the people who work at the hotels and resorts rely on tips to supplement their wages, tipping is not only common but expected. Bartenders expect a $1 or more per round of drinks; bellhops expect $1 to $5 per bag, depending on the hotel and kinds of items you have; hotel concierges expect to be tipped if they render you a service (usually $5 or more); hotel maids expect $1 to $3 per day (it's best to tip your maid daily in cash because the cleaner may be different on different days of your stay); taxi drivers expect 15% to 20%, but round up the fare to the next dollar amount; waiters expect to be tipped at about the same rate they would receive in a major city (15% to 20%, with 20% being the norm at upscale restaurants).

INDEX

Photo Credits

1 and 2–3, Douglas Peebles/eStock Photo. 6, Richard Genova/viestiphoto.com. **Chapter 1:** Experience Maui: 8-9, Pacific Stock/SuperStock. 10 (top), Photodisc. 10 (bottom), Dana Edmunds/Starwood Hotels and Resorts. 11 (top left), Ron Dahlquist/Maui Visitors Bureau. 11 (top right), Chris Hammond/viestiphoto. com. 11 (bottom right), Walter Bibkow/viestiphoto.com. 14, David Fleetham/ Alamy. 15 (top left), Jenny Flores. 15 (top right), Robert Holmes/Alamy. 16, Douglas Peebles Photography/Alamy. 17, Rhodesone. 18, Holly52. 19, Dana Edmunds/Starwood Hotels and Resorts. 20, Grand Wailea Resort. 21 and 22, pssandler. **Chapter 2:** Exploring Maui: 23, Michael S. Nolan/age fotostock. 27, Pacific Stock/SuperStock. 32, tmdave. 36, SuperStock/age fotostock. 44, Douglas Peebles/eStock Photo. 52, HMHolly. 58, Chris Hammond/viestiphoto.com. **Chapter 3:** Beaches and Outdoor Activities:61, Brent Bergherm/age fotostock. 64, Robert Simon/iStockphoto. 72, Tomas del Amo/Alamy. 77, David Olsen/Aurora Photos. 84 and 93, Pacific Stock/SuperStock. 96, Michael S. Nolan/age fotostock. 104, Pacific Stock/SuperStock. **Chapter 4:** Shops & Spas: 113, Douglas Peebles/ Alamy. 115, Grand Wailea Resort. 124 (top), Hotel Hana Maui. 124 (bottom), John C. Russell/Four Seasons Maui at Wailea. 124 (bottom right), Grand Wailea Resort. **Chapter 5:** Entertainment and Night Life: 127, Grand Wailea Resort. 133, David Olsen/Photo Resource Hawaii/Alamy. **Chapter 6:** Where to Eat: 137, Douglas Peebles/Alamy. 143, Danita Delimont/Alamy. 150, Polynesian Cultural Center. 160, Douglas Peebles/Aurora Photos. **Chapter 7:** Where To Stay: 163, Renaissance Wailea Beach Resort. 169, Ritz Carlton Kapalua. 180, Peter Vitale/ Four Seasons Maui at Wailea.

ABOUT OUR WRITERS

Nicole Crane recently moved to Maui from New York City, where she worked at a fashion magazine. Being a New York transplant—and an avid shopper—she was happy to check out the shops and spas included in this guide. She also contributes to *In Style Weddings, People,* and *Maui Nō Ka ʻOi* magazines.

Eliza Escaño was raised in Manila, Philippines, and lived in California before falling in aloha with Maui almost three years ago. She is a contributing writer for the Hawaiʻi-based publications *Maui Concierge, Maui Time Weekly,* and *Smart Magazine.* For this edition Eliza updated the Water Sports & Tours and Entertainment & Nightlife chapters.

Bonnie Friedman, a native New Yorker, has made her home on Maui for more than 25 years. A well-published and well-traveled freelance writer, she also owns and operates Grapevine Productions, which celebrated its 20th anniversary in 2008. She traveled around Maui to get the latest news for the Exploring Maui, Beaches, and Where to Stay chapters, adding some of her favorite places.

Heidi Pool moved to Maui in 2003 after having been a frequent visitor for the previous two decades. She works in the visitor publications industry as a writer and production assistant. An outdoor enthusiast, Heidi enjoys playing "tour guide" when friends or family members come to visit. She updated the Golf, Hiking & Outdoor Activities chapter, as well as Lanaʻi and Molokaʻi.

Cathy Sharpe, our Essentials updater, was born and reared on Oʻahu. For 13 years she worked at a Honolulu public-relations agency representing major travel-industry clients. Now living in Maryland, she is a marketing consultant. She returns home to visit family and friends, relax at her favorite beaches, and enjoy island cuisine—and to keep her eye on the latest tips for travlers.

Carla Tracy hails from the Mainland (she was born in Ohio), but she has called Maui home for the past 30 years. She's been with the *Maui News* for 27 years, and for much of that time has served as the dining editor. The Where to Eat chapter was her Fodor's beat. Carla is also a James Beard Awards panelist and writes freelance articles for numerous island magazines.